THEY NEVER HAD A CHANCE TO SPIT

Rick Vaccarelli

BookLocker

Trenton, Georgia

ISBN: 978-1-64438-097-0

Published by BookLocker.com, Inc., Trenton, Georgia.

BookLocker.com, Inc.
2025

Second Edition

Library of Congress Cataloging in Publication Data
Vaccarelli, Rick
They Never Had a Chance To Spit by Rick Vaccarelli
Library of Congress Control Number: 2019913324

To Carol

Who supported my own political adventures including the lower voting age movement that eventually led to the adoption of the 14th Amendment of the Constitution, July 1, 1971

Special thanks and appreciation to ……

Carol my wife who has tolerated my love of politics and many, many election nights

Anita Alfonsi who miraculously donated a kidney to me that added the time to my life to publish this book

To the most terrific medical team of individuals that I will always be grateful to have encountered

Dr. Diana Raub

Dr.Ashutosh Kshirsager

Dr. Nirav Patel,

Dr. Amit Tevar,

Dr. Roberto Carlos Lopez,

Lori Schrall and the

UPMC Transplant team.

…… and the research library staffs at Sewickley Library, Moon Township Library, Robert Morris University Library and *Dana McGrath who took the time to edit my book.*

Introduction

This book has been in the making in my head for over 50 years and was inspired by a book written by Irving Stone and a quote by former Vice President John Nance Garner.

Irving Stone wrote, "They Also Ran," and in that book, Stone wrote about the individuals who ran for President of the United States and lost.

Garner, vice president under Franklin D. Roosevelt, is attributed with the quote he made to then Sen. Lyndon B. Johnson, who was considering an offer to be John F. Kennedy's running mate, "I'll tell you, Lyndon, the vice presidency isn't worth a bucket of warm spit."

Stone looked at individuals seeking the presidency who lost, which made me think about the individuals who ran for vice president and lost. Losing the presidency is one thing, losing a job "not worth a bucket of spit" is another.

In our history, 14 vice presidents went on to become president. History knows about them, and you would probably recognize their names. There have been 48 other individuals who served as vice president, and most of us would be hard-pressed to name who they were. Likewise, some of us could name a few of the 54 individuals who ran for president on a major party ticket and lost, but only a real true-blue political trivia enthusiast would recognize individuals who ran unsuccessfully for the vice presidency.

This book is about the individuals who never even had the "chance" to spit. Who never had the opportunity to create their own "bucket of warm spit." These individuals were never within one heartbeat of the presidency. They are the men and women who had a brief moment on the national stage, and then, in defeat, moved on to other adventures. What happened to them?

I hope you'll find this book interesting, a bit educational, and enjoyable. It is in no way an in-depth biography of these individuals, but rather a quick answer to that question. It's just a small peek at what happens to someone who "doesn't even get the chance to spit."

While I have searched many sources when writing this book, I have acknowledged none of them. I apologize to those who provided bits of the information, and did not mean to slight anyone in any way. Some of the information I have used came from stories I heard way back when. Some information is just from pieces of paper I collected through the years. Other information is from biographies and other sources. Thanks to anyone and everyone who shared information with me. In the end, I hope you will enjoy the thumbnail sketches that clearly show that there is life after a national defeat for a job that "isn't worth a spit." I hope you will have fun learning a little bit about them. I know I had fun writing it.

Contents

CHAPTER ONE

THE ELECTORAL COLLEGE ELECTS DONALD TRUMP AND HILARY CLINTON

When the framers of the constitution created our national system of electing a president and vice president, it seemed only natural to them that the person in second place should become the vice president.

Initially the constitution stated: "The electors shall meet in their respective states and vote by ballot for two persons, of whom one at least shall not be an inhabitant of the same state with themselves........In every case, after the choice of the president, the person having the greatest number of votes of the electors shall be the vice president."

Note that electors were required to vote for two candidates, so clearly, with two or more candidates interested in becoming president; the "losing candidate" with the second highest amount of votes becomes, by virtue of the original constitution, the Vice President of the United States.

In 1789, George Washington was elected president with 69 electoral votes, and John Adams, receiving 34 votes, the second highest, was elected our first vice president. Washington and Adams were willing to serve well together with a common agenda in stabilizing the new nation. However, over the eight-year period, political factions with agendas began developing among groups so that when Washington decided not to seek a third term, the landscape of what direction the nation should move toward was up for debate.

In the election of 1796, the Electoral College, representing their state constituencies, met to select candidates with specific agendas. Vice President John Adams, a Federalist, received 71 votes for president. Thomas Jefferson, a Democratic-Republican, received 68 votes for president. By virtue of the constitution, Adams was elected president, and his chief political rival, Jefferson, was elected vice president.

If this constitutional system remained intact, we would have some interesting administrations in recent times. Richard Nixon would have served as John F. Kennedy's vice president, and would have assumed the presidency in 1963. Bill Clinton, who defeated President George H. Bush, would have had the pleasure of having the defeated president serve as his vice president. Certainly, the administration of Donald Trump would have had new dimensions with Hillary Clinton, who came in second in the Electoral College vote, serving as his vice president.

Obviously, between 1789 and 1800, the handwriting was on the wall that change was needed in this "second place" vice presidency system. It had been shown that political rivals serving together could be inconvenient way for national leadership. As you can imagine, as elections became competitive and agenda-driven, having a rival serve as your vice president was not going to be in the best interest of the country.

The union of two rivals was not advantageous to the building of the nation, and as political parties began to develop, it would show more flaws in the system could develop. In 1800, electors thought they could solve the issue by casting votes for the respective party candidates only, but this resulted in a tie for the presidency between Aaron Burr and Thomas Jefferson. Jefferson was eventually elected after 36 ballots were cast in the House of Representatives for him for president, but the waiting and political maneuvering showed that a constitutional change would be necessary to avoid such elections in the future. On December 9, 1803, Congress proposed an amendment to change the process of election of the president and vice president. It was ratified by three-fourths of the state legislatures on June 15, 1804, as the 12th Amendment of the Constitution.

This new constitutional amendment provided for the separate election of President of the United States and Vice President of the United States, respectively. Furthermore, it clarified circumstances where a candidate without sufficient electoral votes for president or vice president would be chosen to serve in their respective offices. Moving forward, electors would now cast ballots separately for the office of President of the United States and Vice President of the United States. Candidates supported by specific political parties would now be designated specifically for the office they were seeking on behalf of their respective party.

CHAPTER TWO
THE FIRST DEFEATED OFFICIAL VICE
PRESIDENTIAL CANDIDATE

Rufus King had the distinction to be the first U.S. Senator elected for the state of New York after the establishment of the official government. He also had the distinction to be the first official vice presidential candidate to be defeated after the adoption of the 12th Amendment. He may not have known the job wasn't worth the spit because he pursued it more than once.

Rufus was very active in the formation of the republic and represented the state of Massachusetts in the Congress of the Confederation. He was Harvard educated and was an officer in the Revolutionary Army.

He was an active Federalist and worked actively for a strong national government with fellow party members Alexander Hamilton, John Adams, John Jay, and John Marshall. George Washington, while not actively supportive of political factions, believed strongly in a national government and centralized authority, and had he been an active party member, he too would have been a Federalist. The party's loyal opposition came from Thomas Jefferson and the Democratic-Republican Party. In addition to being the first official candidate to be defeated for the vice presidency, Rufus King had the honor of also being the final presidential candidate of the Federalist Party in 1816.

King was active in Massachusetts politics before moving to New York and being elected one of the two first U.S. Senators. King served in the Senate from 1789 to 1796. He was appointed as a Minister to Great Britain in 1796 and served in that office until 1803.

In 1804, the Federalist candidate for President was Charles Pinckney, and Rufus King was the vice presidential candidate. They were opposed by the Democratic-Republican ticket of President Thomas Jefferson and George Clinton. In the first official election where the Electoral College cast separate ballots for president and vice president, George Clinton defeated Rufus King by a vote of 162 to 14. George Clinton would go on to be re-elected vice president in 1808, becoming the first vice president in history to serve two different presidents, Jefferson and James Madison. He also was the first vice president to die in office.

In his defeat for vice president, Rufus would again be a candidate for the office in 1808, along with Charles Pinckney who was the presidential candidate. Both again would be defeated, with James Madison being elected president, while Vice President Clinton was re-elected, defeating King 113 votes to 47.

Slavery had always been an issue for King. After his defeat for the vice presidency, he continued to speak out against slavery and believed that it would become a critical problem for states in the north and the south. His forecast was correct, and he would remain active in politics, returning to the Senate in 1813 and fiercely opposing slavery for the state of Missouri.

In 1816, Sen. Clinton was the Federalist Party candidate for president. He would be their last official candidate and was defeated for the presidency in a landslide by James Monroe by an Electoral College vote of 183 to 34.

He served in the Senate for a second time until 1825 when President John Quincy Adams appointed him the Minister to Great Britain. He died on April 29, 1827, and is remembered as the first official Federalist candidate for vice president and the party's last official candidate for president.

CHAPTER THREE

IT'S GOOD TO ENJOY YOUR LEGAL
CAREER IF THINGS DON'T WORK OUT

1812 was not the best of times to run a national campaign as a Federalist. Jared Ingersoll would learn this as the second individual who never had a chance to spit.

The Federalist Party was in serious decline nationally, being viewed more as a regional party representing the interest of the New England states. The country continued to grow under Jefferson and the Louisiana Purchase, but the Federalist Party did not grow with it. It may have been influential with Washington and Adams, but it was now in disarray. It did not field a presidential candidate in 1812 but instead chose a vice presidential nominee only, Jared Ingersoll.

Jared studied law in Philadelphia and was a graduate of Yale University. He returned home to England but returned to America believing in the cause of Independence for the colonies. He became active in the independence movement and was elected a delegate to the Constitutional Convention. As the national government became established, it was obvious that the Federalist Party would be a natural path for political participation for him. Jared was a strong believer in the power of a central government. George Washington, the new president, and John Adams held similar views, along with members of the Federalist Party.

As the new country began setting its course, two political parties began to emerge. The Federalist, led nationally by then Vice President Adams, and the Republicans, led by then Secretary of State Thomas Jefferson. It became a clear case of centralized government versus more states power. With that Electoral College twist, Jefferson would eventually become vice president under Adams due to his second place finish and then four years later defeat Adams for the presidency. Ingersoll rose to prominence by calling Jefferson a "great subversion" to the national government.

While remaining active in the ongoing development of the country and political affairs, Ingersoll seemed to love the law and being involved with it. Before his ill-fated national campaign, he was the Attorney General of Pennsylvania from 1790 to 1799. He also served as the Solicitor for Philadelphia from 1798 to 1801, and District Attorney of Philadelphia from 1800 to 1801.

In the election of 1812, Jared Ingersoll was the candidate of the Federalist Party for vice president without the benefit of presidential running mate. The party could not agree on a national candidate to lead the ticket. James Madison was elected President, and Elbridge Gerry defeated Ingersoll for the vice presidency by an electoral vote of 131 to 86.

After his defeat, Ingersoll never ran for national office again. He never had a chance to spit, but did return to the legal world he enjoyed. He would go on to serve as the Attorney General of Pennsylvania from 1811 to 1817 and as a presiding Judge in Philadelphia District Court from 1821-1822.

Jared lived to see the Federalist Party become extinct as a national force when it fielded its final presidential campaign in 1816. He died in 1822 and is buried in Philadelphia.

CHAPTER FOUR

THE FINAL FEDERALIST PARTY TICKET

John Edgar Howard was the perfect vice presidential candidate in terms of background. He had it all: He was wealthy, a war hero, and a socialite with political connections. He also was the last official vice presidential candidate as part of a national Federalist Party ticket. He had the distinction to be on the ticket with the very first Federalist vice presidential candidate under the new rules of the 12th Amendment. If he wanted to know how it felt to never "get a chance to spit," his running mate, Rufus King, the presidential candidate of the Federalist Party, could help in that department because he was a candidate for vice president, twice, and lost.

John Howard owned much of the land that is Baltimore today and as a plantation owner was very well off. He had a very distinguished military career serving in the Revolutionary War as a commissioned officer. He was awarded a Silver Medal by Congress for his service in the Continental Army. His was viewed as a hero and public servant. He was very much recognized for his military leadership, and George Washington offered him a position in his cabinet as Secretary of War, but he declined.

Howard went on to become a member of the Continental Congress and also served as the Governor of Maryland for three one-year terms 1788 to 1791. In 1791, he was elected to the state Senate and served until 1795 when he became a member of Congress. He served as a U.S. Senator from Maryland from 1797 until 1803. He retired from active politics and returned to his home in Maryland where he and his wife would host many social affairs at their mansion.

In the 1816 election, the Federalist Party was slowly losing all influence. Members of the party would nominate Howard to run with Rufus King. King now had the distinction of being the standard bearer of a failing national effort that fielded its last official presidential candidate as well. King lost the presidency in a landslide to James Monroe. Howard, his running mate, did not actively campaign for the job and was defeated for the vice presidency by the Electoral College vote of 195 to 22.

The Federalist Party never rebounded, and Howard returned to his life in Baltimore. He is recognized for his philanthropy, military career, political service, and, of course, those social events. He has the unique distinction to be recognized by name in the Maryland State song, "O Maryland, O Maryland." The city of Baltimore has immortalized him with an equestrian statue in the heart of the city.

CHAPTER FIVE

LESSONS LEARNED. IT'S BETTER TO HAVE A RUNNING MATE

Richard Stockton was another unique vice presidential candidate who ran in 1820. He also was a candidate who did not run with a presidential running mate. The Federalist Party was at an end and did not field a national candidate. Recognizing that it would be virtually impossible to defeat President James Monroe, the party supported a vice presidential candidate only. This was the final time a candidate for president ran unopposed, and it was the third and final time there would be virtually no opposition to the presidential candidates. The first two were the elections of George Washington in 1788 and 1792.

Stockton, who was born in 1764, was the son of a signer of the constitution. He studied and practiced law and was appointed to the U.S. Senate, serving from 1796 to 1799. He obviously enjoyed politics, serving later as a member of Congress and then became the first U.S. Attorney from the New Jersey District. A political position that remained out of reach for him in New Jersey was the governor's office, for which he made three attempts to win in 1801, 1803, and 1804. Before becoming the nominee of the Federalist Party for vice president, he had served a term in Congress from 1813 to 1815.

Stockton ran as vice president when the country was somewhat very satisfied with the Monroe administration. The Federalist Party and Stockton appeared to be doomed from the start. The party had no candidate for president and little national support. It was a feel-good era for the country, and with no real national opposition Monroe easily coasted to a second term.

Stockton was handily defeated by Monroe's running mate, Vice President Daniel Tompkins, by an electoral vote of 218 votes to 8. Never getting the chance to spit, his political career over, he went on with his life practicing law until he died in 1828.

CHAPTER SIX

A CAREER POLITICIAN DEFEATED BY A POLITICAL LEGEND

By all accounts, Nathan Sanford was a "career politician" who was part of one of the most controversial elections in American history. The election of 1824 had a far-reaching impact on the country, not only for 1824, but for the two national elections that followed.

Sanford was a Yale Law graduate, started his government involvement as U.S. Bankruptcy Commissioner, and then became the U.S. Attorney for New York. The high-profile position led to his election to the New York Assembly, where he also served one year as Speaker before being elected to the U.S. Senate in 1815. When he was defeated for re-election in 1821, he went on to serve in a state judicial position in New York as a Chancellor, a position he served in from 1823 until 1826.

In 1824, Sanford was one of six candidates receiving electoral votes for the vice presidency. All the candidates, including Sanford, were soundly defeated by John Calhoun, who had the support of both national candidates for president, John Quincy Adams and Andrew Jackson. Adams and Jackson would become the final two candidates considered by the House of Representatives for the presidency, after they and two other national candidates, Henry Clay and William Crawford, failed to receive a majority of electoral votes to be elected president.

Andrew Jackson received the plurality of votes cast nationally, as well as a plurality of electoral votes for president. Speculation is that a back door deal was brokered that would lead to John Quincy Adams being elected president. He was the first son of a former president to be elected in a controversial election, but certainly not the last son of a former president to experience a controversial outcome. The "deal making" became fodder for discussion in that election and served as the primary motivation of a successful Jackson campaign four years later, which would make Adams a one-term president. On the other hand, the landslide and lopsided Electoral College victory by Calhoun in the 1824 election led to his re-election for the vice presidency, giving him the unique opportunity to serve as the Vice President of the United States for both President Adams and President Jackson.

In 1824, Calhoun received 182 votes, while Nathan Sanford received a mere 30 votes. Perhaps over the years Sanford took solace in the fact that Calhoun was supported by both major candidates.

Sanford would not be a candidate for national office again, but he would go on to be elected again to the U.S. Senate, succeeding one of the other famous names who never had a chance to spit, Rufus King. When his term ended, he opted not to seek re-election and returned to practicing of law. Sanford died in 1838.

CHAPTER SEVEN
PUBLIC SERVANT FAILS TO
BECOME VICE PRESIDENT

We often read about individuals entering politics to be "public servants," and Richard Rush, who ran for the vice presidency with John Quincy Adams, was one of those characters in early American history. Rush, a native of Philadelphia, was enjoying his legal career and started his political career as the Attorney General of Pennsylvania in 1811. That same year, he was appointed by President James Madison to serve as the Comptroller of the Treasury.

In 1814, he was appointed as the Attorney General of the United States and then became the acting Secretary of State under President James Monroe until his appointment as the Minister of Britain. He succeeded John Quincy Adams in this job, who returned from that position to become the Secretary of State. Rush helped to develop the Monroe Doctrine as well as set up the 49th parallel, which served as the boundary between the United states and Canada.

Rush was able to get along well and communicate effectively. The man he replaced, John

Q. Adams was elected president and named Rush to be a member of his cabinet as the Secretary of Treasury. Rush was effective, handing his successor a surplus with the federal treasury once he left the role.

Rush earned his stripes as an individual who "never had a chance to spit" when he became the vice presidential running mate of President Adams. Vice President Calhoun, who was elected with Adams, opted to support the candidacy of Andrew Jackson and run with him. The election of 1828 was extremely bitter on both sides because it was a repeat of the 1824 election, in which Jackson and his supporters had already contentiously contested as a deal-making election. This go-around, Jackson easily defeated Adams by a landslide, and Vice President John Calhoun was re-elected, defeating Rush by an electoral vote of 171 to 83.

Rush continued to have an interest in public affairs after his defeat. His international negotiating skills were well known, and the cities of Georgetown and Alexandria, Virginia, along with the city of Washington, actually hired him to seek funding from England and the Netherlands for the Chesapeake & Ohio Canal they were building for business development in that region. With his contacts, he was able to secure funding for the development of that project from the Dutch Bank of Crommelins.

Remaining active and interested in politics, he was offered the top of the ticket in the 1832 campaign by the Anti Masonic Party, but he turned it down and opted to use his skill set to successfully settle a serious border dispute between the states of Ohio and Michigan, which teetered on war between both states. Those negotiating skills would once again come into play when word reached President Andrew Jackson that James Smithson, a British citizen and scholar, who had never been to the United States, left a sizable bequest that involved the country. Smithson had left money in his will for his nephew and his nephew's heirs. However, he stipulated that, in the event his nephew would die and have no heirs, he then wanted the money to be bequeathed to the United States of America for the "increase and diffusion of knowledge." President Jackson worked with Congress in the creation of a committee to secure the funds from England, and Rush was tapped for the position. It took two years involving the English court system, but he successfully returned to the United State with a half million dollars to help secure the creation of the Smithsonian Institution. Rush would go on to become one of the first Regents for the institution and enjoyed his service as it began to grow into the national institution it is today.

Rush returned home to enjoy the peaceful life as a private citizen in Philadelphia, but President James

Polk called him back into public service, naming him the Minister to France. He arrived for his new job at a time when King Louis Phillipe was in the throes of the revolution. The revolution was successful in deposing King Louis, and Rush was quick to formally recognize the new French Second Republic on behalf of the United States.

After returning back to his Philadelphia home, he continued to remain interested in public affairs and was concerned that the Union would fall due to the issues of slavery. He was supportive of his fellow Pennsylvanian, President James Buchanan, and died in 1859.

While Rush, "never had a chance to spit," he certainly made a significant contribution to the country both before and after his failed vice presidential bid.

CHAPTER EIGHT

THE CONVENTIONAL CHOICE

Without any major network news coverage that we have become accustomed to today, the 1832 election witnessed the dawn of political conventions, as the Anti-Masonic Party held the first national convention to nominate their presidential and vice presidential nominees. The party held the convention in Baltimore in September 1831. The National Republican Party and the Democratic Party also joined the "convention era" and followed with their own party conventions as well.

President Andrew Jackson was by his party for re-election, but they dumped his current vice president, John Calhoun, and nominated Martin Van Buren as his running mate. Van Buren would eventually climb the ladder to success, but the candidate nominated to run against him, John Sergeant, would never get a "chance to spit." Sergeant was a former congressman from Pennsylvania who won the nomination of the National Republican Party as the running mate to a well-known leader of his day, Henry Clay.

President Jackson won re-election over Henry Clay by the electoral vote of 219 to 49. Jackson's running mate, Martin Van Buren, easily defeated

Sergeant for the vice presidency in the Electoral College by the vote of 189 to 49. In that election, three other candidates received electoral votes for the second spot as well - William Walker with 30 votes, Henry Lee with 11 votes, and Amos Ellmaker with 7 votes.

While not winning national office, Sergeant had a long history of service in the government prior to his nomination and also after his defeat. He was from Pennsylvania and, before his national candidacy; he had been elected to the state House of Representatives. He was elected to congress in 1815 and served until 1823. He spent an additional term in Congress but was defeated for another term after his election in 1827. After his defeat, as the vice presidential candidate, he left the National Republican Party and joined the Whig Party. He was elected back to Congress in 1837 and served four years. While remaining active in politics he practiced law and would not return to national office politics, although he was mentioned briefly as a vice presidential possibility to Henry Clay's bid in 1844 as the Whig presidential candidate. The Whig convention selected another nominee and future "no chance to spit" candidate, Theodore Frelinghuysen. Sergeant died in 1852.

CHAPTER NINE
THE ONLY VICE PRESIDENTIAL CANDIDATE DEFEATED BY A VOTE OF THE SENATE

Francis Granger was an active politician with roots in the state House of Representatives from New York. He was nominated as the vice presidential candidate of the Whig Party in a very odd strategically planned election of 1836.

The Whig Party was determined to defeat Vice President Martin Van Buren's presidential bid and decided to nominate regional tickets under their party label in order to drive the election to the House of Representatives, where they could elect the next president. Although planned to succeed, it failed. Granger would actually have two running mates; both would lose as well, but in the process he would also become the only vice presidential candidate defeated for the vice presidency by the U.S. Senate.

Granger, a congressman who had been elected in 1835, was nominated to run with Daniel Webster and William Henry Harrison as part of the Whig regional strategy. John Tyler, another Whig, was selected as the running mate with Hugh White. In the end, Van Buren defeated Harrison overwhelmingly for the presidency by an electoral vote of 170 to 73. Hugh White and Daniel Webster received 26 and 14 votes, respectively.

Richard Mentor Johnson was considered a shoe-in for vice president based on the Van Buren result but, since the Electoral College is not bound by a state votes, Johnson would fall one vote shy of winning the second spot. The Virginia delegation casts its 23 electoral votes for Sen. William Smith. To this day, members of the Electoral College are not bound to vote as their state votes. The lack of a majority vote needed would lead to initiating the process as outlined by the 12th Amendment of the Constitution adopted in 1804, clearly stating that, if the vice presidential candidate did not receive the required majority, then the vice president would be elected by a majority vote of the U.S. Senate. The amendment spelled out that the top two contenders would be considered by the senators. When the Senate met, they easily selected Van Buren's running mate, Richard Mentor Johnson, over Francis Granger by a vote of 33 to 16. As of this writing, no other vice president in the history of the country has been elected this way. Francis Granger will go down in history as the only vice presidential candidate considered by and rejected by the U.S. Senate.

After his loss, he remained active in Whig politics, and continued to serve the remainder of his original congressional term. He was defeated for re-election to the seat, but would be re-elected to the seat after that defeat and serve in congress from 1839 to 1841. He was named the Postmaster General by his former running mate, President William Henry Harrison. This gave him the unique opportunity to follow in the family business, so to speak, since his father, Gideon, also had served as the Postmaster General under President Thomas Jefferson.

Granger stayed active in Whig politics, supporting the Compromise of 1850 and President Millard Fillmore in his efforts to hold off what would become the Civil War. He even helped to encourage the Whig Party to join efforts with the Constitutional Union Party in promoting peace and unity candidates in 1860. That movement led to a peace convention that would eventually fail to keep the country from splitting apart over the issue of slavery and states' rights.

He did not serve in elective office again and died in 1868.

CHAPTER TEN

TRAINED IN THE LAW BY AN INDVIDUAL WHO ALSO NEVER HAD A CHANCE TO SPIT

Technically speaking, before moving to the 1844 election, it is important to note that in the 1840 election no official vice presidential candidate was selected by the Democratic Party, so no one earned the opportunity to "not have a chance to spit."

Theodore Frelinghuysen ran for vice president in 1844 as the running mate of Henry Clay on the Whig Party ticket. Frelinghuysen was trained to be a lawyer by Richard Stockton, who ran for vice president without a running mate in 1820 as the Federalist Party candidate. They worked together in the law and enjoyed the same vice presidential fate.

Frelinghuysen entered politics in New Jersey and served as the Attorney General of that state for 17 years before his election to the U.S. Senate. He served in the Senate from 1829-1835, and then would leave the Senate to run for and be elected the Mayor of Newark. He had a strong religious background and was always described as being a notable Evangelical Christian. While it did not endear him to Catholics, he never shied away from his Christianity, even after being nominated for vice president by the Whigs. The election of 1844 was close in terms of the popular vote. Clay and Frelinghuysen would lose to Henry Polk and his running mate, George Dallas, even though they had a clever branding campaign slogan; "Hurray, Hurray, the country is arisen, vote for Clay and Frelinghuysen." Dallas defeated Frelinghuysen for vice president in the Electoral College by a vote of 170 to 108.

Frelinghuysen as a candidate had been serving as the Chancellor of New York University in 1839, and in defeat he continued in that capacity until 1850. He then went on to serve as the seventh President of Rutgers University. He also taught courses in international and constitutional law, as well as moral philosophy rhetoric. He served there from 1850 until 1862.

Frelinghuysen died in 1862 and, while he may never be remembered as a vice presidential candidate, he will always be known in the U.S. Senate where he served as the Christian politician who opposed Andrew Jackson and Indian Removal Act.

CHAPTER ELEVEN

AN UNUSUAL PATH.....FROM POLITICS TO POETRY

William Butler was the Vice Presidential candidate of the Democratic Party in the 1848 election. While he never "had a chance to spit," he ended his career relaxing and writing poetry.

The election of 1848 was the first national election that occurred on the same day throughout the country. It continues to this day to be held on the second Tuesday of November.

He was the running mate of Lewis Cass, a former Michigan Governor and U.S. Senator. Cass also served as the Secretary of War in the Andrew Jackson administration and as the Ambassador to France. Unfortunately, while perhaps more qualified to be president, he and Butler were opposed by a very poplar war general, Zachary Taylor. Butler was very familiar with Taylor, as he served under his command in the Mexican War, the war that propelled the Taylor candidacy.

Butler loved Kentucky and, after graduating in 1812 from Transylvania College, volunteered for military service in the War of 1812 to fight the

British and Indians. He was captured at Fort Niagara and eventually released, but this would prove to be a mistake since he quickly rejoined the military and fought the British and Indians in the victory at the Battle of the Thames in Canada. The battle helped American forces gain control of the Northwest Corridor. In politics, Americans love their generals as potential presidents, and Butler had two close ties to two generals who went on to be elected president. The victory at Thames, where Butler served, helped to secure hero status for a General William Henry Harrison, who went on to win the presidency. In the War of Mexico, Butler served as second in command to the future candidate that would defeat his ticket, General Zachary Taylor.

After the War of 1812, Butler returned to Kentucky set up a law practice and dabbled in politics. He served two terms in the state House of Representatives in 1817 and 1818. He was elected to the U.S. Congress in 1839 and served until 1843 when he was defeated in his campaign for the office of Governor of Kentucky. Butler returned to military service in the War of Mexico, serving as a Major General with General Taylor and was honored for his service in that war.

Butler would be nominated as the vice presidential candidate at the Democratic Party convention over a few other candidates that included the future President of the Confederacy, Sen. Jefferson Davis. In the election of 1848, the ticket of Cass and Butler stayed away from the slavery issue and were defeated by the Taylor-Fillmore ticket. Fillmore, who would become President on the death of Taylor, defeated Butler for vice presidency in the Electoral College by a vote of 163-127.

In defeat, Butler remained hopeful that the Union would remain united and, while owning slaves himself, he seemed opposed to the expansion of slavery. He was offered the political post to serve as territorial Governor of Nebraska in 1855 but declined the offer.

Butler would never return to national politics but did serve in 1861 as a delegate from Kentucky to the 1861 National Peace Convention that made a failed attempt at preventing the Civil War. He enjoyed being home after his military and political services, and remained a popular member of the community until his death in 1880.

Political people pursue interesting hobbies after politics, and Butler was no exception. He began writing poetry. His most popular poem was The Boatman's Horn:

O boatman! wind that horn again,
For never did the listening air,
Upon its lambent bosom bear
So wild, so soft, so sweet a strain!

What, though thy notes are sad and few,
By every simple boatman blown,
Yet is each pulse to nature true,

And melody in every tone.

CHAPTER TWELVE

LAST WHIG STANDING (FOR VEEP)

William Alexander Graham had the honor of being the final Whig vice presidential candidate, as both he and his presidential running mate, General Winfred Scott, were defeated in the landslide victory by the Democratic Party nominees Franklin Pierce and William King.

Graham had quite a political career going before his nomination on the national ticket. He had served in the North Carolina State House of Representatives, the U.S. Senate, Governor of North Carolina, and Secretary of the Navy under President Millard Fillmore. President Fillmore was denied his party's nomination at a split Whig convention that took 53 ballots to nominate General Winfred Scott. Unfortunately, the Scott-Graham ticket, in a losing effort, carried only four states out of 31, and the Whigs in disarray nationally would never field a ticket again.

After the defeat, Graham continued to be very active in politics, returning to North Carolina and winning election to the state Senate. As the nation began to divide with the Civil War, he did try to help lead the Constitutional Union Party in an effort to keep the country together. With those efforts failing and remaining active in North Carolina politics, he went on to be elected to the Confederate Senate, and in that role would eventually oppose the administration of President Jefferson Davis. When the Civil War ended and reconciliation of the nation took place, Graham would be "re-elected" to the U.S. Senate. Unfortunately, based on his previous service in the Confederate Senate and the slow process of readmitting North Carolina to the Union, Grahams' credentials were delayed and he never took his seat in the U.S. Senate, effectively ending his political service to the country.

While his "political career" ended, he did stay involved in working toward reconciliation and improving education after the disruption the war caused. He became an active member of the Board of Trustees of the Peabody Education Fund. This fund was created to give financial aid in schools for children of southern states. The Peabody Education Fund was created by George Peabody in 1867 to promote moral, intellectual, and industrial education.

Graham died in 1875 still being of service and respected by his community. He was elected as a delegate to the 1875 Constitutional Convention, but died before being able to serve.

CHAPTER THIRTEEN

THE FIRST REPUBLICAN VICE

PRESIDENTIAL CANDIDATE

William Dayton was the first nominee of the newly organized Republican Party for the vice presidential nomination in 1856. Dayton defeated Abraham Lincoln for the vice presidential nomination. Four years later, that defeated vice presidential candidate would win the Republican Party nomination for president and become the first Republican president.

Dayton was born in New Jersey. He launched his political career in 1837 as a member of the New Jersey legislature. He was appointed to the U.S. Senate in 1842 to fill a vacancy, but would win election to the seat on his own in 1845. He was, however, defeated for re-election in 1851.

President Franklin Pierce was not re-nominated by the Democratic Party, as the delegates selected James Buchanan, from Pennsylvania, as their nominee for president. The Republicans, meeting for their first national convention in Pennsylvania, selected James Fremont as their nominee for president. This election also featured a former president, Millard Fillmore, as the nominee of the

American Party. The vice presidential candidate of the Democratic Party was John Breckinridge, a former member of the U.S. Congress and U.S. Senate representing Kentucky. He would go on to become the youngest Vice President of the United States. Oddly enough, after his term as vice president, he would go on to become a member of Jefferson Davis' cabinet, as the Secretary of War for the Confederate States. The American Party nominated Andrew Donelson to run with Fillmore. While the American Party ran a distant third, it did take votes away from the other candidates and many politicos believe had they not been in the race, the Fremont-Dayton ticket would have been elected. Dayton was the running mate of John Fremont, a military officer and one of the first U.S. Senators from California.

The Republican Party was only a year old. Fremont was a controversial military man, an individual who did not win re-election to his California Senate seat and a Catholic. Dayton was part of the ticket of the new party that was committed to opposing the Kansas–Nebraska Act and the growth of slavery in America. Timing was not in favor of the Republicans, who would be accused by the Democratic Party of leading America to a possible civil war. Overall, the Fremont-Dayton team did well in the north by winning the 11 states. Unfortunately, Fremont did not win his home state of California, and Dayton did not carry his home state of New Jersey. Both states accounted for 11 electoral votes. The ticket did not win any southern states. When the electoral votes were counted, the Democratic ticket won, and Dayton was defeated for his chance to be vice president. Breckinridge would become the youngest Vice President of the United States, winning 174 electoral votes to Dayton's 114. Donelson collected eight votes.

After the election, Dayton would serve as the Attorney General for New Jersey from 1857 to 1861. The man he defeated for the vice presidential nomination at the Republican Party convention, Abraham Lincoln, would name him to the post of Minister of France in 1861. In his role as Minister to France, Dayton would serve Lincoln well, as he is credited with persuading Napoleon III not to recognize the Confederate States of America. Had he done so, it would have given the Confederate Sates a major boost and allowed them to use French ports for commerce. Dayton died in Paris in 1864.

CHAPTER FOURTEEN

THREE NATIONAL LEADERS VIE FOR THE OPPORTUNITY TO SPIT

The election of 1860 set in motion the Civil War and four distinct presidential candidates, along with their running mates. The four argued for the soul of the country. In the end, the country would break apart after a very spirited campaign, and the three defeated vice presidential candidates would go on without the opportunity to spit.

The Republican Party nominated the man they had not accepted as their vice presidential candidate in 1856, Abraham Lincoln, for President. The "Southern" Democratic Party nominated the youngest vice president in American history, John Breckinridge, as their presidential candidate. The "Northern" Democratic Party nominated an old nemesis of Lincoln, Andrew Douglas, for president and the Constitutional Union Party nominated John Bell, a presidential candidate who thought the country could still remain neutral over the issue of slavery.

The vice presidential nominees for all four parties were all active in the issues facing the country and would have served well in the office if elected. Hannibal Hamlin would eventually win with Lincoln but is often forgotten since he did not run for a second term with Lincoln. He was not very happy serving in the vice presidential role that would have led to his succession to the presidency had he been re-elected with Lincoln for that second term.

The Southern Democratic Party nominated U. S. Senator Joseph Lane for vice president. The Northern Democratic Party nominated Herschel Johnson. The Constitutional Union Party nominated Edward Everett. Oddly enough, all three had impressive credentials to be elected, and all three defeated men went on to various paths as the Civil War erupted in America.

The popular vote ended with the Lincoln-Hamlin ticket being elected with close to 40 percent of the vote, followed by Douglas-Johnson with 30 percent, Breckinridge-Lane with 18 percent and Bell-Everett with 12 percent. In theory, Johnson came close to having the opportunity to spit, but in reality with the Electoral College, it was Joseph Lane, with 72 electoral votes who came in second to Hannibal Hamlin.

When the Electoral College met, Hamlin was elected vice president by a vote of 103 to Lane's 72, Everett's 39, and Johnson's 12 electoral votes.

Based on the popular vote, history gives us a picture of a very spirited Lincoln-Douglas race. Herschel Johnson, who ran with Douglas, served previously as a U.S. Senator and Governor of Georgia. As a slave owner and southern political owner, he was added to the ticket because of the strength he could bring from southern voting states. After his defeat, he would go on to serve as a delegate to the Secession Convention of Georgia. In that role, he actually opposed secession from the Union. Eventually when Georgia did secede from the Union, he would go on to be elected as a Confederate Senator from the state. When the Civil War ended, Johnson would be very active in the reconstruction efforts and also was re-elected back to the U.S. Senate to represent Georgia. Unfortunately, he was not permitted to serve in the U.S. Senate due to his support and active government role in the Confederate States of America government. He would return to Georgia unseated as a U.S. Senator and serve as a Circuit Court judge. He died in 1880, remaining committed to reconstruction efforts and the unification of the United States of America.

Joseph Lane was elected to his first political office in 1821 and continued his political adventures through his candidacy for the vice presidency in the 1860 elections. Lane was first elected to the Indiana House of Representatives, serving there and in the Indiana State Senate. He served in the state senate position until 1846 when he resigned to enlist in the Indiana Regiment to fight in the Mexican-American War. His national presence was felt when, after he returned from his military involvement in the war, President James Polk named him the Territorial Governor of Oregon in 1849. He would seek and lose the presidential nomination for president in 1852 and won election to the U.S. Senate from Oregon in 1859. Lane was in favor of slavery and very supportive of the Confederate states. This support eventually would cost him his reputation in Oregon, as well as his political career in the U.S. Senate in 1861. The Senate is on record as noting a heated debate Lane had with future President Andrew Johnson, who was the senator from Tennessee at that time. Lane, in 1860, as senator from Oregon, accused Johnson of selling his birthright as a legitimate southerner because he was opposed to the breakup of the Union. Johnson, in turn, called Lane a traitor to the country. Four years later, Johnson would become the President of the United States on the death of Abraham Lincoln.

Joseph Lane, who ran second in electoral votes for the vice presidency, was finished politically after that race for his support of the Southern cause. He never re-entered politics after the loss of the vice presidency and did not actively participate in the Civil War in any capacity. He died in 1881, as a known slave holder, never having the opportunity to spit.

Historically speaking, many recognize the name of the Constitutional Union Party candidate for vice president, Edward Everett. He has been described as one of the greatest orators of that era, and he brought with him, as a candidate, an impressive resume to be elected. Leading up to his run for vice president, Everett, of Massachusetts, had served as the Minister to Great Britain, a U.S. Congressman, the Governor, and a U.S. Senator. He was a political giant and the main speaker at Gettysburg in 1863. The supposed headliner for the event spoke for two hours, but most Americans can actually recite the speech that almost was given by the man who spoke so briefly, President Abraham Lincoln. While Everett would continue to be noted as a great orator, even he would admit to Lincoln that his two-hour remarks were nothing compared to the short speech by Lincoln.

After his vice presidential defeat, Everett would not hold any elective office but would continue to tour the country giving lectures and speeches. He was supportive of Lincoln and died in 1865. America was blessed to have three unique candidates for the role of vice president who never had a chance to spit.

CHAPTER FIFTEEN

THE CIVIL WAR ELECTION THAT BRINGS

A SOUTERHNER TO THE WHITE HOUSE

The election of 1864 proved that American democracy and the constitution were still intact. Citizens today are somewhat surprised that in the midst of a civil war, the country did move forward with national elections for the White House. Two candidates would emerge in an election that observers thought would not happen because of the war. President Abraham Lincoln would again be the nominee of the Republican Party, temporarily renamed the National Union Party and Civil War. General George McClellan would be the Democratic Party nominee.

History is clouded due to the assassination of Lincoln, but at that time, Lincoln was not so assured of his renomination for a second term. He was challenged within the party due to the Civil War and circumstances surrounding it. Eventually, the party, as the National Union Party, did nominate him, along with a southerner, Tennessee Sen. Andrew Johnson. Johnson replaced Lincoln's vice president, Hannibal Hamlin, who did not relish the office and was very pleased to vacate it. Johnson was selected in a bold move to pick up support for a unified country. The

Republicans gambled on the Border States to the Confederacy to support the effort to reunite the country. As history shows, the unity plan somewhat worked, and with the war over an assassin's bullet put a "Southerner" in the White House.

The Democratic Party nominated Gen. George McClellan for president and a strong anti-war congressman, George Pendleton, as his running mate. The election itself was very much influenced by the direction of the war, as well as some political maneuvering by a temporary third-party campaign waged by Sen. John Fremont from California. His quick withdrawal from the race and support for Lincoln doomed Pendleton's opportunity to have a chance to spit.

George H. Pendleton served as a Congressman and U.S. Senator from Ohio. As the nominee in 1864, he opposed the war. The election did not go well for the McClellan-Pendleton ticket, as they lost in a landslide in the Electoral College. Andrew Johnson would be elected vice president by the Electoral College by a vote of 212 to 21.

Pendleton suffered a double loss that year, not only losing the vice presidency but also losing his congressional seat. His political fortunes kept slipping as he would lose the Democratic Party nomination for president in 1868. He would also lose a race for Governor of Ohio in 1869 to future President Rutherford B. Hayes.

After these losses, it was assumed his political career was over. But, as is often the case, there is life in politics after you lose a national campaign. He would become President of the Kentucky Central Railroad and seemed to be enjoying his private life. However, the political bug was too much to handle, and he re-entered politics after staying away for 10 years. In 1879, he was elected to the U.S. Senate. Unfortunately, he did not endear himself to his Ohio political cronies in that role and was not re-elected by the legislature to that position. The reason for his unpopularity was the famous legislation that he proposed and shepherded through the Senate. The people were very supportive of the concept that the political patronage system of awarding jobs to political supporters was not a good idea. The concept of developing a civil service system grew in popularity with everyone except the politicians, who would promise political jobs to supporters. The Pendleton Act, named for George Pendleton and still in force today, was designed to employ people in government jobs based on merit and capabilities. It also ensured that government workers would not simply be replaced based on who was elected. Again, the people supported the concept but the politicians not so much.

Once defeated for reappointment to the Senate, his political career was again assumed to be over and, for the most part, in terms of national politics, it was. However, his courageous act was rewarded by President Grover Cleveland, who appointed Pendleton as the Ambassador to Germany. Never again having the opportunity to spit, he served as ambassador until his death in 1889.

CHAPTER SIXTEEN

A REAL MODERN DAY CAMPAIGNER

Andrew Johnson's term was coming to an end. He failed to get his party to endorse him for a second term due to his impeachment process, as well as lingering issues from the Civil War reconstruction plan. The "United States" would now have the opportunity to elect a new president and vice president, and Francis Blair would join the ranks of those who would never have a chance to spit.

Blair was a candidate for vice president on the Democratic ticket that nominated, virtually against his will, Horatio Seymour for president. The ticket faced a formidable ticket nominated by the Republican Party, Gen. Ulysses S. Grant, and Speaker of the House, Schuyler Colfax.

Blair became involved in politics when he was appointed the Attorney General for the New Mexico Territory following his active participation in the Mexican-American War. After serving in that capacity, he returned to Missouri where he was elected to the U.S. Congress. He was defeated for re-election to that seat, won it back, and then resigned to become active in the Civil War. Even though he had been a strong supporter of Abraham Lincoln and the Republican Party, he left the party and became an active Democrat because of the Reconstruction policy.

This election was the first election to take place after the Civil War ended. Blair wanted to be vice president and worked very hard to secure the nomination. Generally, candidates did not actively participate in campaigns at that time, but Blair was very aggressive in campaigning for the ticket and did participate in many events to make a case for why Reconstruction would ruin the Union. At the time, he was characterized as very racist in terms of how he portrayed what Reconstruction would do to the country. Oddly, vice presidential candidates are given very little credit for helping to win or lose elections, but most Democratic Party leaders of the time believed that the aggressive campaign style of Blair and his anti-Reconstruction rhetoric caused the ticket to lose the election.

Schulyer Colfax was elected vice president over Blair by an Electoral College vote of 214 to 80. The Seymour-Blair ticket did win approximately 47 percent of the popular vote, but the electoral results were quite lopsided.

Blair enjoyed politics and remained active in politics following his national defeat. He would eventually be elected to the Missouri state legislature and was also appointed by the legislature to the U.S. Senate to fill an unexpired term. In 1872, he had a stroke and was not reelected to the U.S. Senate. He was appointed to serve as the State Superintendent of Insurance, a post he held until his death in 1875.

CHAPTER SEVENTEEN
A MAN OF MANY PARTIES FAILS TO WIN
THE VICE PRESIDENCY

The 1872 losing candidate for vice president loved to change political parties. Generally, most candidates do not shift positions or change parties very often. He did it six times. He also was involved in a duel, which again, makes him a very interesting candidate to observe.

In an odd set of circumstances, Benjamin Brown, a former newspaper man, ran on the Liberal Republican ticket with Horace Greeley, a famous newspaper publisher from New York. This election process had twists and turns to the very end, including the decision by the Democratic Party not to offer a candidate but to support a Republican alternative. Also, Greeley, who ran with Brown, died before the Electoral College would meet, so that added a mystery as to how the popular vote candidates differed from the final electoral vote count.

President Ulysses S. Grant was nominated for a second term by the Republican Party. His vice president, Schulyer Colfax, was not renominated. The party chose U. S. Sen. Henry Wilson to run on the ticket with Grant. Opponents within the party not happy with the Grant selection organized and supported a Liberal Republican ticket of Greely and Brown. Meanwhile, the Democratic Party members, frustrated within their own party, decided to support the Liberal Republican movement thinking it would be the only way to defeat Grant and capture the White House to serve their agenda.

Brown had an interesting political career that began with his return to Missouri after law school to join his cousin's law firm. They were two famous politically savvy lawyers, Frank Blair and Montgomery Blair. He won election to the Missouri state legislature in 1852, 1854, and 1856. He joined the Missouri Democrat as the editor and was very active in expressing political views on slavery. In an odd case, his political views clashed with the Lt. Governor of Missouri, Thomas Reynolds, which resulted in a duel in which he was wounded. Brown always seemed to be controversial in his opinions, which caused him not to be re-elected in 1858. That would also cost him his job as the editor of the Missouri Democrat. Brown would fight in the Civil War, believed in freeing the slaves (an opinion which differed earlier), and became involved in the Radical Republican Party. He returned to Missouri where he was elected to fill a vacated U.S. Senate seat. Not a candidate for a full term, he would flip parties again, and would become a Liberal

Republican candidate for Governor of Missouri. Winning the office of governor, propelled him to national politics, where he would be the vice presidential running mate of Horace Greeley.

The election was notable for a variety of side events that were going on. The Democratic Party did not officially field a candidate but supported the Greeley-Brown ticket. The Women's Suffragette movement, organizing as the National Woman's Suffrage Association, nominated a woman, Victoria Woodhull, for president. Her vice presidential running mate, who never accepted the nomination, was Frederick Douglass. Some members within the Democratic Party organized their own convention, nominating a candidate who refused to be a candidate. However, their vice presidential candidate was John Quincy Adams II. Adding additional chaos to the political side-shows going on, Horace Greeley, who was soundly defeated in the popular vote, died before the Electoral College could meet to cast their votes.

With this political circus going on, President Grant easily won re-election, winning 31 of the 37 states. Benjamin Brown would go on to lose the vice presidency to Sen. Henry Wilson by a vote of 286 to 47. Nine other candidates would share 19 other votes. (John Quincy Adams II, of the Straight-Out Democratic Party, did not receive any electoral votes for vice president).

The vice presidential campaign effectively ended his political career. He would return to his law practice and change his political party affiliation yet again by joining the Democratic Party. He died in 1885.

CHAPTER EIGHTEEN

A SUCCESSFUL BUINESS LEADER REJOINS THE POLITICAL ARENA

With the wounds still healing from the intense 1876 election, President Rutherford Hayes, as promised, decided not to seek re-election, leaving the country with a fresh election to choose their new president and vice president. The Democrats nominated James Garfield. His running mate, who defeated William Hayden English for the second spot, would become President of the United States due to the assassination of Garfield.

English served briefly in Congress representing Indiana, before leaving office to pursue a successful career in the business world. His entry on the national scene was quite unexpected due to his very successful lifestyle "after politics." He had a very interesting brush with history when, as a congressman, he teamed up to work on a critical piece of legislation, the Kansas-Nebraska Act, with a fellow congressman, William Stephens, the future (and only) vice president of the Confederate States of America. This legislation would allow western territories to vote on accepting or rejecting slavery within their state boarders and repealed the original Missouri Compromise legislation. English would serve in Congress until 1860, before giving up political life for a more lucrative business career.

Before being nominated for the vice presidency, English became the first president of the First National bank in Indianapolis. He was extremely active in the business community. He would begin accumulating real estate in the area and helped to develop the theater district within the area. The "Grand Opera House," which he helped to build and develop, opened in 1880. At the height of his business success, he was nominated to return to politics and run for the vice presidency with Gen. Winfield Hancock. The popular vote was rather close, as the Hancock-English ticket would lose nationally to the Garfield-Arthur ticket by less than 2,000 votes. However, as is often the case, the Electoral College vote was dramatic as Chester Arthur was elected vice president over English by a wide margin vote of 214 to 155.

English would again "exit the political word," this time for good, and returned home to continue with his business development programs. He would build a major hotel, as well help to finance a Soldiers and Sailors Monument. He became well known as a business leader in the community. He would serve as an Indiana historian and publisher of two historical books about the region. His hotel that was connected to the Opera House was a major development in the area known as the "Circle" and stood there until it was demolished in 1948. While never having the opportunity to spit, in the state, he is recognized for his political service and, in the city of Indianapolis, he is recognized for business growth and development. English died in 1896.

CHAPTER NINETEEN

NEVER HAD A CHANCE TO SPIT BUT

REMEMBERED IN STATE SONG WITH

ABRAHAM LINCOLN

The 1880 vice presidential candidate, one of those who would have made the "never had a chance to spit" list, Thomas Hendricks, was elected vice president running with Grover Cleveland. Since he captured the second spot eventually, he is not part of this book.

In 1884, the Cleveland-Henderson ticket defeated the Republican ticket of James Blaine and John Logan. Logan was a well-respected military and political leader from Illinois. Anyone traveling to Washington D.C. can see the remarkable sculpture honoring Logan. The monument is of Gen. Logan riding a horse on what is now Logan Circle.

John Logan, an attorney, served in the Mexican-American War and was elected to the state Senate of Illinois. He would go on to be elected to the U.S. Congress. He would leave congress to serve actively in the Civil War. After the war, he was elected to serve in Congress, and then elected to serve the state of Illinois as a U.S. Senator. Due to his service in the war, as well as his political stature, he is well known for leading the efforts to create "Memorial Day," previously called, "Decoration Day." This day was dedicated to taking time to decorate cemeteries and honor those who died in serving the country.

Logan had made losing attempts at being the presidential nominee of his party in the past before being selected to run for vice president on the ticket headed by former Speaker of the House and U.S. Sen. James Blaine. It was a very politically experienced ticket.

The election between the two major parties did turn in to personal attacks, with Cleveland being elected by a close popular vote. The final count showed both candidates collecting 48 percent of the vote, with two minor parties collecting the other 2 percent. When the electoral votes were counted, the ticket of Grover-Hendricks was elected over Blaine and Logan. Logan would lose the vice presidency in the Electoral College by a vote of 219 to 182 votes. After his defeat, he would return briefly to the U.S. Senate, dying in 1886, less than two years after the national campaign.

In addition to being honored with the Logan memorial, he is also honored with his name being included in the Illinois state song. The song mentions only two other individuals, Ulysses S. Grant and Abraham Lincoln.

CHAPTER TWENTY

THIS FUTURE VICE PRESIDENTIAL LOSER HELPED ELECT HIS OLD OPPONENT PRESIDENT

Allen Thurman was defeated for the vice presidency, running with President Grover Cleveland. He was nominated as Cleveland's new running mate because Vice President Thomas Hendricks, who was serving with President Cleveland, died in office. At that time in our history, there was not a constitutional procedure in place to fill the vacancy in the event of the death of a vice president while serving in office.

Allen Thurman was a career politician with a good political reputation for working with both political parties. This ability to work on both sides of the aisle earned him the respect of the Senate members with whom he served. He was first elected to Congress, representing Ohio, in 1845, serving one term before being selected to serve as a member of the Ohio Supreme Court. As fate would have it, he had two interesting encounters with a future President of the United States, Rutherford B. Hayes.

In 1867, Thurman ran a losing campaign for governor against the Republican Hayes. Thurman would move on and be elected by the legislative branch to be elected to the U.S. Senate. Two years later, in 1875, as a senator, he ran for governor again against Rutherford Hayes with the same losing result. Hayes would become the Republican Party's nominee for president, and the man he defeated for governor twice would play a key role in the constitutional crisis that would eventually elect him the President of the United States.

Thurman had become the leader of the Democrats in the Senate. In the intense election of 1876, the Electoral College was deadlocked on its votes for the presidency between Democratic candidate Samuel Tilden and Rutherford Hayes due to major challenges from four states on their electors. Without a settlement, neither candidate would receive the required 185 votes to be elected president. This was a serious crisis that had to be resolved. It was Thurman, as one of the leaders of the Senate, who proposed the creation of an Electoral College Commission to review the disputed electoral votes not counted, so that a major constitutional crisis could be avoided. Oddly, that was the election that had Thomas Hendricks, the future vice president under Grover Cleveland, on the ticket with Tilden. The "Compromise of 1877," which Thurman is credited for helping to organize and implement, was made up of five U.S. Senators from each party, five members of the U.S. Congress from each party, and five members of the Supreme Court. This "Compromise Committee," supposedly an unbiased group, had the responsibility to review the disputed 20 electoral votes of Oregon, Louisiana, South Carolina, and Florida. In reality, the commission was made up of eight Republicans and eight Democrats who would eventually vote on party lines that resulted in the election of Hayes over Tilden by an Electoral College vote of 185-184. The compromise Thurman worked so hard to create rewarded his old gubernatorial opponent the presidency, even though Tilden actually won approximately 51 percent of the popular vote in the election.

Thurman would serve in the Senate until 1881. The Republicans in Ohio took control of the legislature and did not re-elect him. He would return to his law practice in Ohio and remain active in politics, even turning down an additional opportunity to be the Democratic nominee for governor in 1887. He was nearing the end of his life when the Democratic Party nominated him to be the running mate of Grover Cleveland in 1888. He would not be overly active in the campaign, and would lose the vice presidency to Levi Morton by a vote of 233 to 168. In this election, President Cleveland was defeated for re-election to the presidency by the same electoral vote to Benjamin Harrison. Of course, as history shows, Cleveland would go on to become the only president ever defeated for re-election and then eventually re-elected president. Thurman, who did not run with Cleveland in his successful bid in 1892, retired from the political arena, returning to his law practice in Ohio. He died in 1895, never having the opportunity to spit.

CHAPTER TWENTY ONE
PROOF THAT THERE IS LIFE AFTER NOT
GETTING A CHANCE TO SPIT

The election of 1892 was an interesting one in that the president who was defeated four years earlier was re-nominated for president and would become the only president to have served, been defeated, and then subsequently be re-elected president. Grover Cleveland, who actually won the popular vote four years earlier in his re-election bid, this time around won both the popular and electoral vote to win the office, defeating President Benjamin Harrison.

Whitelaw Reid would have the honor of being part of this unique history by being the running mate of Harrison. Reid was nominated to replace the incumbent Vice President, Levi Morton. Depending on a variety of sources, some indicate that Harrison did not want his vice president to serve again, and Morton seemed to be disinterested in another term as well.

Reid was the former Ambassador to France, but a journalist at heart. He was the powerful owner of the New York Tribune, a paper he purchased after the death of Horace Greeley. As the owner of the publication, he was quick to purchase the important technology of the day to streamline the publication. Journalism was his roots. He actually was a war correspondent during the Civil War and did reports on the Battle at Gettysburg and Shiloh. He eventually joined the Tribune, the paper Greeley owned, to further Republican causes and interests. He had no problem, after purchasing the paper, to do the same. His active role in promoting Republican issues certainly would bring him political recognition that not only led to the vice presidential nomination but future government appointments as well.

The rematch election was focused on economic issues, and Harrison had proved to be unpopular during the term. Reid picked an inopportune time to seek the vice presidency. In the end, the Harrison-Reid ticket would lose to Cleveland and Adlai Stevenson by a margin of over 390,000 popular votes. They would lose the Electoral College vote by more than 132 votes. Several minor parties also fielded candidates, with one of the parties, the Populist Party, collecting some electoral votes as well. Technically, Stevenson defeated Reid and Populist candidate James Field for vice president. Stevenson received 277 votes, Reid 145, and Field 22 votes.

Following his election defeat, Reid did not go in to the woodwork. He continued his partisan networking with meetings and social events. He was a modern day networker before it was fashionable. While he would not seek national office ever again, he did enjoy political appointments. In 1897, he represented the United States at the Diamond Jubilee of Queen Victoria. Five years later, he was supposed to represent America at the Coronation of King Edward VII. (The coronation was delayed.) In 1898, he would serve as a member of the Peace Commission for the Spanish-American War. His national and international recognition would continue with honorary degrees from Oxford, Manchester, St. Andrews, Victoria, Dartmouth, Princeton, and Yale. In 1905, he was named the U.S. Ambassador to Great Britain. Reid was first selected for the position by President Theodore Roosevelt and would retain the position during the administration of President Howard Taft. Reid died in office as the ambassador in 1912.

CHAPTER TWENTY TWO

TWO RUNNING MATES TRY TO GET A CHANCE TO SPIT

The election of 1896 was unique in that a major party candidate and political legend had actually two running mates for the vice presidency. Williams Jennings Bryan, who ran for president three times, was nominated by both the Democratic Party and the Populist Party.

It is historically odd that Bryan, as the candidate of both the Democratic Party and the Populist Party, never really announced who he preferred as a vice president. Obviously, at Democratic rallies he supported Sewall. At Populist gatherings his choice was Thomas Watson.

Arthur Sewall was the nominee of the Democratic Party for vice president, and Thomas Watson was the Populist nominee for vice president. Both men would receive electoral votes for the office, but neither would get elected.

Sewall was an odd choice for a running mate. It seemed he won the nomination based on his wealth, not his political experience. His political resume includes a losing run for the U.S. Senate. His very limited political resume does include service as a councilman from his home town in Maine. He is best known for his wealth and business background, which was far more impressive. He and his brother Edward launched the E&A Sewall Company, a ship building company, in 1854. He would become president of the Sewall Company in 1884. His company built the ship, "Vigilant," which captured the "Sumter," the infamous Confederate ship during the Civil War. Sewall amassed a fortune, and certainly his money was an added advantage to the Bryan-Sewall ticket. He would also become the president of Maine Central Railroad and the Bath National Bank.

Sewall actually ran second in the vice presidential Electoral College vote. He won 149 votes in a losing campaign to the eventual vice president, Gary Hobart. He would not run for national political office ever again, returning to his business world by serving as president of the Bath National Bank until he died in 1900.

Thomas Watson was quite the opposite of Seward. Watson had a powerful political resume by comparison. He was extremely active in politics before and after his national run for vice president. He would also run in a national campaign as the nominee of his party for president.

Watson was a politically active individual who would run the spectrum of political beliefs over time. He is probably most famous for leading the effort to get free mail delivery to rural areas. Up until the enactment of the legislation he supported and would see signed in to law, many citizens within rural areas either paid for mail delivery or had to travel to their respective town to pick up their mail. Watson initially was considered too liberal in his political outlook when first elected to Congress in 1890. He strongly supported government ownership of steamship lines, telephone companies, and telegraph companies. He was against national banks and thought Blacks should have the right to vote. He was a big supporter of the concept of direct elections by the people of U.S. Senators. He was a "real populist," so much so that after being elected to Congress, he joined up with the Populist members, rejecting his own Democratic Party. He was the Populist choice for Speaker of the House, which of course, he was not elected to since they had less than 10 members in the Congress that year. His choice to join them cost him is re-election.

Watson was nominated to be William Jennings Bryan's running mate as a member of the Populist Party. He was defeated for vice president, winning only 27 electoral votes, running third in the national campaign.

After his defeat, Watson continued to remain extremely active in politics. His political views began to shift from his original liberal thoughts. He ran for president as a White Supremacist in 1908, and was viewed as anti-Black, anti-Semitic, and anti-Catholic as the years went on. He would leave the Populist movement and return to the Democratic Party, and was elected in 1921 to the U.S. Senate as a Democrat. Unfortunately for him, he would not serve the term as he died in 1922.

CHAPTER TWENTY THREE
YOU'RE NEVER TO OLD TO RUN
FOR VICE PRESIDENT

Henry Davis was nominated for vice president when he was 80 years old. He still holds the record as the oldest vice presidential candidate on a national party ticket. The 1904 election leap frogs the 1900 election, which re-elected William McKinley to the presidency. The defeated candidates for president and vice president were William Jennings Bryan and former Vice President Adlai Stevenson. Apparently, Stevenson didn't mind the office he once held and decided to give it an unsuccessful try. Having already served in it, he did in fact get his chance to spit.

In 1904, the Democrats, after failing twice with Bryan, decided to nominate Alton Parker to run against incumbent President Theodore Roosevelt. Roosevelt succeeded to the office after the assassination of McKinley. They nominated Charles Fairbanks for vice president, who would face the very wealthy and well connected Harry Davis.

Davis was born very poor, but through hard work he rose through the ranks and would eventually create the Potomac and Piedmont Coal and Railway Company. He also created the Harry W. Davis Company. As a businessman he stayed very connected to politics and, even though he was a Democrat, he was very impressed with Republican President Abraham Lincoln. During the Civil War, Davis was not supportive of his home state of Virginia's decision to support the Confederacy and worked very hard to encourage a split that created, in 1865, the state of West Virginia. Lincoln wrestled with the idea to create the state of West Virginia and is immortalized with a famous statue that sits in front of the West Virginia capitol wearing slippers and a robe pondering the decision. When the state was created, Davis was elected to the West Virginia House of Delegates. In 1869, he was elected a state senator, and in 1870, with his political connections and wealth, was elected to the U.S. Senate. Davis, having completed two terms in the U.S. Senate, actually had the support of many party members to be the vice presidential candidate of the Democratic Party in 1884 but decided not to be a candidate.

Davis would continue to be very active in politics and business when he left the U.S. Senate. He and his son-in-law, Stephen Elkins, partnered to build the Davis Coal and Coke Company. Staying active in business and politics, and with substantial wealth, Davis was the perfect vice presidential candidate for Parker in that he could help fund the campaign. When most people are looking at life as ending,

Davis was willing, at age 80, to join the national ticket as his running mate.

The election was not close, as the Roosevelt-Fairbanks ticket defeated Parker-Davis with 56 percent of the popular vote. Davis would collect 140 electoral votes for vice president, losing to Fairbanks who won 336 electoral votes. Although defeated at age 80, he remained active in politics and business. He would be a key player on the Pan American Railway Committee, linking North and South America for continued economic growth through the rail system. He also used his wealth to finance the Davis & Elkin College of West Virginia. He has grown to be well respected in West Virginia historical circles for his political involvement, business acumen, and philanthropic efforts for the college. Davis, who "never had a chance to spit," died in 1916, 12 years after his defeat for the vice presidency.

CHAPTER TWENTY FOUR
NEVER FIGHT FOR A LAW THAT COULD COME BACK TO BITE YOU

John Kern, a U.S. Senator and a man destined to miss an opportunity to spit, has the dubious distinction of fighting to change the law on how U.S. Senators were elected. He strongly believed and championed legislation to allow the people to directly vote to elect their U.S. Senator. It seemed like a good plan and a great idea. Unfortunately, when the law was enacted, the "people" voted to send Kern into political retirement, as his opponent defeated his re-election bid.

Kern was nominated by the party convention to run with William Jennings Bryan. Historically, the New York Times had fun with their nominations in saying that the Democrats nominated a two-time presidential loser for president and a two-time loser for governor for vice president. Apparently, they knew their eventual ticket for national office would also suffer the same fate.

John Kern started his political career as an Indiana state senator in 1893. He served for four years and unsuccessfully ran for governor in 1900 and 1904. He lost both elections, but being a political activist led him to be chosen at the national convention for the vice presidential nomination. The ticket of Bryan and Kern was defeated in a landslide by Howard Taft and James Sherman. The Electoral College gave Sherman 321 votes for vice president and 162 to Kern. This was the third and final defeat for Bryan for president.

You would assume, after two failed elections for governor and the defeat for the vice presidency, that the political career of Kerns would be over. However, that was not the case; in reality, it seemed it was just the start of a new political life. Kerns continued to show political strength and would be elected to the U.S. Senate in 1910, and technically become the first Senate Majority Leader in the Senate. He was a strong leader and led legislation that created the effort for approval of the amendment to the constitution for an income tax. He also became actively involved in leading the fight for child labor laws, as well as better working conditions in West Virginia coal mines. He led the efforts for the adoption of the 17th amendment, allowing the people to directly elect their U.S. Senators, instead of party legislatures. He was a major proponent of voters deciding directly who should represent them in the Senate. In 1916, the voters decided he should not represent them, and Kern was defeated for re-election to the Senate. He died in 1917, a mere five months after leaving the body where he played such an active role in national legislation and law.

CHAPTER TWENTY FIVE

VICE PRESIDENTIAL CANDIATE OF A

THIRD PARTY COMES ON STRONG

In the United States, third parties never fare well in national elections, but Hiram Johnson, running with Theodore Roosevelt, proved the exception. Nicholas Butler, who ran on the Republican ticket with President Taft, suffered the loss as a major party vice presidential nominee.

Hiram Johnson was a dynamo. He left his mark on California and the nation. He started his career in 1873 as an attorney and would be elected to the State Assembly 1894. He served a term but would return and serve again in 1907. Johnson, as a progressive Republican, was elected Governor of California and started his progressive agenda immediately. Johnson was a key leader in the reform movement that helped to launch the Progressive Party nationally. He became a major leader of this new party effort, and the Progressives would impact elections locally, statewide, and nationally in America for a brief period. The Progressive Party he built in opposition to the incumbent president, Howard Taft, organized and nominated Theodore Roosevelt and Johnson as a national ticket that shook what appeared to be a safe two-party system dominated by the Republicans and Democrats.

In the 1912 election, the efforts of the Progressive movement took on the Republican Party that was suffering with major splits within its ranks. With the three-way race that included Republicans crossing over, Woodrow Wilson would win the presidency running with Thomas Marshall as his running mate. Wilson and Marshall would only capture 41 percent of the national vote; however, they did win the majority of popular votes in 40 states. The Electoral College would give Thomas Marshall 435 votes for vice president, the third-party candidate Johnson received 88 votes, and the major party nominee, Nicholas Burton, an embarrassing eight votes.

In defeat Hiram Johnson would not be silenced. He was the Governor of California and the leader of the Progressive movement. He used his political power to launch major reform legislation in the state. He targeted successfully major efforts in California for workman's compensation laws, child labor laws, and laws impacting public utilities. He won two terms as governor and would go on to be elected to the U.S. Senate, where he was re-elected five times. He returned to the Republican Party after the Progressive Party began to wither away. Johnson would seek and lose the Republican Presidential nomination in 1924. Although he failed to win the GOP nod, he continued to remain in the Senate and proved to be a major national leader. He maintained the attitude throughout his political career never to be beholden to political parties or bosses, and viewed his political service as personally representing the people who elected him to office. He served in the U.S. Senate until his death in 1945, and remains the longest U.S. Senator to serve the state of California.

CHAPTER TWENTY SIX

YOU WOULDN'T ELECT MY BROTHER PRESIDENT, HOW ABOUT ME FOR VICE PRESIDENT

Before we talk about the brother of a famous political leader running for vice president, please note that the election of 1916 and 1920 are not covered in this book. The reason for eliminating both losing vice presidential candidates is because one had already served as vice president and the other would go on to be elected president, a step above the right to spit.

In 1916, former Vice President Charles Fairbanks was nominated on the Republican national ticket to run again for vice president with the only U.S. Supreme Court Justice ever nominated for president, Charles Evans Hughes. Since Fairbanks had served and had his chance to spit, he is not covered in the book. The same goes for the 1920 election, in which the only person ever elected president four times, Franklin D. Roosevelt, was defeated as the vice presidential nominee of the Democratic party, running with James Cox. While Roosevelt "never had a chance to spit," he certainly managed to win the grander prize of the presidency and, therefore, is not part of the book.

In the 1924 election, the Democrats nominated the brother of their famous three-term losing presidential nominee, William Jennings Bryan. Obviously, history books seldom speak of Charles Bryan, but he had a great love for politics and entered the national arena following the death of his brother William.

Charles and William enjoyed politics. Charles was elected to City Council and subsequently Mayor of Lincoln, Nebraska, in 1915. He would make a losing effort to run for Governor of Nebraska in 1916 before joining his brother William, a congressman, as his secretary and business agent. As his brother's national campaigns all failed, Charles would run for Governor of Nebraska and be elected. In 1924, Charles, with outstanding political contacts and great name recognition, would be nominated by the Democrats as the vice presidential nominee to run with John Davis. Davis, of West Virginia, was nominated on the 103rd ballot to be the nominee. The weary long vote of those in attendance at the convention signaled a disastrous campaign to follow. Davis would face Calvin Coolidge, who became president upon the death of President Harding. Coolidge was elected in a three-way race by a landslide vote, winning 52 percent of the vote over the two campaigns of the Democratic and Progressive party nominees. The electoral vote shows that Bryan was defeated for vice president by an electoral vote of 382 votes for Charles Dawes, Bryan with 136, and the minor party campaign of Burton Wheeler who had 13 votes.

After his defeat for the vice presidency, Charles Bryan returned to politics in Nebraska. He took over the Commoner, a national newspaper his brother created for his political views, and threw himself back in to campaigning. He ran for his old gubernatorial job and lost in 1926 and in 1928. Not to be deterred, he ran again and was elected back to the old job as governor, serving from 1931 to 1935. He 1934, as his term was ending; he ran a losing campaign for the U.S. Senate, followed by a loss for governor in 1938, a loss in 1940 for Congress, and a final losing race in 1942 for governor. Obviously, both Bryan brothers enjoyed the sport of a political campaign. Charles died in 1945.

CHAPTER TWENTY SEVEN

A POLITCAL RESUME FIT FOR THE OFFICE, BUT NOT TO BE

If any candidate seemed fit to be vice president, Joseph "Joe" Robinson was the man. His political experience would be selected by any computer today as a match for the job.

Robinson had the dubious honor of being the running mate to the first Roman Catholic nominated for the presidency by a major political party, Alfred Smith. Smith, Governor of New York, would find being a Catholic in America was not a national political asset in 1928, and the campaign would suffer an incredible landslide defeat to the father of the depression, Herbert Hoover.

Robinson was a political rising star from day one. He was elected a state senator from Arkansas in 1895, and would go on to be elected to the U.S. Congress four times. He resigned from Congress when he was elected Governor of Arkansas in 1913, but served only briefly when elected to the U.S. Senate to fill a vacancy of Sen. Jeff Davis, who had died in office. Robinson, known as a fighter in the U.S. Senate, would eventually win four consecutive terms in the Senate. In 1923, he would become the

Democratic Party leader in the Senate, a position that he relished and used to pass legislation within the body. This national prominence would obviously propel him on the national scene, and in 1924 he sought but lost the Democratic Party nomination for president. However, in 1928, being a presence on the national stage, backed up with impressive political service, Robinson would be nominated to run for vice president with Governor Alfred Smith. Anti-Catholic feelings abounded in that era, and Robinson was not afraid to take on the fight to defend his running mate. The same pugnacious attitude he had as a senator carried with him in the campaign. He was not afraid to challenge fellow senators concerned with the Pope and the Catholic Church.

The Smith-Robinson ticket seemed doomed from the get-go, and Herbert Hoover and his running mate, Charles Curtis, would win in a landslide. The Electoral College vote for vice president gave Curtis 444 votes and Robinson 87. The popular vote had the Hoover-Curtis ticket winning with 58 percent of the vote to 41 percent. After losing the race, Robinson would continue serving in the Senate, and was elected the Senate Majority Leader. As leader, he ruled with an iron fist, and history records he was not afraid to yell, kick, punch, and fight for causes he believed in or votes he expected his colleagues to make. Robinson was the leader who helped marshal into law the key legislation that Franklin D. Roosevelt proposed to get the country back on track after the depression.

Franklin D. Roosevelt ushered in remarkable bills supported by the Democrats that did help America get back on its feet economically. Roosevelt used the strong leadership of Robinson to make this happen. Robinson in his final days would find himself in a key role that supported Roosevelt in his efforts to stack the U.S. Supreme Court with additional justices. This stacking of the court debate was extremely intense in the Senate. Some historians indicate that the additional fire and brimstone that Robinson brought to the argument was because he was promised a seat on the court by the president. No one knows if that is really true; the battle was intense and the argument raged on in the Senate. The arguments took a toll on Robinson, and before that vote took place, he died of a heart attack in 1937, a "fighting" senator to the end.

CHAPTER TWENTY EIGHT

REPUBLICAN VP CANDIDATE COMES UP

SHORT BUT SERVES THE NATION

AS A DEMOCRAT

Before moving on to the 1936 election, it is worth noting that the man who was elected vice president in 1932 is the reason for the title of this book. It was John Nance Gardner, elected vice president with Franklin D. Roosevelt, who said the vice presidency was not worth a warm bucket of spit. Interestingly enough, he ran for re-election anyway and defeated Frank Knox, who wanted a chance to spit.

Frank Knox was a newspaper man with a military past. He served as a rough rider with Theodore Roosevelt in Cuba during the Spanish-American war. He would serve as a Major in the U.S. Army, and when he returned to get involved in newspapers he would eventually actively support, as a Republican, the Progressive Party candidacy of Teddy Roosevelt for president.

Knox was the founding editor of the New Hampshire newspaper that in our day plays such key role in the first presidential primary, the

Manchester Leader. He would eventually go on to become the publisher and part owner of the Chicago Daily News. In 1936, he was nominated to run with Alf Landon who, up until George McGovern, suffered the most notable presidential loss by carrying only two states. Knox was a bit more active in the race for the ticket than Alf Landon, who seemed to disappear from the campaign scene after being nominated. The Electoral College would re-elect John Nance Gardner as vice president over Knox by a vote of 523 to eight. The Landon-Knox ticket would win 36 percent as Roosevelt and Gardner coasted to a 61 percent popular vote victory winning 46 states. After the loss, his career was not over.

As early as 1933, Knox was very suspicious of the Japanese Americans living in the country and actually thought more surveillance should be put in to place to secure America against possible sabotage in the country. After Pearl Harbor was bombed, he was a major voice to ensure internment camps were created. Knox, a strong Republican, would become the Secretary of the Navy, appointed by Democrat President Franklin Roosevelt. He added bipartisan support to Roosevelt's war efforts and was instrumental in expanding the naval forces of the country. It actually proved to be his second stint at supporting the Roosevelts, after having supported Teddy over the Republican nominee Howard Taft for president. Knox would never serve America as

Republican vice president but did serve a Democratic president and America as a loyal Secretary of the Navy. Knox died in 1944 while the Secretary of the Navy but is known for carrying out FDR's directions faithfully.

CHAPTER TWENTY NINE

HE LOST THE VICE PRESIDENCY IN ONE

OF THE MOST HISTORIC ELECTIONS

OF OUR TIME

George Washington set a precedent that presidents would serve only two terms. It was never a law until after Franklin D. Roosevelt won his fourth term. Charles McNary was hoping that enough anti-third term sentiments would rally behind him and his running mate, Wendell Willkie, to be elected.

Charles McNary was an attorney from Oregon who launched his political career working for his brother, who was the District Attorney from their home county. He was appointed to the Oregon State Supreme Court in 1913, a position he held for two years before being defeated for re-election to the position. He would become the chairman of the Republican Party in Oregon, which was instrumental in his appointment, by the governor, to fill the U.S. Senate left vacant by the death of Sen. Harry Lane. McNary, who had lost that Supreme Court bid in Oregon by a narrow margin, was elected by the citizens to the U.S. Senate. They would re-elect him five times to that Senate seat, giving him a dynamic political career even after his defeat for the vice presidency.

In the Senate, McNary was elected the minority leader of the Republicans. He was very supportive of the United States entering the League of Nations and in opposition to the Ku Klux Klan. With the depression and the election of Franklin D. Roosevelt, McNary would do his best to be supportive in his efforts to get the country up and running again. He put America first and, in a strange political twist, McNary opposed the nomination of Wendell Willkie for president and was supportive of Roosevelt's efforts, and was actually nominated by the Republicans for vice president to run with Willkie.

There were very mixed emotions going on in America in 1940 when McNary ran. Some pundits actually believed the ticket of Willkie and McNary would win because of FDR's decision to seek a third term. Vice President John Garner was not on the ticket, so McNary's opponent was Henry Wallace. Wallace was the Agricultural Secretary and even after the vice presidency would have a very interesting political career, including a run for the presidency against FDR's successor, Harry Truman. The election focused on two emotional issues. One issue was the question of whether a president should be elected a third time. Clearly, it was legal, but George Washington set the precedent for two terms. The other emotional issue was the impending possible involvement of the United States entering the World War. The idea of "changing horses in mid steam" was circulating throughout the country. It was the idea that this was not a time for change.

In the end, the president and his new running mate, Wallace, easily defeated the Republican ticket, capturing 54 percent of the popular vote. The Electoral College elected Wallace vice president over McNary by a vote of 449 to 38.

Wallace would go on to be miserable about the position that McNary would lose. He was not a happy vice president, finding the job very boring as the president of the Senate. McNary, on the other hand, enjoyed the Senate, and even as the opposition minority leader would be very supportive of Roosevelt in his plans. He died in 1944 as a senator of the United States. In a very odd twist of fate, Wendell Willkie would die six months after McNary. Historically, it is the only time on record that a national ticket would die during the term for which they sought the presidency and vice presidency.

CHAPTER THIRTY

THIS VEEP CANDIDATE CHALLENGED THE MAN WHO DEFEATED HIM CONSTITUTIONALLY

John Bricker of Ohio loved the law and politics. He spent the beginning of his life in law, the middle in politics, and rounded out close to 26 years at the end of his life as a very active attorney.

President Franklin Roosevelt was seeking an unprecedented fourth term when the senator from Ohio was selected to run with Gov. Thomas Dewey for vice president. No president had ever sought a fourth term, and it appeared almost certain that with the war going on, Roosevelt would win another term. Americans still seemed conflicted about a "president for life" scenario, but the climate in the country was about the war and less about politics. Dewey and Bricker did their best to make it about big government, but with the war going on, Americans decided no change was needed.

Bricker was an attorney in Ohio before becoming Attorney General of the state. After running unsuccessfully for governor in 1936, he would go on to be elected to three terms as governor and then be elected to the U.S. Senate. He served with Robert Taft, and when Taft opted out of running for president himself, Bricker became the Ohio conservative voice at the convention that would eventually nominate him to run with Dewey. The ticket was no match for FDR. Bricker proved to be one of the most aggressive vice presidential candidates to that time; however, in the end, Bricker would be defeated in the Electoral College by Harry Truman by a vote of 432 to 99. Truman, selected by FDR after Vice President Henry Wallace was dumped from the ticket, would succeed to the presidency and would find Bricker once again a very active opponent as he served in the Senate.

There was life after a failed run for the vice presidency for Bricker. He returned to the Senate, a conservative and big proponent of smaller government. He was also seriously mentioned as a possible candidate for the Republican nomination for president in 1948, He decided not to seek the presidency and support his fellow Senate colleague from Ohio, Robert Taft. He became known for his fierce defense of the constitution and became a nemesis of President Truman by supporting what came to be known as the Bricker Amendment. This amendment, which failed, was in direct opposition to the man who defeated him for vice president, Harry Truman. He became upset, when without congressional authorization, Truman sent troops to

Korea. The amendment would have prohibited presidents from being able to negotiate agreements with any foreign power without the direct consent of congress. Additionally, his time in the Senate is noted for an odd and bizarre event occurred in 1947, when a disgruntled Ohioan tried to assassinate him.

Bricker most likely would have played a major role in national politics, but in a major political upset in 1959, he was defeated for re-election to the Senate by a 70-year-old Democrat. The pundits were stunned and his political career ended. This defeat led to his return to his law practice, which he enjoyed for an additional 26 years, dying in 1986.

CHAPTER THIRTY ONE

THIRD CHOICE FOR THE VICE

PRESIDENTIAL BUT IMPACTS

AMERICA FOR DECADES

Earl Warren was not the first choice of Thomas Dewey to be his running mate, nor the second. Third choice is more like it and, although he lost, he would enjoy an incredible career after the defeat. His career following the vice presidential election continues to impact America to this day. Most speculation is that Dewey wanted Gov. Dwight Green of Illinois to be his running mate, while his campaign team wanted U.S. Senator Charles Halleck of Indiana. In the end, Dewey selected an equally popular governor. He selected Earl Warren, the Governor of California. Put in political perspective, the two candidates were popular governors from two of the largest states in America, New York and California. It was a strong winning combination. Even the media agreed, not only for that reason, but because the Democratic Party split at their convention. President Harry Truman was renominated as the official candidate, but two major factions bolted the convention and nominated their own candidates. Gov. Strom Thurmond and former Vice President Henry Wallace decided to run separate campaigns for president. It was the perfect storm for the Democrats and a Republican victory seemed assured, with technically three well-known Democrats running national campaigns for the presidency. In the end, it proved to be one of the biggest upsets in modern political history, and three vice presidential candidates would fail to get an opportunity to spit.

Earl Warren was destined to be vice president. He looked like a vice president, and he was running with the dynamic Governor of New York, Thomas Dewey. The Democrats nominated Sen. Alben Barkley from Kentucky as their vice presidential choice. The States Rights Party, splitting from the Democrats, organized and nominated the Governor of South Carolina, Strom Thurmond, for president and Governor of Mississippi, Fielding Wright, for vice president. The Progressive Party nominated former Democratic Vice President Harry Wallace for president and Sen. Glen Taylor of Idaho as his running mate.

Fielding Wright, an avowed anti-segregationist and governor of Mississippi, carried four states as the vice presidential nominee of the States Rights Party. He and the presidential nominee, Strom Thurmond, had hoped that capturing the southern states would ensure that the election would be deadlocked. That, of course, did not happen. After

Wright lost the vice presidential campaign as a third-party candidate, he served as governor until 1952, and would return to practice law. His running mate, Thurmond, would go on to continue to serve in the U.S. Senate for 48 years and was a major political force in American politics.

The media wrongly assumed that the Dewey-Warren ticket would win. If it had, it is possible that major rulings that have impacted, and continue to impact America, may never have come about. Warren, an attorney, rose through the ranks of county government, becoming the District Attorney of Alameda County in California. In 1938, he was elected the Attorney General of California, and in 1942 he successfully ran for Governor of California. As the governor he supported the internment of Japanese citizens during World War II and was very progressive in terms of education, health care, and prison reform. He was re-elected in 1946.

Warren was a very active campaigner for the ticket in 1948. The campaign was dramatic, with basically three Democrats running against the assumed winner, Thomas Dewey and Warren. Truman and Barkley stunned America by winning the election. Major newspapers were reporting that Dewey had been elected and had to run retractions in their next editions.

In the end, Warren would be defeated for the vice presidency by Alben Barkley by a 303 to 189 vote. Fielding received 39 votes. The Progressive Party candidate, Glen Taylor, running with former democratic vice president Wallace, received no electoral votes.

By far, Warren, historically speaking, had one of the most impactful political careers after his defeat for the vice presidency. He and Franklin D. Roosevelt both had impressive post-vice presidential careers. Warren remained popular throughout America. He was re-elected Governor of California in 1950 and with this win and national contacts became a serious contender for the 1952 Republican Party nomination for president. At the 1952 convention, a fellow Californian, Richard Nixon, had promised him support for president, but threw his support elsewhere, causing him to lose the nomination to Dwight D. Eisenhower. This act would forever cause a rift between the two that lasted up to the day Warren died. He never trusted Nixon after that and was not shy about believing that Nixon was not a good person.

The election of 1948 was the only election that Warren would lose, but life was not over after his vice presidential defeat; his national imprint on America would be forthcoming. In 1953, he was nominated by President Eisenhower to be the Chief

Justice of the Supreme Court. This court would initiate interpretations and rulings that impacted America for decades. In 1954, the Warren court issued the Brown vs. Brown ruling that declared it was unconstitutional for separation of public school children according to race. The 1962 Warren court, Engel vs. Vitalie, prohibited mandatory prayer in schools. The Warren court also ruled in the Peterson vs. Greenville case that struck down local ordinances prohibiting racial segregation in public places, such as hotels and restaurants. In the 1964 Supreme Court case Watkins vs. United States, the court gave the right of a witness to refuse to testify at a Congressional committee. Also in 1964, the Warren court ruled in the Reynolds vs. Sims case that legislatures must do their reapportionment on the basis of population and not geography. The landmark Warren court case Miranda vs. Arizona in 1966 made it necessary for police to advise criminal suspects of their rights.

Warren will always be associated with shepherding the court in these major rulings, but he is also known for heading the commission to investigate the assassination of President John F. Kennedy. The Warren Commission ruled, to the dismay of many that Lee Harvey Oswald acted alone.

Warren would resign from the court in 1969 and watch his nemesis, Richard Nixon, appoint his successor. He actually advised President Lyndon Johnson in 1968 that he was planning to retire, expecting Johnson to fill the seat, which due to political maneuvering did not happen. Warren would continue to give speeches and actively comment on issues around the country. In one of his final acts in opposition to President Nixon, it was comments made by the former Justice Warren that actually encouraged the court and Congress to successfully push for the resignation of Richard Nixon as president. He died July 9, 1974. Nixon resigned one month later, August 9, 1974.

CHAPTER THIRTY TWO
THIS VEEP CANDIDATE WALKED FOUR MILES BACK AND FORTH TO ATTEND HIGH SCHOOL

John Sparkman was Alabama through and through. He never received less than 60 percent of the vote in any U.S. Senate race he ran in Alabama, and he was the longest serving senator in Alabama history.

Sparkman grew up poor in Alabama but went on to be an attorney in his home state. He was appointed a magistrate, and also was a key member in his community and eventually became the president of the Chamber of Commerce in his community. He would be elected to Congress in 1936, serving as a congressman until his election to the U.S. Senate in 1946. Sparkman, representing Alabama, was a segregationist who strongly condemned racial integration. He was a strong opponent of the Brown vs. Board of Education Supreme Court ruling that allowed integration in schools. He would be one the senators who signed the Southern Manifesto in opposition to Civil Rights legislation in 1965.

In the 1948, he was opposed to President Harry Truman being nominated for a full term, but lost that battle. In 1952, Truman would lose a presidential primary to Estes Kefauver, and decided to withdraw as candidate for re-election. Kefauver, an extremely popular southern senator from Tennessee, won several presidential primaries but failed to get the nomination. With Kefauver defeated for the presidential nomination and not considered for the second spot on the ticket, the path was open for the Democratic nominee Adlai Stevenson to consider a southern running mate. Initially, Sparkman had supported a fellow southerner for president over Stevenson, Georgia Senator Richard Russell. As often happens in politics, political reality sets in, and the Democrats knew they needed a southern vice presidential choice if they were to compete in the election. Stevenson, the governor from Illinois, selected Sparkman from Alabama, a strong southern choice to balance the ticket. Unfortunately, for both Stevenson and Sparkman, the Republicans nominated the very popular Gen. Dwight Eisenhower. At the Republican convention, a future president would be selected as his running mate, U.S. Sen. Richard Nixon. The election was a foregone conclusion, as the Governor of Illinois, Adlai Stevenson, was no match against Eisenhower. Both running mates, Nixon and Sparkman, would actively campaign for their respective tickets, but Eisenhower's popularity would win out in the end.

Even with Nixon under a veil of ethical financial credibility questions, Sparkman would lose the vice presidency to the future president by an electoral vote of 442 to 89. Stevenson and Sparkman carried only nine states. Eight states were southern. They won less than 44 percent of the popular vote in the landslide defeat. The Republican ticket of Eisenhower and Nixon was the first to use television commercials promoting their candidacy. Stevenson and Sparkman did not, but all that changed four years later.

After his defeat for the second spot, Sparkman would return to the Senate. He was a major voice in that body and actively served on the Senate Banking and Currency Committee. He eventually, based on his seniority, became chairman of the Foreign Relations Committee. He remained a strong advocate for segregation. He strongly opposed key Civil Rights legislation throughout his career. He was a southern liberal to some extent, as he became known for being a major proponent for government public housing. Both 1961 and 1964 would see major investments made in public housing, which he supported.

As a senator from Alabama, he was labeled for the "Sparkman Act," which allowed women physicians to be commissioned officers in the Army, and he also brought Wernher von Braun, the

German scientist, and his team to Huntsville, Alabama, which was a boom for his constituents. The group was organized as the NASA Marshall Flight Center.

Sparkman, to the end, remained very popular with Alabamians and, while opposed by politicians within his party, he was never defeated as an Alabama senator. He opted to retire and not run for re-election in 1978 and died in 1985 believing that politics is about talking with people and trying to reason with them.

CHAPTER THIRTY THREE
CLOSE TO BRASS RING, BUT NOT A CHANCE TO SPIT

Politics can be very strange. The man nominated for the second spot on the ticket was so close to being president, before ever being considered for the second spot. Estes Kefauver was a strong national figure on the political scene. Four years before being selected to be his running mate, Kefauver had defeated Adlai Stevenson in the primaries for the presidential nomination. He, of course, would learn that in that period, the people did not select nominees, party conventions do, and Stevenson would have enough party support to win the nomination from him. Kefauver had actually won over 3 million voters in those 1952 nominating primaries compared to Stevenson's 100,000 votes, but they did not translate to delegate support. Four years later, both men would face each again.

Estes Kefauver was the U.S. Senator from Tennessee. He was an original anti-establishment kind of politician, concerned more about the people than the party bosses. It helped propel him into the national limelight for consideration for the presidency in 1952, 1956, and 1960. However, the party organization still ran the behind-the-scenes operations and, throughout his political career, he would find that would be the reason for keeping him out of the top spot. He would come close to having an opportunity to spit, if elected vice president, but, once again, the timing of running with Stevenson would end that possibility.

Kefauver launched his first congressional campaign running against the party choices. This race was the first of many encounters of opposing the party organization. He would serve in Congress for 10 years before being elected to the U.S. Senate. His Senate position launched him in to American media and the homes of thousands when he chaired the committee shining a light on organized crime in America. He had the opportunity as the chairman to travel throughout America, probing organized crime activities and their impact. The term of "taking the fifth" became a mainstay in the American language, as many individuals brought before the committee to answer questions would use the term referring to the Fifth Amendment to avoid answering questions.

In 1952, Kefauver would stun the party machine by traveling to New Hampshire and winning the primary against incumbent President Harry Truman. Truman bowed out of the race shortly thereafter, and Kefauver would go on to win 12 primaries throughout America, capturing more than 3 million votes from the people. As he soon would learn, winning the popular vote in the primaries hardly guaranteed him the nomination, since the party machines he opposed controlled the delegates. Those delegates in 1952 would go on to nominate a candidate who captured less than 100,000 votes in the primaries, Adlai Stevenson.

In 1954, Kefauver was re-elected to the Senate, which made him a natural to run for president in 1956. He stunned party bosses again by winning both New Hampshire and Minnesota primaries over the favored candidate, Adlai Stevenson. The political machine pulled ranks, lined up behind Stevenson, and, eventually, not having the same success due to financial reasons, Kefauver would withdraw his candidacy. Many things would go on at the convention that nominated Stevenson, including a move by former president Truman to push for another candidate to be nominated for president instead of Stevenson. That effort failed, but Stevenson realized he had to do something to get attention and positive momentum back for the party, so he opened the convention to nominate his running mate. It was a popular move that gave Kefauver the nomination over a not so well known senator from Massachusetts, John F. Kennedy. That convention gave Kefauver the vice presidential nod that would end his national political career, while at the same give the defeated Kennedy the momentum that propelled him to national recognition and eventually the nomination of his party for president four years later.

While the campaign was a rematch for Stevenson and Eisenhower, it simply was not a match. Eisenhower, even with a heart attack the year before, remained steady and popular. Vice President Nixon, still somewhat not as popular within party circles, would win re-nomination to oppose Kefauver. As was the case four years earlier, both running mates were active campaigners and remained popular with their party base of supporters. Nixon would be re-elected vice president, winning 457 electoral votes to Kefauver's 73. The Republican ticket was re-elected with over 58 percent of the vote, winning 42 states. Stevenson would be defeated a second time and not seek national office again. Kefauver would return to the U.S. Senate and go on to be re-elected to the Senate in 1960. He was mentioned as a possible presidential candidate in 1960 but decided not to run and remained in the Senate with his own re-election bid coming up.

As a U.S. Senator, he continued to work very hard on legislative matters. He remained popular with his constituents and is known for the legislative actions he supported throughout his career. He is known for supporting labor causes, civil rights legislation, term limits, fighting organized crime, fighting monopolies, and supporting the efforts for reducing prescription cost and prescription safety. In August 1963, while taking on the monopoly of AT&T and fighting to have them pay for the benefits they were getting from NASA for development and research activities, he suffered a heart attack and died. He did his homework, and no doubt many think, that the independent investigative tenacity he applied to being a senator would have served him well in either the presidency or vice presidency.

CHAPTER THIRTY FOUR
THE RIGHT PEDIGREE AND CREDENTIALS DIDN'T TRANSLATE TO BEING VICE PRESIDENT

It is very odd when the vice presidential nominees of both parties have more credentials to serve as president than the person who eventually is elected president. That was the case in the 1960 election, when two well-known political leaders in America served their parties by being the vice presidential nominees of their respective tickets.

If a computer were selecting the candidates, then of the four top spot nominees, John F. Kennedy would have come in fourth to Richard Nixon, Lyndon Johnson, and Henry Cabot Lodge.

The election of 1960 is known for its television appeal to America. In addition to the debates between the two major party candidates, it was also a full-blown arena for television commercials that would set the stage for years to come.

Henry Cabot Lodge was destined for greatness, and many historians believe that he could have been president if he wanted to be. His grandfather was a friend of Teddy Roosevelt, the Republican establishment, and a U.S. Senator. Lodge Jr. was well connected and grew up in a wealthy atmosphere. He was elected to the Senate from Massachusetts in 1936, and re-elected in 1942. In 1944, he resigned his seat to join the military and would return in a year to win a special election for the Senate. Lodge began to flex some national muscle with the Republicans when he organized a draft Eisenhower movement for president for the 1952 elections, and some think his distraction on the national scene led to his defeat to the future President of the United States, John F. Kennedy. Very notable, Kennedy defeated Lodge for the U.S. Senate and, less than seven years later, they would be political opponents on the national stage.

After his defeat for re-election, Lodge went to work for the Eisenhower administration and continued his government involvement. Eisenhower named him the Ambassador to the United Nations. When Vice President Nixon received the Republican nomination for president, he was an ideal running mate for him based on his government service, as well as the fact that he was from Kennedy's home state. Lodge was very popular with the Republican elite establishment. His background and financial worth no doubt left Nixon a bit uneasy. In any case, Lodge enjoyed government service but did appear to enjoy the campaign trail. Historically, the election will go down in history as one that included voting fraud that defeated the Republican ticket. Votes from Illinois gave Kennedy and his running mate, Lyndon Johnson, the victory. The Nixon-Lodge ticket actually won 26 states to their 22, and the percentage of victory in the popular vote was 49.7 percent to 49.5 percent. The electoral vote count that would give Lyndon Johnson the vice presidency over Lodge was 303 votes to 219.

Lodge was financially connected and had little or no worries after the defeat. He remained popular with the Republican Party base, and after a brief stint with Time magazine, accepted a position in the Democratic administration of Kennedy, working with Secretary of State Dean Rusk. Eventually, President Kennedy, his political opponent but friend, named him the Ambassador to Vietnam. In that role, accepted within six months of Kennedy's assassination, Lodge almost immediately urged that President Diem of South Vietnam be removed as president. After Kennedy was killed, President Johnson asked Lodge to remain Ambassador to Vietnam, which he did throughout the remainder of his term as well as in his new term as president. While he was ambassador, the Republican Party, in an effort to stop Barry Goldwater from being nominated, ran a write-in campaign for him for president. Lodge did defeat Goldwater and Nixon in the New Hampshire primary as a write-in candidate.

Even with this win, Lodge did not seem to have any desire to run for the office, even though many thought the nomination was his for the taking. He stayed on as ambassador and did not support Goldwater, the Republican nominee. Lodge would resign as ambassador in 1967 and be named an Ambassador at Large by Johnson. He would eventually be named by Johnson to serve as Ambassador to Germany. His 1960 running mate, Richard Nixon, who was elected president in 1968, would ask him to head up the Paris Peace Talks, putting the Vietnam War to end. He would then serve Presidents Nixon, Gerald Ford, and Jimmy Carter as the Envoy to the Vatican.

In 1977, he officially retired from government service. He would become a lecturer and was well respected as a statesman throughout the country. He served in Congress, the U.S. Senate, and six presidents as a diplomat. He died in 1985.

CHAPTER THIRTY FIVE
VICE PRESIDENTS USUALLY VANISH FROM THE POLITICAL WORLD, SO DID THIS CANDIDATE

William Miller was the brunt of many jokes, including his own, after virtually disappearing from the political landscape after this defeat for vice president. Miller was as conservative as Barry Goldwater when he accepted the second spot on the ticket that would lose by a landslide to Lyndon Johnson and Hubert Humphrey in 1964.

The election of 1964 came within a year of the assassination of President John F. Kennedy, and it was highly unlikely that voters were going to make a change. Surprisingly, before the death of President Kennedy, polls had indicated that he was going to have a tough re-election campaign ahead. Barry Goldwater, a staunch conservative, was going to give voters a real choice of moving the control to the left or to the right. The assassination changed the political landscape dramatically, and Lyndon Johnson rode the wave of Kennedy's New Frontier program, his Great Society idea, the split of the Republican Party, and sympathy to an astonishing landslide victory.

With the liberal and conservative wings of the Republican Party split at the nominating convention, Barry Goldwater made no gesture of uniting the factions when he selected a congressman from New York to be his running mate. William Miller, an attorney, had a conservative background and did nothing to unite the two factions. After law school and brief military service, he started his career in government serving a future U.S. Supreme Court Justice, Robert Jackson, as an assistant prosecutor for the Nuremburg Trails. He would eventually be appointed by Gov. Thomas Dewey to serve as the District Attorney of Niagara County in New York. He would go on to win election on his own to the post. As a congressman, he managed to make contacts nationally when he had served as the chairman for the Republican Congressional Campaign Committee. The successful campaign of Republican candidates in the congressional campaign would lead him to be elected the National Chairman of the Republican Party. In that role, he proved to be very aggressive in making ongoing verbal attacks of President Kennedy and the Democratic Party. His wit and snide remarks served to annoy those supporting the new programs. Miller would serve seven terms before joining Goldwater on the ticket.

The ticket did very poorly, as Johnson was re-elected with over 60 percent of the vote, carrying 44 states out of 50. The Electoral College would elect

Hubert Humphrey vice president over Miller by a vote of 486 to 52. The man with the sharp tongue would end his political career and disappear from national politics. The former seven-term congressman, former National Chairman of the Republican Party, and national candidate just seemed to blend in to the woodwork, avoiding interviews and any conversations regarding political matters. He would return to practicing law locally, becoming more local than national with life.

In a stroke of marketing genius, Miller would have one final opportunity to enjoy the national spotlight after disappearing from public view. In 1975, American Express, aware of the mystery of whatever happened to William Miller, ran a national advertising campaign featuring William Miller asking the public if they knew who he was. He would then point out that he could not be recognized without his American Express card. In later years, William Miller would point out that he was known more for having an American Express card than being the running mate of one the most famous conservatives in American history. Miller died in 1965, and Barry Goldwater praised him for the person he was.

CHAPTER THIRTY SIX

THE SENATOR WHO SERVED HIS COUNTRY WELL AFTER HIS VEEP LOSS

The election of 1968 featured a former vice president, an avowed segregationist, and the current vice president who could not shake himself away from the Vietnam War or the president leading the fight.

Edmund Sixtus Muskie of Maine, an often mentioned presidential contender himself, was selected by Hubert Humphrey as his vice presidential nominee at a national convention in Chicago that was marred by violence and riots. It was a difficult start for the ticket that would remain far behind in the polls until the final month of the campaign. Muskie, as part of the ticket, would lose the vice presidency to a man who would later resign from office as the vice president. The Electoral College would elect Spiro Agnew vice president by a vote of 301 to 191. Curtis LeMay, who ran as a third-party candidate with Gov. George Wallace would receive five electoral votes. With heavy anti-war sentiment and national protest in a year that would see the assassination of the Rev. Dr. Martin Luther King, Jr. and Sen. Robert Kennedy, it was difficult for the Humphrey-Muskie ticket to win. However, the ticket with Muskie joining Humphrey in aggressively campaigning came within 600,000 votes of winning the popular vote, losing to Nixon and Agnew by less than 1 percent of the vote. Muskie is one of the vice presidential candidates who would discover that there is political life after losing the vice presidency.

Edmund Muskie started his political career as a state representative in Maine. In 1954, he would become the Governor of the Maine, actually winning two terms before being elected to the U.S. Senate in 1958. The voters would return him to office for three additional terms. His Senate career would be marked by liberal causes, supporting Johnson and the Vietnam War plan, and leading the efforts for environmental issues. Muskie's service in the Senate was briefly interrupted when selected as Humphrey's running mate in the losing effort. After the defeat, Muskie would return to the Senate and, in 1972, would be the front runner for the Democratic presidential nomination. Unfortunately for the senator, an incident where he appeared to be crying at a rally because of the attacks on him and his wife would force him out of the race. It was a campaign trick that caused Muskie to bow out of the race when the Manchester Union had accused him of using a derogatory term to describe Canadians, and also accused his wife of being a heavy drinker. In an effort to deny the remarks, the tears only made him look weak, and Muskie withdrew from the race because he believed America wanted a strong president, not one who appeared to be weak. It was only later during the Nixon debacles that the Nixon campaign organization planted the story with the conservative newspaper.

After this brief appearance on the national stage, Muskie would return to the Senate representing Maine. Leading up to the 1980 re-election campaign of Jimmy Carter, a Draft Muskie movement was set up for him to seek the nomination against the sitting president. Muskie had no desire to oppose President Carter, dashing the efforts of the draft movement. Muskie would serve in the Senate until 1980, when President Carter named him the Secretary of State. In the final week of the administration he served, President Jimmy Carter awarded him the Presidential Medal of Freedom for his work during the Iran hostage crisis. As is tradition, he resigned as Secretary of State when President Ronald Reagan was elected.

Believing that his government service had ended as governor, senator, Secretary of State, and Presidential Medal of Freedom awardee, he returned to be a private citizen. Muskie would find out that there is also political life after you enjoy a stint as a private citizen. In 1987, a special review board led by Sen. John Tower would ask him to serve as a committee member to review the actions of President Reagan in the Iran-Contra affair. Muskie actively served on the Tower Commission and was critical of the activities going on within the Reagan administration. In the Clinton administration, the president asked him to serve as his special representative to Cambodia in helping to stabilize the new government. Even though he never had a chance to spit, Muskie lived a very active political life after losing the vice presidency. He died in 1996.

CHAPTER THIRTY SEVEN
MANY ARE ASKED, AND EVENTUALLY
SOMEONE GETS CHOSEN

John Nance Gardner would have enjoyed the amount of individuals who said no to the opportunity to get a chance to spit. It was his point exactly. The job isn't worth it. However, 1972 was filled with far more reasons to say no to the nominee than to the office. The re-election of Nixon was never in doubt, although as history shows, apparently his campaign teams were not reading the news of the impending landslide victory. Based on the facts, it appeared Richard Nixon would have no chance of losing, but his campaign committee was so paranoid they set in motion what caused the only American president in history to resign from the office.

Most political historians say that George McGovern asked a minimum of seven other individuals to be his vice presidential nominee before R. Sargent Shriver stepped in to replace his previous fifth choice, who actually won the nomination. Shriver jokingly acknowledged that he did believe he was the "seventh asked" and jokingly named his airplane "Lucky 7."

The 1972 Democratic nominee for president was South Dakota Sen. George McGovern. Most experts agree that it would be an impossible campaign to defeat the sitting president, Richard Nixon. At the convention, after winning the nomination for president, historians believe that McGovern offered the second spot to Sen. Ted Kennedy of Massachusetts, former Vice President Hubert Humphrey, Sen. Abraham Ribicoff of Connecticut, and Sen. Walter Mondale of Minnesota. All four declined, before Missouri Sen. Thomas Eagleton accepted.

The Democratic convention, although not completely happy with the choice, went on to nominate Eagleton, and within three days, McGovern was asking those four who said no previously and a few others, including Democratic Chairman Larry O'Brien and Florida Gov. Reubin Askew to join his ticket. The reason for the new ask was based on the fact that Eagleton was previously treated for depression with electro shock therapy. The "shock therapy" concept, accepted medically, was suspect in terms of whether Eagleton would be capable of serving as president if, by chance, he would have to succeed McGovern. McGovern, who originally said after the story was revealed that he was "1,000 percent behind Eagleton," would ask him to step aside, which was the reason that, after so many "no's", R. Sargent Shriver was named to the ticket and approved by a special session of the Democratic Party Committee.

The likelihood of Shriver having to serve was extremely remote. When the votes were counted, the polls were correct and the Nixon-Agnew ticket was re-elected by a landslide vote. They carried 49 of the 50 states, winning over 60 percent of the vote. The stand-in vice presidential nominee, R. Sargent Shriver, was defeated by Vice President Agnew for the vice presidency by an electoral vote of 520 to 17.

Shriver was no stranger to politics. Politically, he was the brother-in-law of President John F. Kennedy, as well as former Attorney General and U.S. Sen. Robert Kennedy and U.S. Sen. Ted Kennedy. Shriver had married Eunice Kennedy in 1953. He coordinated the Wisconsin and West Virginia primary campaigns for Sen. John F. Kennedy, who would be elected in 1960. Kennedy would name Shriver the first director of the Peace Corp, a position he held even under Lyndon Johnson until 1966. He would then serve President Johnson as the first director of the Office of Economic Opportunity under the War on Poverty mandate.

In 1968, he was being considered by Johnson as a potential running mate before Hubert Humphrey was selected and he was named the Ambassador to France. He returned to the states in 1970 to lead a project in electing members to Congress. The group he founded was the Congressional Leadership for the Future organization.

In the losing effort to the Nixon-Agnew ticket, Shriver was not ready to go away quietly from the political arena. In 1976, he ran a brief campaign for the presidential nomination himself before withdrawing to support Jimmy Carter. The loss to Carter ended his national presence on the stage, and he would go back to private legal service with the firm of Fried, Frank, Harris, Shriver & Jacobsen in Boston. Shriver would be honored with the Presidential Medal of Freedom for his service to America in 1994. He died in 2011, and was warmly remembered for the service he provided to the country without ever being elected to any political office.

CHAPTER THIRTY EIGHT
SERVICE TO AMERICA, THE
CORNERSTONE OF THIS CANDIDATE

The election of 1976 featured an appointed Vice President of the United States who would run for president. His appointed vice president, a political icon, chose not to seek the vice presidential nomination and ended his political service to America. It was the first time in American history that the serving president and vice president were not chosen by designated electors, the Electoral College or the American electorate.

Gerald Ford was appointed the Vice President of the United States in 1973, when then Vice President Spiro Agnew resigned from office. In 1974, when President Richard Nixon resigned, Gerald Ford would become the President of the United States. Ford then appointed Nelson Rockefeller, a major Republican Party leader, to serve as his vice president. In less than four years, the political landscape had dramatically changed, and neither Nixon nor Agnew were on the political stage that they previously dominated.

Vice President Nelson Rockefeller declined to run for the office, and Ford selected Republican

Senate Leader Robert Dole from Kansas to serve as his running mate. Dole, a wounded war veteran, started his own political career in Kansas as a state representative in 1950. After serving two terms, he was elected the County Attorney for Russel County in Kansas before winning a seat as a U.S. Congressman in 1961. He held the seat until 1969, when he would win the first of his five terms in the U.S. Senate and go on to serve as the leader for his party in the Senate.

The election of 1976 was overshadowed by the demise of the Nixon presidency. The Democratic nominee, a little known Governor of Georgia, Jimmy Carter, capitalized on the weariness of the Nixon-Agnew administration to present a fresh alternative to government in Washington. While Gerald Ford was looked upon as an honorable man, his decision to pardon Richard Nixon proved to be a detriment to his re-election bid. While the Ford-Dole ticket would win a majority of states, carrying 27 out of 50, they lost the popular vote by a percentage of 50 percent to 48 percent. The Electoral College elected Walter Mondale over Bob Dole for vice president by a vote of 297 to 241. Dole actually collected one more vote than his running mate, Gerald Ford, as he was defeated by Jimmy Carter in the Electoral College by a vote of 297 to 240. One member of the Electoral College voted for Ronald Reagan, the Governor of California, for president.

Dole did not let his political career or ambitions end with his defeat for vice president. He would return to the Senate and serve there until 1996. Twenty years after running for vice president, he would run for and lose the presidential nomination of his party in 1980 and 1988 before becoming the nominee of his party for president in 1996. Dole would lose to Bill Clinton, and his presidential ambitions and Senate career ended in 1996.

Dole, as of this writing, continues to play a role in veteran activities. He most recently attended the funeral of President George H.W. Bush. Bush had defeated him for the Republican presidential nomination in 1988. Although they had been political rivals, they were both American war veterans and Dole honored him by standing up and saluting his casket as it laid in state. On most Saturdays, Dole will travel to the World War II Memorial in Washington D.C. and greet World War II veterans and other veterans who come to visit the memorial. Dole never won the big prize or a chance to spit, but he did make the most of his national loss by playing a key role in American politics after that vice presidential run. He continues to be respected for his service in the war and service in the Senate.

CHAPTER THIRTY NINE
THE FIRST WOMAN ON A MAJOR PARTY
TICKET FOR VICE PRESIDENT

The election of 1980 is not part of this book because Vice President Walter Mondale was defeated for re-election with Jimmy Carter. There was a third-party candidate, Patrick Lucey, who ran for vice president with John Anderson as the presidential nominee that year. Their joint campaign did receive an impressive 6 percent of the vote, but Lucey received no electoral votes, so I have not included him in the book.

The election of 1984 would have been historic for the incredible landslide of a sitting president, but it became more historic because the Democratic Party became the first major political party in history to nominate a woman to their national ticket.

Congresswoman Geraldine Ferraro was selected by former Vice President Walter Mondale to be his running mate against incumbent President Ronald Reagan and Vice President George H.W. Bush. The reality is that, defeating the Reagan-Bush ticket would have been virtually impossible regardless of who was selected as the nominees of the Democratic Party. In leading up to the election, the economy was strong and national security issues, including a strong military, were key elements for the American voter. The polls indicated that President Reagan and Vice President Bush would be re-elected, and in a major landslide the they won 49 of the 50 states.

Ferraro was a member of Congress from New York. After a stint as a teacher and working in the Queens County Attorney's Office, she was elected to Congress in 1978. She made key contacts during her congressional service and supported major legislation involving equal rights and pay for women. Former Vice President Mondale, well aware that he would need something major to bring attention to his candidacy for president, selected her to be the first woman, as well as the first Italian-American to run on a national ticket. After the nomination, there were key questions involving her husband's business dealings and personal finances. This did not help the campaign. Ferraro did not slow down her efforts to work for the election of the team. She campaigned aggressively, but nothing could stop the Reagan-Bush train. They won the election with almost 60 percent of the vote, and the Electoral College re-elected George Bush to a second term for vice president over Ferraro by a landslide margin of 525 votes to 13.

Name recognition, a national campaign, and the first woman on a ticket would have seemed to be a natural that only good things could happen for Geraldine Ferraro after this election. It would seem that major political office would await her. Unfortunately, in terms of an elected political career, this defeat would be the end of elected political office for her. Her personal and family finances came under question and her husband was convicted of financial fraud. Her son was arrested for cocaine possession. With all this going on, her personal political career was put on hold. She did organize an effort to help elect other women to Congress. She also decided to seek the U.S. Senate nomination in 1992, but lost in the primary election. President Clinton named her to serve as a United Nations Ambassador in 1993 and she served in that role until 1996. She became a political host for CNN in 1996 and took another run for the U.S. Senate in 1998, losing again in that primary. She would never again seek elective office after that primary defeat. She would become a political commentator for the conservative network, FOX News, and then went into business as a management consultant in 2000 to help develop women in their careers. She would remain politically involved, including coming aboard quickly to work for Hillary Clinton's presidential campaign.

Geraldine Ferraro made history. She blazed the way that made it acceptable to select Sarah Palin as a running mate and Hilary Clinton as a presidential nominee. Along with her and them, each political party from that race in 1984 now finds it natural for women to be considered for the first or second spot on a ticket. Ferraro died of cancer in 2011.

CHAPTER FORTY

HE LOST THE VICE PRESIDENCY BUT WON THE DEBATE WITH A CLEVER QUOTE

In the 1988 election, Vice President George Bush would select a young senator from Indiana, Dan Quayle, as his running mate. The young senator often would compare himself to another young senator from Massachusetts, John F. Kennedy, on the campaign trail and did that again during a debate with his vice presidential rival, U.S. Sen. Lloyd Bentsen of Texas. Not much is remembered in terms of the substance of the debate, but the statement Bentsen made to challenge the historical comparison of Dan Quayle remains forever famous. In the heated exchange, it was Bentsen who said; "Senator, I served with Jack Kennedy. I knew Jack Kennedy. Jack Kennedy was a friend of mine. You, sir, are no Jack Kennedy." That was Bentsen's great moment before losing the vice presidency to Dan Quayle by an Electoral College vote of 429 to 111.

That moment was not the only Kennedy reference in the campaign. Michael Dukakis, the Governor of Massachusetts, selected Bentsen as his vice presidential running mate. The media jumped on this selection, citing that in 1960 a Massachusetts presidential nominee selected a senator from Texas as his running mate. The team of Kennedy and Johnson were elected; Dukakis and Bentsen did not enjoy the same outcome.

Lloyd Bentsen enjoyed both a political career and business career before being the nominee of his party for vice president. After his defeat, he would again enjoy the same path. He started his political career by being elected a judge at the age of 25 and would be elected to Congress in 1948 at the age of 27. He would serve until 1955 when he decided to go into business helping to build the American Life insurance company. It was a business career that he would have for over 16 years before selling the company and deciding to return to politics and run for the U.S. Senate. He was re-elected to that office three more times.

In his Senate career, and probably due to his extensive financial background before getting there, he was known for two key pieces of legislation that impacted the financial lives of Americans. ERISA, the Employment Retirement Security Act, protected the pensions of millions of Americans. He also led the efforts for development of IRAs. As a senator in 1976, he made a brief run for the presidency and then returned to work in the Senate. When he was nominated to run for vice president, it was noted that then Vice President George Bush, the

Republican nominee for president, actually was defeated for the U.S. Senate by Bentsen.

The Dukakis-Bentsen team carried only 10 states, as Vice President Bush and Senator Quayle were elected with 53 percent of the vote. While Bentsen had that debate moment, he did not seem to impact the national race as much as expected. In 1992, he considered running for president but dropped those plans. He remained in the Senate until President Bill Clinton asked him to help with the economic recovery plans for the country. He resigned his Senate seat and would be named to the cabinet as the Secretary of the Treasury. President Clinton credited him as the chief architect of the Clinton Economic Plan. He was instrumental in the successful passage of NAFTA, the North American Free Trade Act.

His political life ended as the Secretary of Treasury and he was awarded the Presidential Medal of Freedom by President Clinton in 1999. Bentsen died in 2006, respected as a former senator, business executive and Secretary of the Treasury.

CHAPTER FORTY ONE

FROM FOOTBALL HERO TO

QUARTERBACKING THE COURSE OF

AMERICAN ECONOMICS

Leading up to the 1992 election, it is interesting to note that the previously defeated vice presidential candidate, Lloyd Bentsen, had considered running for president but dropped the plan due to unprecedented popularity of the incumbent president George Bush. Events in history change fast, and in 1992, the sitting president and vice president were defeated for re-election. Much like the 1980 campaign that would see Vice President Mondale defeated, the same is true of this election, so no vice presidential losing candidate is mentioned. Bill Clinton and Al Gore were the nominees of the Democratic Party, and won the presidency and vice presidency, respectively. Ross Perot selected James Stockdale as his running mate on a third-party run, and while the Perot-Stockdale ticket collected an impressive 19 percent of the national vote, Stockdale did not receive any electoral votes for vice president so this work moves on to the 1996 elections.

The election of 1996 would feature incumbent President Bill Clinton and Vice President Al Gore running against a previous losing vice presidential candidate, Bob Dole of Kansas. It would not end well for the Republican ticket of U.S. Sen. Bob Dole and former Congressman and Housing Secretary Jack Kemp, who collected only 40 percent of the vote and won 19 out of 50 states.

Jack Kemp, often referred to as a Jack Kennedy look-alike in conservative Republican clothes, was a football star before joining the world of politics. He played for the National Football League, the Canadian Football League, and the American Football League. He became a hometown hero in Buffalo as he led the Buffalo Bills to two consecutive AFL championships. While football was his dream, he did have early brushes with politics supporting Barry Goldwater for president in 1964 and working to elect Ronald Reagan Governor of California in 1966. Those campaigns molded him as a conservative in his future political plans. In 1980, a strong draft movement for Jack Kemp was made for Ronald Reagan to select him as his running mate over George Bush.

On the coattails of his football success, Kemp was elected to Congress in 1971 as a conservative from a Democratic district in Buffalo. His election proved not to just be a sports fluke, as he would be re-elected to the seat over and over and would serve in Congress until 1989. He made a brief run for president in 1988, losing to George Bush, and Bush did consider him as a running mate that year, before selecting Dan Qualye. President Bush would appoint him to his cabinet as the Housing Secretary, a position he would serve in until the end of his term.

Kemp did consider running for president in 1996, but having now joined the corporate world decided to stay out of the race that would eventually nominate Bob Dole. He did not support Dole for president, which made him a surprise selection to some degree, when Dole asked him to be his running mate. President Clinton knew that elections were about the economy, and while Kemp was extremely youthful and active in the campaign, the re-election of the Clinton-Gore team was inevitable. The Electoral College would elect Al Gore to a second term as vice president over Jack kemp by a vote of 379 to 159.

Like several other recently selected vice presidential losers, Jack Kemp would discover that there is still life after a national defeat. He was considered a potential presidential contender in 2000, but instead would support George W. Bush for the office. His career would focus on business and charitable efforts. He would be called on to make speech appearances throughout the country. He continued to be likable and energetic and served on many corporate and charitable boards. He formed his own company, Kemp Partners, a major consulting firm for business and policy issues. Kemp would remain very active in political issues and serve in advisory roles to political leaders on government issues.

Kemp is known nationally for the Kemp-Roth Tax Cut bill that was the hallmark of the Reagan administration and died in 2009. He was awarded the Presidential Medal of Freedom posthumously by President Barack Obama. Kemp proved that even in losing the vice presidency, you could remain relevant in the course of political history. He helped to change the economic direction of the country and forever remains a key player in the conservative thought of supply side economics.

CHAPTER FORTY TWO

THIS VEEP CANDIDATE LOST THE LOVE OF HIS OWN PARTY

The election of 2000 continues to haunt Americans to this day. No presidential election since has been the same due to the ongoing issues that occurred in the state of Florida. Eventually, after days of ballot counting, legal battles, and a Supreme Court ruling, George W. Bush and Dick Cheney were elected over Vice President Al Gore and U.S. Sen. Joe Lieberman. Florida's 25 electoral votes picked up by Bush-Cheney would give them the electoral victory, despite their loss in the popular balloting.

Republicans nominated the son of former President George H. W. Bush for president. He selected former Congressman and Defense Secretary Dick Cheney as his running mate. Actually, since Cheney was in charge of the committee to find a running mate for Bush, many believe he recommended and selected himself. Vice President Gore selected the independent-minded Lieberman as his running mate. Lieberman would become the first Jewish nominee of a major party ticket.

Lieberman started his political career in the State Senate of Connecticut. He served 10 years in the State Senate before losing a race for Congress in 1980. He would be elected Attorney General of Connecticut in 1983 and serve until his election to the U.S. Senate in 1988. He would be re-elected three more times, but his last re-election would be the strangest of all and forever set him on a course of true independence from the same party that would honor him with the vice presidential nomination.

In the 2006 Democratic Primary, Lieberman would be defeated for re-election to the Senate. He did not accept the defeat well and would file as an independent candidate for the Senate seat. In a major split for the state party that would also impact fellow Democratic senators throughout the country, Lieberman would run an aggressive campaign and surprisingly defeat the official nominee of the Democratic Party to win a fourth term. When he arrived to the Senate, even as an independent, he did agree to side with the Democratic Party, but he would display independence in supporting some efforts of the Republican Party. This started the path that would continue, even to the end of his political career. Leaders of the party would forever question his loyalty over personal gain.

In the 2000 campaign, Lieberman, because of his Jewish faith, would not actively campaign on Saturdays in order to honor the Sabbath. The ticket would win 20 states and over 500,000 more popular votes than Bush and Cheney. What followed those results became a battle over how one state, Florida, counted its votes and the subsequent electors who would be seated. In the end, the Supreme Court would settle the disputed vote issue and the Bush-Cheney ticket would win the election. The Electoral College would elect Dick Cheney vice president by a vote of 271 to 266 over Lieberman.

All was not over for the senator from Connecticut. The November election that defeated him for vice president was also the election that re-elected him to his Senate seat. Lieberman was re-elected to his fourth term. He would return to the Senate and become an advocate for supporting President Bush, including the war in Iraq. This decision, more than any other, would put him in a difficult position with many Democrats, including those at home, and effectively lead to the presidential primary races that denied him of his party nomination for president.

Lieberman was not endorsed for president by Al Gore, his former running mate. Gore would not comment on the loyalty factor of Lieberman in the 2004 primaries. After failing to win any primaries, he withdrew from the 2004 presidential sweepstakes that would nominate John Kerry. He again would find himself at serious odds with

Democratic Senate leadership and the national party when, in 2008, he would publicly abandon the party nominee for president by actively supporting Republican Sen. John McCain. Lieberman, a lifelong Democrat and now independent senator, would speak at the GOP convention for McCain. Lieberman himself said that McCain had asked him to run with him for vice president in the hopes of creating a national unity ticket, but Lieberman turned him down because of his Senate committee chairmanships. McCain would go on to lose the presidency and, with eroding support at home, Lieberman would retire from national politics. He went to work for the law firm of Kasowitz, Benson, Torres, and Friedman. He serves as a lobbyist today and is involved with a conservative think tank. He was considered by President Donald Trump as the possible Director of the FBI. He remains staunchly independent in his thinking and knows he will never again have an opportunity to spit, or become President of the United States.

CHAPTER FORTY THREE

THIS VICE PRESIDENTIAL CANDIDATE

LOST THE ELECTION AND

HIS REPUTATION

By all measures, the rise and fall of John Edwards in political history is incredible. The senator with the good looks and charisma appeared destined to be part of American life far longer than the 10 years he had on the national stage.

In 2004, George Bush and Dick Cheney were re-elected over the two Democratic Party running mates of U.S. Sen. John Kerry of Massachusetts and Sen. John Edwards of North Carolina. The vote margin was approximately 51 percent to 48 percent. Cheney was re-elected vice president over John Edwards by the Electoral College vote of 286 to 252. In one of those oddities that sometimes occur within the Electoral College, John Edwards received one vote for president. A Minnesota member of the Electoral College, possibly in error, voted for him for both president and vice president.

Edwards, who was selected by Kerry, spent his early career as a very successful trial lawyer and medical malpractice attorney. He managed to gain incredible financial settlements for his clients. In 1996, his son Wade was killed in an accident, and Edwards started to re-evaluate his legal career and decided without ever holding political office before to run for the U.S. Senate from North Carolina. He defeated an incumbent senator and became an instant rising star on the national scene. He was not known for legislative achievements but was charismatic enough to position himself in national political affairs. Al Gore had considered Edwards as a potential running mate before selecting Joe Lieberman. Edwards decided within that the Senate was not his future and launched his own campaign for the 2004 presidential nomination. He would eventually bow out of the race and endorse John Kerry, who after winning the nomination selected Edwards as his running mate.

With a close election and his appeal, the future seemed bright for him. Shortly after the campaign ended, he and his wife announced that she had cancer. Sympathy and support came in across America. After losing the vice presidency, he became the Director for the Center on Poverty, Work and Opportunity at the University of North Carolina. He remained active in his own One America Committee, which kept him front and center on national issues. He also eventually joined a Wall Street firm, Fortress Investment Group, which provided a very substantial income until he could make what everyone suspected would be another bid for national office. He did seek the presidency in 2008, but would withdraw from the race and endorse Barack Obama.

Edward's political future still looked bright as the media mentioned him as a possible Obama running mate or future member of his cabinet. Unfortunately, all the expected political stardom would dramatically begin to unwind with the news that his wife's cancer had returned, and information began to surface that, at the time of her ongoing treatments, he was having an affair. He denied the affair for two years but eventually would admit that it was true. Word surfaced that he also had a child as a result of the affair, and his wife Elizabeth filed for separation. While waiting to file for divorce, his wife died in December 2010. All the negative press over the situation effectively ended his political career. As his political activity unraveled, he was indicted by a grand jury for multiple campaign contribution violations. He was never convicted, but it seemed to seal his fate as never having the possibility to return to public office. Today, out of the limelight, Edwards works as personal injury attorney in North Carolina.

CHAPTER FORTY FOUR

A CANDIDATE OF FIRSTS, BUT NOT THE

FIRST WOMAN VICE PRESIDENT

The 2008 presidential campaign was going to be historic anyway. The selection of Sarah Palin as a running mate just added to the flavor of this history-making election. The Republicans knew it was going to be an uphill battle, and nominating Palin at least gave them potential historic bragging rights. Many within the party believed it added an additional dimension to be competitive in the race.

In the 2008 election, America was going to elect a new president and vice president. U.S. Sen. Barack Obama and Sen. Joe Biden were the nominees seeking to succeed President George Bush and Vice President Dick Cheney. Obama was the first African-American nominated for president by a major party. Not to be denied a shot at history, the Republican Party nominated U.S. Sen. John McCain and Gov. Sarah Palin of Alaska. McCain decided to give the campaign a boost with his surprise selection of a female governor to be his running mate. The results, regardless of the winning ticket, would be historic. Either the first female would be elected vice president, or the first African-American would be elected president. History was made, but McCain and Palin were defeated. The ticket would lose the election, capturing less than 46 percent of the votes and winning 22 of the potential 50 states.

Sarah Palin was the first Republican female on a national ticket and the first Alaskan to win a spot on any major party ticket. She was well known in Alaska but not nearly as well known in the neighboring mainland states. She would rise to prominence in Alaskan politics by winning a seat on Wasilla City Council in 1992 and then be elected mayor of the city in 1996. She was re-elected mayor and had a failed attempt at being elected the lieutenant governor of the state. In her loss, she became part of the Alaska Oil & Gas Conservation Committee and used the role to highlight unethical activities, which would bring her to the limelight of Alaskan state voters. She was Governor of Alaska in 2006. She became the state's youngest governor and the first female to be elected Governor of Alaska.

She was an unorthodox choice for the vice presidential nomination, and she proved to be a very aggressive campaigner, winning the hearts of conservative voters during the campaign. When all the votes were in, the Electoral College would elect U.S. Sen. Joe Biden to be the vice president by a vote of 365 to 173 over Palin.

Controversy always seemed to follow Palin around as an Alaskan politico, and it was no different when she lost the vice presidency. After her loss, she made an attempt to deliver a concession speech, which the McCain campaign disallowed. She embarked on a political tour espousing her strong-willed conservative statements that carried her through the campaign. She resigned as Governor of Alaska, organized a political action committee to help elect Republican woman to office, and became a television celebrity as well as political commentator. Many viewed her as a potential candidate for president in 2012. She decided not to run and would capitalize on her "moment of fame" with a book and political speeches. She was the keynote speaker at the First Tea Party convention and a popular figure at conservative political events. In the 2016 election, she endorsed Donald Trump for president.

As of this writing, she seems to have withdrawn from major political activity and seemed to be hurt when it was learned that she would not be invited to attend U.S. Sen. John McCain's funeral. She maintains respect for McCain and has taken the high road in describing her relationship with him. She has continually expressed gratitude to McCain for having the courage to nominate her as his running mate. McCain wrote in his final auto-biography that he had regrets about selecting her as his running mate and wished that he would have had the opportunity to run with Joe Lieberman instead. The political future of Palin is unclear at this time, but she was a person of political firsts, just not the first female vice president.

CHAPTER FORTY FIVE

FROM VICE PRESIDENTIAL CANDIDATE

TO SPEAKER OF THE HOUSE

TO RETIREMENT

President Obama and Vice President Biden would be re-elected to the presidency and vice presidency, respectfully, in the election of 2012. Mitt Romney, former Governor of Massachusetts, would select Paul Ryan, a congressman from Wisconsin as his running mate. The Republican ticket would carry 24 states and win 47 percent of the vote in a losing cause that at times looked winnable.

Paul Ryan grew into politics early on as he worked in Washington as a legislative aide. He would also become a speech writer for a previously defeated vice presidential candidate, Jack Kemp, being baptized in being pro-business and free market conservatism. Ryan, after remaining involved in conservative causes, would run for Congress from Wisconsin and was elected to his first term in the 1998 elections. Wisconsin would re-elect him to 10 terms, including re-electing him to Congress at the same time he was being defeated for the vice presidency. The Electoral College would elect Biden for a second term by a vote of 332 to 207.

In defeat, Ryan's political life would go on. He returned to Congress as a congressional conservative leader within the party. He was mentioned as a potential presidential candidate in the 2016 elections but decided against running. That year, the Republicans nominated Donald Trump, a controversial GOP candidate to say the least, and a candidate who did not quickly win the support of the Republican leadership. Ryan, himself, was not quick to endorse Trump, and even after a cool endorsement, found it difficult to campaign with him based on a series of comments, tweets, and remarks. In 2015, leading in to the new administration of Donald Trump, Ryan was elected the 54th Speaker of the House after the party was seeking a unifying leader. As Speaker of the House, he worked with the administration to usher in a tax reform bill. Also as the Speaker of the House, he failed in the attempt to overhaul the health care legislation, which was a key agenda item of the Republican Party. Ryan opted not to seek re-election to Congress and ended his 20 years of service in 2019. He has consistently been mentioned as a future presidential candidate and currently serves on the board of the FOX Corporation. He also served as professor at the University of Notre Dame. As speculation continues to swarm that his political career is not over, he did tell CBS News in an interview that now that he is out of politics, he simply wants to hunt, fish, and ski with his family. His party may have other plans for him.

CHAPTER FORTY SIX

THIS VICE PRESIDENTIAL CANDIDATE KNOWS HOW DEWEY MUST HAVE FELT

As the 2020 election unfolds, the stories of the 2016 elections will resurface many times. U.S. Sen. Tim Kaine of Virginia, the Democratic nominee for vice president, almost certainly can explain the feelings Thomas Dewey had when he ran for president in 1948 against President Harry Truman. Virtually every poll and every pundit assumed that Hillary Clinton would be the first woman elected President of the United States. Kaine, part of that ticket, was the assumptive vice president. When the results were in, Clinton and Kaine did, in fact, win the popular vote, and carried 20 of the 50 states. Winning the popular vote does not assure election, and the Electoral College vote would give Donald Trump and Gov. Mike Pence a clear victory. Mike Pence was elected vice president over Kaine by a vote of 304 to 227.

The election remains controversial to this day and will continue to be rehashed for quite some time. The polls were clearly out of step with the results. Speculation and issues continue to remain about vote tampering and foreign meddling. The bottom line is that Donald Trump and Mike Pence were elected.

Kaine had a very natural rise in politics. His political resume was well suited for the job. He was elected Mayor of Richmond in 1998 and served until 2001. He was elected the lieutenant governor in 2002, serving until 2006 when he was elected governor of the state. He would serve as the chairman of the Democratic Party in 2009 and would run for the U.S. Senate in 2012. Based on the polling and his political rise, including a perfect record of campaign wins, most assumptions were that he would serve with Hilary Clinton. Many experts assumed he would eventually run for the presidency at the conclusion of the Clinton presidency. He did well in the debates and was an effective campaigner in a losing effort. After the election, he returned to the U.S. Senate.

In 2018, Kaine would be re-elected to his Senate seat. Politics is a game where "never say never" is a cliché, but Kaine has publically said he would not run for president or vice president again. He currently serves on the Foreign Relations Committee; the Budget Committee; the Armed Services Committee; and the Health, Education, Labor Pension Committee.

When U.S. Sen. John McCain died, Kaine told the story that McCain came to him shortly after his defeat and said that he, McCain, was the only one person currently in the Senate who knew how he felt after the loss, since they were the only current members to be on a national ticket that lost. He advised him to get back to work. Kaine said he took the advice to heart and made the decision to get to work on Senate matters. He is expected to represent Virginia until his term ends in 2024.

-.-

CHAPTER FORTY-SEVEN
TWO OUT OF THREE AIN'T BAD

Meatloaf, the singer, had a hit record, "Two out of three ain't bad" and that certainly seems an appropriate tune for Minnesotans waking up to the election results in 2024.

Tim Waltz, governor of Minnesota, fell short of joining fellow Minnesotans Hubert Humphrey and Walter Mondale in getting a chance to spit in the 2024 elections.

Oddly enough, while Minnesota has never seen a native son elected President, the state has had the privilege of seeing two of its own reach the vice presidency of the United States. It also has seen them become the nominee of a major party for President of the United States.

In 1964, Hubert Humphrey was elected vice president of the United States as the running mate of Lydon Johnson. Humphrey defeated William Miller for the vice presidency and would go on to be the 1968 nominee of the Democratic Party for President of the United States. Humphrey would lose to Richard Nixon and eventually returned to the United States Senate where he had previously served the state.

In 1976, another Minnesotan, United States Senator, Walter Mondale, was elected vice president of the United States. Mondale, running with Jimmy Carter, defeated Senator Bob Dole for the office, who ran with the only person never elected to the office of vice president or president, Gerald Ford. Mondale would be defeated for reelection to the office of vice president in 1980 by George H. Bush, who was elected in a landslide victory as the running mate of Ronald Reagan. Mondale would go on to win the Democratic nomination for President in 1984, becoming the second Minnesotan to accomplish such a feat. He too, like his former mentor, Hubert Humphrey, would be defeated for the presidency. One side note worth mentioning is that the election had historic significance because Mondale selected as his running mate, the first woman, Congresswoman Geraldine Ferraro, to be nominated by a major party for the office of vice president. After his defeat, Mondale would become the Ambassador to Japan and did try to return to the United States Senate but was defeated.

In 2024, America featured an unusual upheaval in politics, which opened the door for one of the major party candidates to become the next person who would "never have a chance to spit".

The nominee of the Democratic party seemed assured when President Joe Biden announced he would run for a second term with Vice President

Kamala Harris. The Republican Party nominated former President, Donald Trump who selected Senator J.D. Vance of Ohio, as his running mate. At that moment, only Senator Vance appeared to be the individual with an opportunity to become a person who would not get a chance to spit.

However, fate would step in, when an exhausted looking President Biden debated former President Trump in a nationally televised debate. Soon after the debate, various leaders within the party called on the President to step aside as the nominee, which he did on July twenty first. The party quickly and surprisingly rallied behind Vice President Harris, who accepted the nomination as the "certified" candidate on August sixth before the national party would meet later in August. In doing so she became only the second woman in history to be the nominee of a major party for the office of President of the United States.

On August sixth, after being certified by the Democratic delegates, Harris asked the Governor of Minnesota to be her running mate and Tim Waltz was formally nominated for the office by the Democratic Party at their convention on August twenty first. Unlike Hubert Humphrey and Walter Mondale, Waltz was not a national household word at the time of his nomination. Several other potential running mates for Harris were clearly known better with deeper political connections.

The Waltz background for national politics in modern times is different. His earning level does not rival some of the major contenders in major political circles. His background also has a few varied twists and turns that again, many more focused national contenders have managed differently. At age 17, he enlisted in the Army National Guard. He retired after 24 years as a Command Sergeant Major. He spent a year teaching in China and speaks Mandarin. He spent 16 years in the education system as a high school teacher and it appears that experience propelled him into a political career. He had his first encounter in the political world by doing some volunteer work, which led to official work for John Kerry's 2004 presidential campaign. The official line is that he was inspired to pursue a pollical career when his high school students were questioned by a security detail at a Bush for President event with Kerry campaign material. Within two years, Waltz, with the support of many of his former high school students, would go on to be elected to Congress, a position he held for 12 years before deciding to run for Governor of Minnesota. He won that election and would win reelection as Governor in 2022. While he was front and center in the media for the George Floyd incident his first real taste in national politics came in 2023 when he was elected as the chair for the Democratic Governors Association. Little did he know that in less than six months, he would be on a much bigger stage as the nominee of his party for vice president. As the hurried campaign went on, his lack of national exposure and the lack of political experience created some small issues for the campaign particularly with his military service, a DUI incident, the debates and political appearances. His biggest campaign statement came when he said he thought the Republicans were "weird". This statement played throughout the campaign and inspired voters on both sides of the ledger to react. Most pundits agree that the statement fired up the opposition to their campaign. He was often overshadowed by the intense campaign of the two candidates at the top of the ticket. The loyalty of both Trump and Harris followers would often leave their running mates as simply surrogate campaigners.

When the votes were tallied, the Trump-Vance ticket would defeat the Harris-Waltz ticket in the electoral college and popular vote. Waltz would go back to Minnesota to continue to serve as Governor.

About the Author

AJ Rick Vaccarelli enjoys politics and is a big fan of biographies. He earned his degrees from Geneva College and Duquesne University. He was the first male resident from Beaver County, Pennsylvania under the age of 21 to register to vote. He spent over 40 years in the corporate world of advertising sales and management and has served as an Adjunct Professor for the past 24 years. He enjoys politics like other people enjoy sports. He and his wife Carol live near Pittsburgh, Pennsylvania. He welcomes your comments or letters and you may reach him at www.rickvac@comcast.net or www.neverhadachancetospit.com

Updates to this book will appear on:
www.neverhadachancetospit.com

desenvolver o caráter, ao ajudar a aprender e a apreender virtudes como paciência, humildade, perseverança e dependência Divina (COSTA, 2024):

Capítulo 1
1.1. A subjetividade e psicoterapia

Segundo Freitas (2021), para melhor compreensão dos modos de subjetivação para um tratamento eficaz é necessário entender algumas dimensões referentes à subjetividade.[7] Embora ela é passível de parte da;

---

[7] A idéia de produção da subjetividade pode ser enriquecida pela noção de subjetivação (FAUCALULT, 1990; DELEUZE, 1992). Sempre precedida das palavras "formas", "modos", "processos", que apontam que a subjetivação nunca está acabada, mas se constitui como um processo contínua. A partir dessa perspectiva, há múltiplas maneiras diferentes de se subjetivar no decorrer da história, em que o sujeito pode fixar, manter ou transformar sua identidade (Foucault, 1990). Dito em outras palavras, a suposição é que a sub subjetividade hoje se produz diferentemente do que se produziu, por exemplo, no início do século XX, aspectos humano também estudado por Bauman (2019), através das sua obre sobre modernidade líquida. De modo não casual, a instituição escolar fez e faz parte dessa produção, uma vez que, se por um lado ela é um lugar fundamental na constituição da subjetividade, por outro ela também está inserida num amplo contexto. Nesse sentido, a engrenagem da escola é atravessada e marcada pela configuração social, mas também tem o papel de definir o sujeito, seja por meio. das relações de poder entre professores e alunos, seja na forma pela qual concebe a aprendizagem e transmite o saber. A identificação da subjetividade com a consciência e suas consequentes derivações, um "eu" racional, autônomo, e individualizado, parece ser um ponto inabalável da filosofia moderna, a partir das meditações cartesianas. Em termos esquemáticos e simplificados, a consciência como subjetividade estaria referida e se constituiria através destas instâncias, eu, pessoa, cidadão e sujeito, e seria ativa, sede da razão e do pensamento, capaz de identidade consigo mesma, sujeito de direitos, virtude e verdade (*Seminário 4* de LACAN). Criam-se assim duas esferas autônomas e interativas, cortadas de suas realidades políticas, culturais, produtivas - um sujeito a um só tempo pensante e autobiografável, que conhece

descentralização e, ou, centralização no indivíduo; visto que a subjetividade implica uma produção incessante de efeitos, modelados a de encontros que vivemos com o outro. Ao se falar em produção de subjetividades, não a compreendemos como algo pré-concebido, pois ela se caracteriza por um processo social constante. A partir dessa perspectiva, há múltiplas maneiras de se subjetivar; de modo que a subjetivação presentes no no decorrer da história, em que o sujeito pode fixar, manter ou transformar sua identidade. Conquanto, para realizar a

---

o mundo, e um objeto dado a priori que espera ser desvelado em sua intimidade pelo primeiro. A subjetividade como um fluxo contínuo de sensações, modos de existir, amar e comunicar, de imagens, sons, afetos, valores e formas de consumo literalmente fabricadas no entrecruzamento de instâncias sociais, técnicas, institucionais e individuais, estamos radicalizando as possibilidades dos engendramentos de subjetividades. No limite, é possível talvez considerar que todos os sujeitos e coletivos humanos, institucionalizados ou não, com maior ou menor grau de instrução e de conhecimento tecnológico, são produtores de subjetividade. Conquanto, as condições de produção evocadas nesse esboço de redefinição implicam, então, conjuntamente instâncias humanas intersubjetivas manifestadas pela linguagem e instâncias sugestivas concernentes à teologia, interações institucionais de diferentes naturezas, dispositivos maquínicos, tais como aqueles que recorrem ao trabalho com computador, Universos de referência incorporais tais como aqueles relativos à música e às artes plásticas. Essa parte não-humana pré-pessoal é essencial, já que é a partir dela que pode desenvolver sua heterogênese. Chega-se, então a uma definição provisória do o que estamos chamando aqui de subjetividade: tudo aquilo que concorre para a produção de um "si", um modo de existir, um estilo de existência. Mas, outras perguntas se fazem necessárias para a continuidade da problematização apresentada a subjetividade como modo de se relacionar com o mundo, considerado fruto de uma "engenharia de altas interações" de componentes heterogéneos, é produzida, o que (ou quem), então, de fato a produz.

análise dos modos de subjetivações individuais e coletivas tem-se a religião como instrumento da obrigatoriedade aplicada à subjetividade das pessoas, acarretando a determinação de comportamentos com base em julgamentos morais que visavam o controle dos sujeitos. Esta lógica adiverte que,

> "a subjetividade enquanto processo de constituição do psiquismo possibilita ao homem apropriar-se das produções da humanidade (universalidade), a partir de determinadas condições de vida (particularidade), que constituem indivíduos únicos (singularidades), mesmo quando compartilham a mesma particularidade" (SILVA, 2009, p.174).

Com isso, é possível apontar que a subjetividade é construída através da cultura, das relações sociais, das vivências e do contexto histórico. Sendo silva (2009), geralmente, subjetividade é entendida como aquilo que diz respeito ao indivíduo, ao psiquismo ou a sua formação, ou seja, algo que é interno, numa relação dialética com a objetividade, que se refere ao que é externo. É compreendida como processo e resultado, algo que é amplo e que constitui a singularidade de cada pessoa. A ideia de que a subjetividade é algo, mas sem definir claramente o que vem a ser esse algo, é bastante recorrente, como podemos verificar na citação abaixo. É um fenômeno psicológico deve ser entendido como construção no nível individual do mundo simbólico que é social. O fenômeno deve ser visto como subjetividade, concebida como algo que se constituiu na relação com o mundo material e social, mundo este que só existe pela atividade humana. Subjetividade e objetividade se constituem uma à outra sem se confundirem. Ela faz com que, vivenciando uma mesma situação, pessoas possam interpretar e tomar atitudes diferentes. Além disso, o processo pelo qual, também de forma singular, algo é apropriado e se torna pertencente e constitutivo do indivíduo é igualmente compreendido como subjetividade (SILVA, 2009). Para tal, o homem é um projeto, que constrói sua subjetividade ao passo em que vive em um determinado tempo histórico, são as ações concretas desse homem em um dado contexto que definem sua subjetividade. Dessa forma, ela seria uma construção humana multifacetada, em constante movimento, criada na relação entre o homem e o mundo, podendo inclusive ser afetada a partir do olhar do outro. Assim sendo, toda experiência que concretiza uma subjetividade envolve modos historicamente peculiares de se fazer a experiência do si mesmo. A preocupação de Foucault (1985, 1988) estava vinculada à exposição da determinação eminente e contingente de nossos modos atuais de subjetivação, assim como à possibilidade de construção de novos processos, numa estética da existência. Se considerarmos que os modos de subjetivação imprimem registros no âmbito psíquico, eles estão ligados aos padrões identitários presentes nas relações entre sujeitos e de acordo com as regras normativas de cada época. Com isso, podem surgir diferentes subjetividades constituídas por práticas de assujeitamento que condizem com o atual capitalismo, favorecendo o surgimento do "sujeito consumidor". Portanto, Lacan (1998) afirmam que as forças sociais que administram o capitalismo atual já entenderam, há muito tempo, que a produção de subjetividades é tão importante quanto a produção material dos bens de consumo.

1.1.2. A psicanálise para as reflexões sobre religião

Este livro trata-se sobre a importância da psicanálise[8] para a ciência tanto da saúde quanto as ciência humanas. Sabe-se que a psicanálise, também conhecida como terapia que utiliza fala como instrumento para análise; um tipo de tratamento baseado nas teorias de Sigmund Freud e de seu sucesso Jacques Lacan,[9] frequentemente

---

[8] Diferente de um médico, a teoria usada por um psicanalista começa com o inconsciente, o aparelho psíquico. É a partir desta teoria e seus desdobramentos que um psicanalista trabalha. Ela considera que somos influenciados por partes profundas de nós mesmos e também por partes que tentam conciliar nosso eu e a realidade externa. Ou seja, somos influenciados por coisas que a gente sabe e coisas que a gente não sabe sobre nós mesmos e também coisas do mundo externo e do outro. Para Freud, a neurose é fruto de um conflito entre partes de nós que sofrem influências distintas e a neurose acontece quando algo é tão insuportável de lidar que ao invés de lidar com isso encontrando caminhos possíveis, o aparelho psíquico recalca o conteúdo como se ele não pudesse procurar outros caminhos de satisfação; isso justifica as razões porque a psicanálise trabalha com a fala e os sentidos humanos.

[9] Jacques Lacan (1901-1981) foi um grande psicanalista, sendo considerado um dos principais intérpretes de Sigmund Freud. Sua obra é considerada como complexa de se compreender. Ele fundou uma corrente psicanalítica própria: a Psicanálise Lacaniana. Em resumo, Lacan é considerado um pensador revolucionário da psicanálise. De modo que tem um lugar próprio na teoria psicanalítica: a psicanálise lacaniana ou linha francesa de psicanálise.

chamado também como sucessor de Freud; "pai da psicanálise". Freud desenvolveu a modalidade psicanalística de tratamento para pacientes que não respondiam aos tratamentos biofisiológicos e mentais médicos disponíveis em seu tempo. Um desses mecanismos surgida na personalístico chama-se de "recalque"; entendido como um sinal de defesa, que mantém afastado da consciência alguma ideia ou situação que pareça ameaçadora. Ou seja, é um mecanismo de defesa mental de algo incompatível com o sujeito. Outro o projeto de trabalho da psicanálise é a ideia de que o ser humano tem direito de falar o que quer, como quer e quando quer; com esta lógica a psicanálise atua analisando clinicamente as informa subjetivava da linguagem do sujeito e, assim, por orientá-lo. Seguido esta menção, Lacan utiliza a noção de subjetivação humana para valorizar a dimensão histórica da sociedade

---

A Psicanálise de Jacques Lacan constitui um sistema de pensamento que inovou a teoria e a prática clínica propostas por Freud. Lacan propôs um retorno a Freud, ampliando e criando novos conceitos, além de ter criado uma técnica de análise e uma abordagem clínica próprias. As dimensões da linguagem, do simbólico, do desejo e o papel do Outro na constituição do sujeito são marcas de Lacan. Lacan apresentou inovações na psicanálise, tanto do ponto de vista teórico, como no ponto de vista prático. Segundo Lacan, a psicanálise tem apenas uma interpretação possível, que é a interpretação linguística. Isso porque os significados atribuídos às coisas são fatores determinantes na vida psíquica de uma pessoa. E esses significados só podem ser construídos ou expressos pela linguagem. Na psicanálise, o inconsciente é tido como fonte dos fenômenos patológicos. Sendo assim, conforme também defendido por outros psicanalistas, é uma tarefa descobrir as leis pelas quais se rege o inconsciente. Leis que são descobertas pelas manifestações do inconsciente, e assim, pode-se tratar essas patologias.

e da psicanálise, com objetivo para desenvolvimento das fórmulas desta área de conhecimento e da qualidade de vida das pessoas. Assim, a religião como instrumento da operacionalização da psicanálise exige histórico do conhecimento referente à subjetividade do indivíduo e da sociedade a qual ele está inserido: isso significa não isolar os planos religiosos na clinicagem ou em pesquisas da psicanálise. A rejeição das linguagens das experiências religiosas passa pela ignorância epistemológica das ciências; isto é, presença de desconhecimento sobre o impacto de religião na vida das pessoas e da sociedade (JAMES, 1991). As funções da religião vão além da linguagem; está presente na cultura, onde o homem está inserido e; há, na miraria, sujeitos com desconhecimento da lei experiências e linguagens (JAMES, 1991). Quanto a tal, sabe-se que no sujeito há pertencimentos pelos seus ascendentes, suas funções, seu futuro, sua cultura, é algo que toca passagem, em função da ideia que acredito desta bastante dever ser bastante sã, de que não se pode desconhecer a filiação simbólica de um sujeito (ELIADE, 2008, CROATTO, 2001). Isso leva diretamente aquilo de que se tratava: religião é uma forma de linguagem aplicada na psicanálise.

1.1.3. A linguagem aplicada na psicanálise e religião

Esta sessão estuda, especificamente, a linguagem aplicada na psicanálise para a religião enquanto um substrato do ser humano. Tara tal, a linguagem está para Lacan assim como a questão sexual está para Freud. Essa é uma frase que não é difícil de ser ouvida entre pessoas que estão conhecendo os dois psicanalistas mais famosos da história. Lacan sempre dizia que o inconsciente é estruturado como uma linguagem; por isto os "os chistes e sua relação com o inconsciente: a interpretação dos sonhos, por exemplo; onde fica é clara a importância da linguagem nos estudos sobre a subjetividade. Neste sentido, Lacan buscou construções histórica de representações da sociedade; visto que

> "o estilo e o próprio homem", repete-se sem nisso ver malícia, e sem tampouco preocupar-se com fato de homem não ser mais uma referência tão segura. Aliem do mais, a imagem da roupa que adorna Buffon ao escrever está aí mesmo para manter a desatenção" (LACAN, 998, p.9).

Inicialmente, Lacan está falando do perfil da linguagem do homem Equivale à ideia ou pensamento da pessoa; movimento que ganha força na década de 1960. Visto que a estabilidade do campo que abordava a problemática do estilo a partir da dualidade entre fundo e forma sofria abalos profundos. Tributo da ideia de que o pensamento e a linguagem são duas operações que se complementam, a conceituação clássica de estilo, pautada na dualidade das figuras de fundo e forma, seria colocada em questão pelos proponentes do estruturalismo. Quanto a confiabilidade do homem, Lacan dizia que para confiabilidade é necessário estreitar relação entre a psicanalítica do homem com a lógica, em regras de análises. Isso porque

> "o homem brandido no adagio já então clássico, por ter sido extraído de um discurso na Academia,

revela-se, nessa escrita, uma fantasia do grande homem, composta em um roteiro tal que ela toma sua casa inteira. Nada ali provem do natural. Quanto a isso, Voltaire, estamos lembrados, generaliza maldosamente" (LACAN, 1998, p.9).

Com isso, "o estilo e homem; vamos aderir a essa formula, somente ao estende la: homem a quem nos endereçamos?" (LACAN, 1998, p.9). Este autor responde que endereça uma "carta" para aqueles que um dia trabalho com a formula da malícia.[10] Lacan está falando metaforicamente para fazer entender que o ser humano é

---

[10] "Melancolia" é um dos termos mais antigos e inespecíficos da medicina mental. É, também, desde sempre, um significante da cultura, que deu ensejo a produções extraordinárias, não apenas na psiquiatria, mas no campo das artes plásticas, da literatura, do cinema e da religião. Sua desaparição na classificação psiquiátrica atual é bastante emblemática do tempo e do tipo de psiquiatria que vivemos, interessada em afirmar um vocabulário imune às imprecisões inerentes à interseção com a cultura e em excluir a subjetividade. Junto com a melancolia, outros termos também desapareceram ou perderam seu estatuto na classificação das doenças mentais: paranoia, neurose, histeria - todos eles termos que realizavam essa incidência recíproca dos significantes da cultura na psiquiatria e da psiquiatria na cultura. A própria categoria de psicose, como entidade nosográfica, foi abandonada, restando o adjetivo "psicótico" para designar a ocorrência de delírio, alucinações e alterações grosseiras de comportamento. A tentativa de fazer do diagnóstico psiquiátrico uma língua sem equívocos representou um empobrecimento discursivo da psiquiatria, implicando uma "superficialização da psicopatologia" e uma tendência a se restringir o campo da intervenção psiquiátrica ao controle farmacológico dos sintomas. Assim, retomar essa entidade é também valorizar uma prática discursiva em torno da psicopatologia, abandonada pela tendência psiquiátrica atual, com graves prejuízos para a clínica e não sem consequências para a própria cultura.

cheio de demandas de recalque pré-consciente e inconsciente. Nesse sentido, Lacan abriu o caminho para se pensar no inconsciente e na pulsão como historicamente adquiridos ao postular que sua gênese e sua natureza são indissociáveis do mundo humano e da comunicação interhumana; mas este autor, também, concebe o inconsciente e a pulsão como ligados a uma dimensão essencialmente humana que aponta para uma ruptura ou um desvio com relação ao inato e/ou instintual. Assim,

> "a linguagem é duplamente estruturada: enquanto "sistema do significante" (é o abc de que falávamos antes, e vê-se que a expressão sistema do significante assume também um estatuto equivalente a língua) e enquanto "sistema do discurso": é o bê- á-bá " que vislumbramos acima, e é a fala que, como se pode perceber nesse momento, é também sistema. O primeiro sistema é de natureza sincrônica, e o segundo, de natureza diacrônica" (KANT, 1999, p.10).

Este ponto de vista de Kant denota que é elementar para ressaltar que Lacan (no seus Seminários) e Saussure (2006) contém interpretações essenciais sobre a língua para os estudos psicanalísticos.[11] Sabe-se que existe uma

---

[11] Nota- que é extremamente representativo de certa apreciação, bastante difundida nos meios analíticos, a propósito da articulação teórica existente entre Lacan e Saussure e, de um modo geral, da associação entre linguística estrutural e psicanálise. Tal ponto de vista participa da ideia segundo a qual haveria na teoria psicanalítica um objeto, o inconsciente, que permanece fora do domínio da

relação subterrânea entre linguagem, psicanálise e religião nas noções saussurianas de diacronia[12] e de linearidade; pois, "na linguagem nossa mensagem nos vem do Outro, e para enuncia-lo até o fim: de forma invertida" (LACAN, 1998, p.9). Ao pensar sobre linguagem enquanto mensagem para o Outro,

> "condescendemo-lhe um patamar na escalada de nosso estilo, dando a carta roubada o privilégio de abrir sua sequência, a despeito de sua diacronia" (LACAN, 1998, p.10).

Outro elemento elencando por Lacan que contribui para compreender o homem é a função da linguagem refletir sobre a realidade, pensar o pensar, comunicar e, com estes aspectos, desvelar recalques. Dentro da psicanálise, temos os mecanismos de defesa, como por exemplo o ego, que são usados de forma inconsciente para suportarmos a angústia do ser (FREUD, 2019; LACAN, *Seminário 4*). Um desses mecanismos denominado "recalque" pode ser entendido como um sinal de defesa, que mantém afastado

---

linguagem e que somente poderia ser abordado através de Saussure com a condição de adotarmos, com respeito à sua linguística.

[12] A sincronia é estudo do sistema da língua. Assim, ocupa-se de descrever os aspectos que regem, em determinado momento histórico, o funcionamento linguístico. Em outras palavras, estuda e descreve o modo como a língua funciona. Trata de fatos simultâneos, ou seja, inseridos em idêntico recorte temporal. Isso significa que ela abstrai a passagem do tempo. Na sincronia, não importam as mudanças, mas um momento. Os fatos sincrônicos, por se referirem a um sistema, apresentam princípios de regularidade. Contudo, esses fatos não são absolutos, uma vez que podem ser alterados caso ocorra uma mudança na língua (SAUSSURE, 2006).

da consciência alguma ideia ou situação que pareça ameaçadora. Ou seja, é um mecanismo de defesa mental de algo incompatível com o sujeito (FREUD, 2019). O recalque, então, é uma forma de negação e rechaço de elementos do psiquismo ideias, emoções, memórias para fora da consciência. O ponto de vista de Saussure (2006) e de Lacan (nos seus Seminários) É um mecanismo que tem um dispêndio de energia capaz de realizar pressão para manter os elementos no Inconsciente. Nesta lógica, a partir da repressão através da subjetividade expressa na linguagem em sua subjetividade, surge o recalque. Significa mencionar que o fato de enviar o conteúdo que está dimensionado do consciente para o inconsciente, causando, assim, sensação de alívio da tensão causada pela repressão. Segundo Freud (2019a, 2019b), é a partir do recalque, engatilha-se o sintoma, que é o retorno do recalcado. O recalque consiste na tentativa do Eu se furtar do desprazer, mas este mecanismo é falho, não poupa o sujeito do desprazer, como prova a formação dos sintomas. Segundo Freud, se o recalque não conseguir impedir sentimentos de desprazer e angustia, pode-se dizer que falhou. De acordo com a psicanálise, o recalque é um mecanismo mental de defesa que protegem a pessoa de pensamentos que sejam contrários ao "eu". Ou seja, uma pessoa recalcada está colocando em evidência as situações, desejos ou problemas em si que não quer admitir, espero ter contribuído. Sendo assim, recalque está intimamente relacionado à realidade tanto subjetiva quanto objetiva. Tanto Freud quanto Lacan abordam o inconsciente como uma forma de linguagem. Visto que, com a linguagem, "tendo constituído seu primeiro núcleo, a repressão começa. Há agora um ponto central em torno do qual poderão organizar-se, em seguida, os sintomas, as repressões sucessivas e, ao mesmo tempo, já que a repressão e o retorno do reprimido são a mesma coisa – o retorno do reprimido" (LACAN, 1975, 215).

Nesta citação nota-se que o inconsciente é o não consciente, sendo que o inconsciente é o ponto central na psicanalise, por nele existir sintomas, organizações, não organizações, confusões de representações vivadas e reprimidas. O termo "recalque" é uso quase que exclusivo da psicanálise, definido como sendo o movimento que o aparelho psíquico promove para despejar da consciência as representações que podem gerar desprazer. Além disso, o aparelho psíquico disponibiliza energia para executar a tarefa de manter o conteúdo que foi despejado afastado da consciência (FREUD, 2010). O mecanismo do recalque não dispõe de força suficiente para erradicar as fontes pulsionais do aparelho psíquico, mas para empurrá-las de volta, "desalojar do centro da cena" (FREUD, 1910, p.363), mantendo-as fora da consciência, no inconsciente. Assim sendo, o recalque mantém-se existente e necessário, pois as fontes pulsionais, uma vez recalcadas, movimentam-se constantemente buscando um caminho para acessar a consciência e o mundo externo, onde irá encontrar a satisfação. A função do recalque é gerar contra-investimentos para manter o material recalcado no inconsciente (FREUD, 1910). Segundo este autor, o recalque é um processo que obriga as idéias e as representações pulsionais a permanecerem no inconsciente. Esse funcionamento se estabelece para evitar o desprazer que pode ser gerado pelo retorno deste material, bem como o desequilíbrio psicológico do sujeito. Neste sentido, a linguagem é uma forma de comunicação do inconsciente com o consciente e, este com as relações sociais, relevante na fábrica de informações do inconsciente. O discurso da linguagem

> "quer nos atenhamos a etimologia que indica um acompanhamento e implica a precedência do trajeto parodiado, que', reconduzindo O termo a seu emprego comum, nela vejamos esconjurada a sombra do maitre à penser, para obter o efeito que preferirmos" (KANT, 1998, p.10).

As ciências da linguagem, como ponto de apoio, é um instrumento de manipulação com finalidade positiva ou negativa; por ela evocar comunicação, tarefas e reponsabilidades, objetivando a promoção dos interesses dos sujeitos; bem como possibilita que o objeto atravessa princípios, uma vez que é o objeto que possibilitas e responde às perguntas. Ressalva-se que a linguagem, ao oscilar, interroga, por si, o outro com palavras. Assim, "o programa que se trava para nós, portanto, e saber como uma linguagem formal determina o sujeito" (LACAN, 1998, p.47) aplicada através das expressões e manifestações religiosas; visto que, o sujeito constrói e é construído pela linguagem através de associações. Enquanto ser social o sujeito precisa da linguagem verbal e não verbal para a expressão, a compreensão, a comunicação, a transmissão de conhecimentos e as reproduções; conquanto, a linguagem está relacionada com a subjetividade do sujeito, pois que a interpelação, colocar algo para uma discussão, provocar confissão, confessar algo intencionalmente para o domínio do outro e sintonizar a diacronia, são aspectos elementares na vida do indivíduo enquanto ferramentas para dá a linguagem verbal e não verbal expressão para transmissão de conhecimento e suas reproduções. Segundo Kant (1999), a linguagem faz parte da experiência dos sujeitos: é

> "instalar no circuito da realidade, como processo primário, a articulação significante da repetição - acaba tomando um sentido ainda mais novo por se prestar a formação de sua barreira tradicional pelo lado de um gozo, cujo ser faz-se então revestir pelo masoquismo, e até mesmo se abre para a pulsão de morte" (KANT, 1999, p.72).

Os circuitos da realidade passam pelo deslocamento de "técnica teórica psicanalítica" para "práxis psicanalítica", que segundo Lacan, sobre sua própria maneira de nomear o campo pelo qual o analista entra na experiência clínica, não é sem razão e consequências.[13] Essa passagem pode

---

[13] Significa mencionar que (LACAN, 1960) a relação terapêutica entre o psicanalista e o paciente é permeada por fenômenos psicológicos complexos, como a transferência e a contratransferência. O psicanalista, por meio de sua formação e experiência, é capaz de manejar essas interações de forma ética e terapêutica, contribuindo para o progresso do tratamento. Portanto, a qualificação do psicanalista é essencial porque ele utiliza uma variedade de técnicas e abordagens terapêuticas, adaptando-se às necessidades específicas de cada paciente. Essas intervenções podem incluir a interpretação dos sonhos, a análise da transferência, o questionamento reflexivo e

ser localizada no Seminário da Ética, momento no qual Lacan propõe, com todas as letras, que a direção da cura deve ser orientada pelo real. Logo no início do seminário diz:

> "iremos, pelo contrário, ao inverso, no sentido de um aprofundamento da noção de real. A questão ética, uma vez que a posição de Freud nos faz progredir nesse domínio, articula-se por meio de uma orientação do referenciamento do homem em relação ao real" (LACAN, 1959, p. 21).

Neste sentido há aproximações de linguagem e realidade. Esse "sentido de um aprofundamento da noção de real" se deve ao fato de Lacan ter verificado a presença do real na clínica para além de sua função exclusiva de limite ao simbólico, posição que vinha orientando suas formalizações até então. O real, dessa forma, passa a ser reintroduzido em seu ensino desde a recuperação da noção de Freud, neste mesmo seminário, até sua reformulação do objeto a no Seminário da Angústia (FREUD, 1976), passando pelo alguma e pela ideia de mancha nos seminários e escritos intermediários. Todos eles, maneiras de abordar o real desde a perspectiva não apenas do objeto perdido, mas de um real como núcleo da pulsão, informe, sem representante e em um lugar de intimidade ao sujeito. Aquilo que estando no núcleo do próprio sujeito é o que lhe é de mais estranho e exterior, avesso às suas coordenadas. Consoante a Kant (1999), a linguagem é condição de ordem mental, como a

---

outras estratégias que visam promover a autorreflexão e o crescimento pessoal.

compulsão. Significa Saúde mental, mal-estar e psicanálise. Vimos a proliferação de uma discussão nos mais diversos setores sobre a temática concernente ao campo da saúde mental. Dentre os diversos assuntos pertencentes a este campo, um que se faz bastante presente é a concepção geral do que seria alguém possuir boa saúde mental. Em documento orientador a países componentes de seu bloco, a OMS[14] afirma que um indivíduo ser mentalmente saudável está articulado não apenas com a ausência de transtorno mentais, sejam eles de ordem psicológica ou psiquiátrica, mas também a fatores socioeconômicos, biológicos, de meio ambiente e de retorno da produtividade (força de trabalho) para com sua respectiva comunidade. Desde a perspectiva da psicanálise, nos perguntamos o que é ter saúde mental na atualidade, em meio a um cenário político-econômico-social instável, agravado por uma situação de pandemia que escancara as três fontes do sofrimento humano apontadas por Freud[2] em "Mal-estar na civilização". A saber, nosso próprio corpo, condenado à decadência e à dissolução, que nem mesmo pode dispensar o sofrimento e a ansiedade como sinais de advertência; o mundo externo, que podem voltar-se contra nós com forças de destruição esmagadoras e impiedosas; e, finalmente, nossos relacionamentos com os outros. Sendo esta última fonte, apontada, como a mais dolorosa entre todas. Nesta obra, o autor recolhe que a tentativa que o humano faz de realizar diversos feitos e progressos é tão somente um esforço em se afastar dos sentimentos infelizes. Podemos interpretar tal ação, como a tentativa de uma conciliação entre o que vem a ser reivindicado tanto por cada sujeito

---

[14] https://www.who.int/pt/about

quanto pela vida coletiva. Ambos possuem interesses distintos. Ainda em "Mal-estar", Freud afirma que o ser humano pode vir a empreender três comportamentos distintos frente ao mal-estar causado pelo atrito sujeito x vida coletiva: uns preferem apostar nos relacionamentos emocionais com outras pessoas, mesmo sendo estes, conforme vimos anteriormente, uma fonte de sofrimento, outros tendem a ser autossuficientes buscando suas satisfações em processos mentais internos e um outro grupo empreende ações onde podem testar sua força. Embora existam estas tentativas, na sentença freudiana, há algo da ordem de um mal-estar, que não nos abandonará. Tal princípio vai na contramão de práticas que prometem felicidade plena e absoluta, sendo que o próprio funcionamento da vida coletiva pede que as pulsões de todos não sejam totalmente satisfeitas. De alguma forma, essa porção de não-realização pode vir a retornar como mal-estar. Dentre alguns dos elementos comuns nos casos clínicos, figura a exacerbação do sentimento de inadequação por parte do sujeito que, por vezes, resulta em dificuldades de manejo com sua própria angústia. Tais situações nos remetem a Freud, com o fenômeno do mal-estar na civilização e seus efeitos para cada sujeito. A chegada de casos com diversas demandas de tratamento e acompanhamento alojadas na perspectiva do campo clínico da saúde mental. Depressão, ansiedade, e outros, são alguns dos nomes na boca dos sujeitos para dizerem do seu sofrimento singular, que embora encontre algum nível de nomeação pela via diagnóstica padrão também esbarram em um algo de cada um não-possível de nomear completamente. O discurso analítico não encontra eco numa prática em saúde mental que pretende "garantir" a todos e que pode vir a estar (mesmo que sem um objetivo direto nisso) aliada a uma prática que irá produzir manobras de engodo subjetivo. Izaguirre[3] localiza que os pilares conceituais do campo da saúde mental, originaram-se no ocidente a partir da burguesia, sob o nome de modernidade. Baseados numa ideia do desenvolvimento indefinido do homem sobre a natureza e determinado pela supremacia da razão, próprios da era do Iluminismo. Vimos tal supremacia encontrar seu limite em fins do século XIX, a partir do limite ideológico de que o homem é determinado de maneira absoluta pela razão, portanto, pela consciência. É neste cenário que vemos surgir a psicanálise. Freud ao diagnosticar que o homem não é senhor em sua própria casa, abre, o que ele mesmo considera ser, uma terceira ferida narcísica (as outras duas abertas por Copérnico e Darwin) em um saber até então pretenso completo: cogito *ergo sum* (Penso, logo sou). E diz, a seu modo, que há algo sobre o funcionamento humano que nos é desconhecido: o inconsciente. A prática analítica vem desde sua origem, debruçando-se sobre esta porção do humano (e isto inclui o sofrimento) que em Lacan podemos ler sendo da ordem de um saber que não se sabe. Saber este que escapa à consciência humana, que não se enquadra e não cede totalmente às nomenclaturas impostas pela civilização. Isto é paradoxal, pois mesmo que em alguma dimensão o sujeito possa valer-se de garantias prometidas por certas práticas em saúde mental, a dimensão do mal-estar estrutural jamais é dominada ou exterminada da vida do sujeito podendo vir a ressurgir, sob diversas facetas. Tal fenômeno marca a impossibilidade de garantia que o discurso do capitalista aliado a certas práticas tenta propor: a existência de um único e permanente bem-estar a todos. Vemos em Freud, que se por um lado, não podemos eliminar todo o sofrimento oriundo da própria condição humana, podemos inventar modos de lidar com ele tornando-o menos intenso. Trata-se aqui de pensar uma prática em saúde mental articulada ao exercício de abarcar o surgimento de um sujeito que, na concepção lacaniana, pensa-se onde não é e é onde não se pensa. Portanto, abordagem sobre o campo da saúde mental tem efeitos singulares que reverberam no coletivo, pois conforme a experiência singular de cada análise prossegue, o sujeito percebe os efeitos de diminuição de seu sofrimento psíquico frente ao mal-estar estrutural. Possibilitando que cada sujeito possa estar na civilização em uma posição repensada e um pouco mais avisada de seu funcionamento. Em uma rápida e breve articulação, em psicanálise, pensar saúde mental é também pensar a inclusão do mal-estar de cada um na dimensão da clínica. A clínica que não é sem ética. Ética que não é sem o desejo de cada um.

1.1.3.1. A função da linguagem religiosa aplicada na psicanálise

Na psicanálise, as tentativas e as possibilidades de comunicar-se estão presentes entre a dupla: paciente e psicoterapêutica; por isso a importância da função da linguagem religiosa aplicada à psicanálise.[15] Seja pela via

---

[15] A linguagem religiosa faz alegações factuais, a saber, se ela faz referências a seres, a objetos, a fatos, a estados de coisas de modo semelhante à linguagem usada nas ciências seja a física, a biologia ou

verbal, não-verbal, corporal, intrasubjetiva e intersubjetiva.[16] A verbalização a oralidade permanecem

a história. A visão tradicional da linguagem religiosa sustenta que sim, desde sua forma mais ingênua e literal como entre as mais sofisticadas. No âmbito religioso não é diferente. O processo de se comunicar – passar uma mensagem e esta ser compreendida por quem a recebe, pode ser entendido, então, como um meio de divulgar a visão de mundo cristão de uma instituição. Comunicação e religião podem ser compreendidas como dois termos indissociáveis.. Como exemplo: os estudo de textos, símbolos, mitos, ritos, práticas das religiões, assim como de sistemas doutrinários a partir de sua linguagem e articulação próprias por meio de métodos das ciências da linguagem, da hermenêutica, da teologia, da filosofia, da história e da antropologia. No âmbito religioso não é diferente. O processo de se comunicar – passar uma mensagem e esta ser compreendida por quem a recebe, pode ser entendido, então, como um meio de divulgar a visão de mundo cristão de uma instituição. Comunicação e religião podem ser compreendidas como dois termos indissociáveis. Assim sendo, a linguagem religiosa é entendida fundamentalmente como imagem e sua finalidade é garantir certo modo de vida que é útil à pessoa religiosa: a lição que se tira dessa discussão é não reduzir a linguagem religiosa à factual.

[16] Quanto a intersubjetividade e a intrasujetividade, Matos (2018) dispõem que: a dimensão da intersubjetividade como constitutiva da subjetividade pode ser considerada aquisição recente da teoria psicanalítica, constituindo-se em uma possibilidade teórica para contornar o solipsismo moderno. No campo filosófico, a problemática cartesiana acarretou o desenvolvimento do estudo da linguagem basicamente em duas direções, resultando em duas concepções dominantes de linguagem contrapostas na contemporaneidade: a objetivista/representacionista e a construtivista/pragmática. Neste artigo, Assim, o conceito de intersubjetividade tal como vem sendo utilizado pela psicanálise, debatendo os usos e as ideologias a ele subjacentes de acordo com essas duas concepções filosóficas de linguagem, por meio de um estudo teórico. Conclui-se que o uso do conceito de intersubjetividade pela psicanálise parece servir mais para contornar

no centro das preocupações da clínica psicanalítica, tornando quase impossível encontrar um lugar para o não verbalizável, o não comunicável, o indizível; visto que o inconsciente recalcado só encontrava via de expressão por meio da verbalização entre o paciente e seu analista, seguindo a regra fundamental da psicanálise. Ao partir das comunicações verbais dos afetos, poder-se-ia chegar até suas representações no inconsciente. Ainda, sem dar a devida importância aos gestos e expressões de alguns pacientes, compreendendo a recusa em falar, de alguns deles, como pura censura ou resistência ao tratamento, no início dos primeiros casos clínicos o inconsciente só

---

a problemática solipsista do que romper com o pensamento moderno. A dimensão da intersubjetividade como constitutiva da subjetividade pode ser considerada aquisição recente das teorias psicológicas, posto que, em sua maioria, elas são herdeiras da tradição moderna cartesiana. Concebem, portanto, o Eu como unidade autoconstituída, independente da existência do Outro, marcando uma oposição entre sujeito e objeto. Na tentativa de se adequar ao modelo vigente, almejando alcançar o status científico, tais teorias psicológicas não se interessaram e até mesmo recusaram a noção de intersubjetividade por bastante tempo. Contudo a Psicologia tem se confrontado cada vez mais com a necessidade de reconhecimento da alteridade na constituição da subjetividade, parecendo não haver dúvidas no cenário contemporâneo a respeito da participação do Outro na constituição subjetiva. No cenário psicanalítico, a tentativa de encontrar soluções para o solipsismo moderno proporcionou modificações na forma como a psicanálise concebe a relação entre o Eu e o Outro, e acabou propiciando a apropriação do conceito de intersubjetividade pelo meio psicanalítico. Apesar de o conceito intersubjetividade ser utilizado pela psicanálise somente há algumas décadas, este tem se apresentado extremamente importante, conforme amplia o foco outrora restrito ao intrapsíquico, possibilitando revoluções na forma como os psicanalistas concebem a mente, as interações e a noção de "outros".

podia ser dizível ou verbalizável, para daí ser analisado e interpretado. Qualquer outra forma de comunicação deveria ser posta de lado:

> "Se a comunicação se encontra no ponto de origem deste processo, a questão é *quem* comunica, já que o eu nasço como *consequência* da comunicação? Freud é muito claro, aqui: é o *desamparo* de origem que *comunica*. Comunicação que desencadeia uma via de alterações internas *no adulto*. O desamparo, porém, faz suspeitar da existência de um eu que sofre deste estado. Entretanto, esta lógica, *psicológica*, deve ser mantida em suspenso" (SILVA, 2002, p.85).

Isto é essencial porque é através da comunicação, que está o centro da relação entre analista e paciente; ponto de origem de todo o processo mental; por desencadear uma seria de alterações internas que havia mantida em suspenso. Operacionalizar a comunicação, verbal e não verbal, mostrar aspectos da subjetividade religiosa da pessoa, sua importância, sua função na prática clínica e; assim, razões porque ela descrever e explicar sequências clínicas, ou um determinado fenômeno psíquico. São aspectos característicos, de certa maneira de exposição do trabalho analítico. Sem a comunicação, a psicanálise é impossível existir; pois a teoria da comunicação, plena da subjetividade. Assim, a teoria da comunicação é de fundamental necessidade para o profissionalismo dos psicanalíticas. Esta abordagem, aplicada tanto a posição de Freud quanto a de Lacan, reconhece o caráter transformador da investigação inerente à *práxis* da comunicação psicanalítica e antecipa elementos epistemológicos da pesquisa científica contemporânea para as ciências. Na condição de *práxis*, propõe-se a escutar o sujeito do inconsciente, que se apresenta no inesperado e fugaz das experiências singulares e, ao mesmo tempo, universais de cada ser humano. Esta intenção epistemo-metodológico representa um vínculo indelével com a instituição socialmente legitimada para a produção do conhecimento canônico da psicanálise aplicada à subjetividade religiosa, tanto individualmente quantos nas relações sociais. Neste sentido,

> "é tão importante para o paciente saber que ele é livre para estar em silêncio, quanto é importante que saiba que é livre para falar. Privilegiar a fala sobre o silêncio, a revelação sobre a privacidade, a comunicação sobre a não-comunicação, parece ser tão não-analítico quanto privilegiar a transferência positiva sobre a negativa, a gratidão sobre a inveja, o amor sobre o ódio" (SILVA, 2017, p.66).

O provérbio Árabe, "a palavra é de prata, e o silêncio é de ouro" remete dizer que a psicanálise é tradutora de mensagens do inconsciente e para a análise de discurso no do silêncio, vazio, mas repleto de sentidos. Atribuir significado ao silêncio é ir além da representação, simbolizando imagens que a memória gravou e inseriu na estrutura psíquica dos sujeitos. Na comunicação verbal, o silêncio, traduzido na pausa. pode ser muito sedutor e tão eloquente quanto as palavras; mas também pode demonstrar segurança, controle e domínio. Com a comunicação verbal não é diferente, pois, às vezes, falamos mais com a eloquência do silêncio que propriamente com as palavras. A pausa silenciosa chega a ser sedutora:

> "O silêncio, quando usado corretamente, é uma das ferramentas mais eficazes para aprimorar suas habilidades de comunicação em público. Ele permite que você capture a atenção, reforce pontos importantes, transmita confiança e evite erros. Incorporar pausas silenciosas estratégicas em suas apresentações pode transformar seu desempenho e tornar sua mensagem mais impactante. Da próxima vez que falar em público, lembre-se: nem sempre o mais importante é o que você diz, mas o que você deixa de dizer."[17]

Isto significa mencionar que o silêncio expressa pensamento, desejos e recalques. Ele, após inflexão de voz apropriada, constitui demonstração de in-segurança, controle e domínio ou não. O momento de silêncio, que pode ser apenas uma fração de segundo, que a comunicação mostra seu encanto; instância em que as informações transmitidas são valorizadas. O ouvinte, psicanalista, tem a oportunidade de refletir sobre a mensagem que acabou de receber. Passa a existir expectativa sobre o que é ou que virá a seguir. Fazer a pausa, conseguir naquele momento de silêncio manter contato visual com o interlocutor, além de não quebrar a linha de comunicação que os mantêm ligados, se

---

[17] Acessado em 19/10/2024: https://exame.com/carreira/guia-de-carreira/como-usar-o-silencio-para-falar-melhor-em-publico/

comporta como se estivesse, silenciosamente, repetindo as informações importantes que acabou de pronunciar é uma das essencialidades da *práxis* psicanalística. Há assim uma valorização da pausa e do silêncio; dinâmica que está em vista a interligação de fatos ditos e, ou, não ditos pelo sujeito. Isto, denota ressaltar que a pausa silenciosa tem tanta influência no processo de comunicação que chega até a funcionar como elemento de transição. Isto é, em vez de ligar as informações importantes com palavras ou expressões, a passagem de uma parte da mensagem para outra é feita com o silêncio da pausa. Esse recurso personalístico, possui valor subjetivo, facilita o entendimento, porque houve uma espécie de aviso de que nova informação estava para surgir, apresentando expectativa e mostrando como o assunto está evoluindo. E isso faz com que as pessoas acompanhem com mais interesse e motivação o que está sendo exposto. Para que alguém saiba desenvolver sua competência oratória, esse é um dos maiores indicadores, a tranquilidade de ficar em silêncio durante os instantes de pausa. E como nos referimos a um dos maiores indicadores, como curiosidade, os outros dois são: ouvir o som da própria voz e conseguir enxergar a fisionomia das pessoas na plateia:

> "Se esse efeito de comunicação apresenta, por vezes, algumas dificuldades, pensem na experiência do mel. O mel ou bem é muito duro, ou bem muito fluido. Se é duro, corta-se dificilmente, pois não há nele clivagem natural. Se é muito fluido - penso que todos vocês fizeram a experiência de absorver mel na cama na hora do

café da manhã -, logo, logo tudo fica melado"
(LACAN, 1959, p,29).

A identificação projetiva ao ser considerada como uma forma de comunicação, consiste em um processo por meio do qual sentimentos próprios ao paciente são projetados no analista, oportunizando um modo de ser entendido tal como "se fizesse parte do outro". Sob esta perspectiva, há um destaque no potencial de comunicação e não no caráter defensivo do mecanismo. Para o psiquiatria Daneiel Delouya, a comunicação se

> "se encontra no ponto de origem deste processo, a questão é quem comunica, já que o eu nasço como consequência da comunicação? Freud é muito claro, aqui: é o desamparo de origem que comunica. Comunicação que desencadeia uma via de alterações internas no adulto. O desamparo, porém, faz suspeitar da existência de um eu que sofre deste estado. Entretanto, esta lógica, psicológica, deve ser mantida em suspenso" (DELOUYA, 2002, p.85).

Assim pois, não é somente por meio da comunicação verbal do analisando ou da comunicação do analista – interpretação, que se promove um conhecimento e a estruturação de si mesmo, isso ocorre também por intermédio de uma relação intensa, íntima, empática e prolongada com o analista. Conquanto, psicoterapeuta é tomada por medo e pavor, pois tem a sensação de que existe alguma arma dentro da mochila "Uma faca ou uma arma" ela pensa. Após dizer algumas palavras, o paciente se inclina em direção a mochila e a psicoterapeuta tem seu medo aumentado, temendo que ele irá retirar algo de dentro da mochila para matá-la. O paciente ainda inclinado, pega uma garrafa de água que estava no bolso lateral da mochila (relato realizado em grupo de estudos de caso clínico. A psicoterapeuta relatava diversas vezes sua falta de vontade, dificuldade e medo de atender esse paciente). A partir da comunicação, destaca que para estar disposto e poder investir no outro, o trabalho de um analista está implicado também em investir muitos anos na sua própria análise, em estudos teóricos, técnicos, fazer supervisões, participar de eventos científicos, da cultura, de entretenimento, produzir, desenvolver seu repertório de sonhos (FREUD, 2019a, 2019b). Trata-se de um processo para si e para o outro, em que os dois lados se beneficiam, a partir de um gesto necessário de amor e de paixão. Atualmente, a psicanálise contemporânea tem se ocupado de aprofundar nos estudos das transformações técnicas e clínicas, em especial devido as novas configurações do psiquismo que vêm se apresentando entre os indivíduos da atualidade (SANTOS, 2019). Note-se:

> "é inegável a relevância das experiências comunicacionais no mundo contemporâneo, mas principalmente da invasão da comunicação audiovisual em diversas áreas e instâncias da vida com um amplo espectro de vídeos que circulam por diversas plataformas, suportes e dispositivos. Com os avanços das pesquisas tecnológicas ligadas à internet das coisas, as pro postas dos Wearables Technologies buscam através dos

materiais eletrônicos ampliar o desempenho humano das funções e dos sentidos corporais e de suas relações com os ambientes e as coisas, mantendo uma constante conectividade, de informações, comunicação e entretenimento" (SANTOS, 2019, p.67).

Ainda:

> "os dispositivos digitais eletrônicos na contemporaneidade assumem o lugar em que os discursos se cruzam, se entrecruzam e são agenciados, assim como aparecem novas formas de manifestação da subjetividade, ao generalizar a partir da ampla classe dos dispositivos foucaultianos e da própria concepção herdada da teologia dos padres latinos, na qual Foucault também havia se referenciado" (SANTOS, 2019, p.68).

A revolução tecnológica trouxe proximidade e velocidade, mas também "empobrecimento" emocional e intolerância a frustração e à espera de realização de projetos. Este cenário se apresenta como um desafio aos aportes clínicos tradicionais, assim como a própria psicanálise, a qual se depara com um indivíduo empobrecido simbolicamente, alheio às emoções e formação da própria mente. Sob este contexto, vale também um destaque para não somente uma ampliação dos estudos de novos e reformulados conceitos e propostas técnicas, tais como o *acting* e o *enactment*. Mas sim de uma ampliação de sua subjetividade e espaço psíquico e de sua capacidade de tolerar o não-conhecido. Elementos estes que se aprende não em estudos teóricos, mas mais especificamente na própria analise (CAVALINN, 2018). Segundo Lacan (1959, p.3) vai dizer que a linguagem nas vias da comunicação é a relação com a realidade. Sabe-se, pois, que a comunicação produz paralelismo. Através dela, pode-se observar e interpretar comportamento através de formações simbólicas (sintomas, sonhos, chistes e atos falhos), via discurso articulado, por meio de atribuições de sentidos partilháveis ou não, ou, ainda, na forma de angústia. Algumas delas, especificamente as que localizamos no cerne da clínica psicanalítica, já podem ser reportadas ao que é mesmo anterior à constituição de uma subjetividade. É o que verificar com Lacan, a partir da inscrição dos signos da percepção (LACAN, 1985), através da incidência, no corpo, do significante enquanto signo. Responsáveis, respectivamente, pela instituição da pulsão ou como causa do gozo as primeiras marcas da linguagem, irredutíveis à representação, funcionarão como mola propulsora da constituição subjetiva e, ao mesmo tempo, como condição de possibilidade da própria clínica psicanalítica. Em outras palavras, nesta irredutibilidade constitutiva da subjetividade encontra-se o fundamento da psicanálise aplicada aos estudos subjetivos através da religião. De modo que,

> "as máquinas sociais podem ser classificadas na rubrica geral de equipamentos coletivos, as máquinas tecnológicas de informação e de comunicação operam no núcleo da subjetividade humana, não apenas no seio das suas memórias, da sua inteligência, mas também da sua

sensibilidade, dos seus afetos, dos seus fantasmas inconscientes. O sujeito, segundo toda uma tradição da filosofia e das ciências humanas, é algo que encontramos como um *être-là*, algo do domínio de uma suposta natureza humana. Proponho, ao contrário, a idéia de uma subjetividade de natureza industrial, maquínica, ou seja, essencialmente fabricada, modelada, recebida, consumida" (MORAIS, 2006, p.45).

Esta acepção está relacionada propriamente à configuração da psicanálise contemporânea. Conquanto, o que Lacan (1976) viria nomear como "gozo opaco, por excluir o sentido", cerne de sua clínica no final de seu ensino, poderia ser pensado como um retorno à pulsão freudiana, conceito sobre o qual Freud construiu o fundamento teórico-clínico da psicanálise. Para Lacan (1959, p.161), "a linguagem (entre elas a tecnológica) enquanto uma forma de consumição é uma confissão e, é comum, quase uniforme". Neste sentido, a linguagem é uma ferramenta para a interpretação dos conceitos psicanalítico e clínico; processo de comunicação que pode ser oral, escrito, digital. Assim, apresenta-se função emotiva, poética, conotativa, referencial, fática ou metalinguística. Isso significa que há diversas formas de linguagem, que pode ser operacionalizada para várias finalidades; porque com a ela é a capacidade que os seres humanos têm para produzir, desenvolver e compreender a língua e outras manifestações, como a pintura, a música e a dança e a interpretações de fatos, eventos e comportamentos das pessoas. Por conseguinte a língua é um conjunto organizado de elementos (sons e gestos) que possibilitam a comunicação; em vista disto, o funcionamento da psicanalise está inter-relacionado. Assim, assiste-se que a

> "comunicação é notável, feita por alguém que não tinha de revoluciona o domínio da histeria, e que não se encontrava na posição de nos fornecer uma experiência imensa, nem mesmo original, já que é alguém cuja carreira psicanalítica está começando, mas cuja exposição, completíssima e talvez, como foi dito, demasiadamente rica, tinha, não obstante, um caráter extremamente articulado. Isso não é o importante; uma comunicação dessa espécie mostra a que ponto as categorias que me esforço há anos em pro- move perante vocês se revelam manejáveis, e permitem articular as coisas com precisão. Elas introduzem uma clareza que está na& próprias dimensões de nossa experiência e, qualquer que seja a discussão que se possa levantar sobre certos pontos de detalhe, vocês. veem as noções teóricas se animarem como que pelo seu próprio movimento, e encontrarem o nível da experiência" (LACAN, 1995, p. 251).

A linguagem provém dos conceitos antropológica e interdisciplinar;[18] cuja ideia central é de que a cultura, através de sua língua, impõe limitações à maneira de o indivíduo pensar, atribuindo com isso à linguagem e à

---

[18] Acessado em 01/10/2024:
https://ea.fflch.usp.br/subcampos/antropologia-linguistica

cultura uma realidade e uma continuidade mais primárias que secundárias, no que diz respeito ao indivíduo.[19] Pois,

> "tudo parece indicar que no campo da mente a herança é rigorosamente de tipo lamarckiano, é derivada de características adquiridas que se transmite de geração em geração, tanto no que diz respeito à forma como ao conteúdo ou, no caso específico da linguagem, tanto em sua sintaxe como em sua semântica" (MELTZER, 1984, p. 100).

Assim, epistemologicamente, um pensamento como está concretude às palavras, ao considerálas continentes de um significado próprio capaz de ser explorado. Daí que dizer que o conhecimento existe e está à espera de ser descoberto é o mesmo que dizer que o espírito divino se manifesta através da palavra. Na psicanálise contemporânea há também um elemento místico que se relaciona com a Teoria do Conhecimento, porém o lugar onde se realizam as transações é outro e a relação com a linguagem é vista, como já foi dito, de modo criativamente mais amplo. Essa é maneira de o indivíduo pensar que reside, para psicanálise contemporânea, é elemento místico:[20]

---

[19] Segundo Oliveira (2017, p.33), "a socialização primária é a responsável por formar a base do indivíduo, é o primeiro contato deste com o mundo exterior. Já a socialização secundária impõe ao indivíduo submundos dos quais ele desconhece, com isso, percebe que existem outras culturas, outras ideologias além da dele.

[20] O místico é aquele que vive a experiência de uma "vizinhança absoluta" com o Mistério por excelência, sendo capaz de romper com o isolamento egocêntrico e perceber a unidade da Realidade numa

"A essência da experiência mística transcende a fronteira psicológica e disso advém que não possa ser explicada através das expressões naturais, da linguagem comum e nem tampouco descrever-se mediante manifestações do estado de ânimo: a experiência mística é inefável, inexpressável e psicologicamente inexplicável" (TORELLÓ, 2010, p.228).

O ser humano reside nos feitos da vida mental que a psicanálise mística entendi (ALVES, 1999, 2005). Assim,

"a psicanálise dá ao termo criativo (na linguagem) um sentido mais amplo do que o que Chomsky lhe atribui (fazer um uso infinito de meios finitos) e que Meltzer define como alcançar um novo nível de ordenamento capaz de perpetuar-se" (MELTZER, 1984, p. 112).

Significa que o conhecimento existe e está à espera de ser descoberto, e quer dizer que o conhecimento e as emoções se manifestam através da palavra. Diante deste panorama, outra função da linguagem na psicanálise é a sua contribuição para interpenetração dos significados dos sonhos. O que Lacan nos diz é que um sonho pode introduz a experiência insondável, sem nenhuma mística.

---

experiência de amor radical. Essa experiência nodal não elimina no sujeito a consciência de sua distinção profunda com respeito ao Mistério maior. O que vigora, porém, é uma sede infinita da busca permanente de união e comunhão com a Energia benfazeja, que é a razão da mais profunda alegria (TEIXEIRA, 2005, p. 18).

A linguagem dos Sonhos fornece verdades empolgantes e desafiadoras sobre a origem dos sonhos e o porquê dessa comunicação. Conforme Freud e Lacan, os sonhos são considerados como uma janela para o inconsciente e uma fonte valiosa de informação sobre o paciente. Eles compreenderam que os sonhos podem revelar desejos reprimidos, conflitos emocionais e traumas não resolvidos que não podem ser acessados durante o estado de vigília:

> "isso não é o importante - uma comunicação dessa espécie mostra a que ponto as categorias que me esforço há anos em pro move perante vocês se revelam manejáveis, e permitem articular as coisas com precisão. Elas introduzem uma clareza que está na próprias dimensões de nossa experiência e, qualquer que seja a discussão que se possa levantar sobre certos pontos de detalhe, vocês. veem as noções teóricas se animarem como que pelo seu próprio movimento, e encontrarem o nível da experiência" (LACAN, 1959, p.251-252).

Lacan (*Seminário 4*) declara que a interpretação analítica está na contra-mão do sentido comum do termo. Ela não seria um esclarecimento, mas apontaria para um enigma que diz respeito à singularidade de cada sujeito, ideia fruto do pensamento proposto por Freud em suas elaborações. No texto "A direção do tratamento", Lacan (1958), aponta não ser possível entender o que Freud concebe como interpretação sem nos voltarmos às linhas de "A interpretação dos sonhos" (1976), uma vez que é nesse texto que Freud lança os alicerces do que chama "uma nova ciência", a psicanálise. Para tal, segundo Nestor Vaz, integrante da escola de psicanálise Freudiana,[21] o sonho é a estrada real que conduz ao inconsciente". Essa frase foi escrita pelo psicanalista Sigmund Freud em seu livro "A Interpretação dos Sonhos", publicado em 1900, obra que consolidou os principais fundamentos da sua teoria psicanalítica. No trabalho de Freud, a interpretação do sonho se tornou um método para formular hipóteses sobre o sentido de determinados sintomas psicológicos, tais como fobias, neuroses obsessivas e a histeria, trazendo luz, por exemplo, sobre os fenômenos psicóticos e os atos perversos. Para Freud, a essência do sonho se traduzia na realização de um desejo infantil reprimido. Na psicanálise, o sonho é analisado com base em uma associação livre, conforme explica o psicanalista Nestor Vaz, integrante da escola de psicanálise Letra Freudiana, no Rio de Janeiro. "Quando a pessoa procura uma análise, em grande parte é devido a um sintoma, como medo, ou alguma dificuldade pontual, seja na vida pessoal, ou profissional. Esse indivíduo pode ter, por exemplo, uma angústia e não saber de onde ela vem, ou que motivo o deixa assim. No processo de análise, o paciente pode trazer um sonho que, talvez, revele algum elemento motivador de sua angústia. A interpretação dos sonhos é baseada no que a pessoa leva para o consultório, nos problemas que levanta durante as sessões de psicanálise. "Podemos ter o caso da

---

[21] Acessado em 05/11/2024:
https://redeglobo.globo.com/globociencia/noticia/2012/07/segundo-sigmund-freud-os-sonhos-sao-manifestacao-do-inconsciente.html#:~:text="O%20sonho%20é%20a%20estrada,fundamentos%20da%20sua%20teoria%20psicanalítica.

pessoa que sonha com uma palavra enigmática, por exemplo. De repente, ela começa a comparar essa palavra com uma série de coisas, e não encontra associação. Quando vai ver, o termo enigmático que sonhou é o nome do namorado, só que escrito de forma invertida. De acordo com o psicanalista, os sonhos têm a função de manter o sono, e começam quando a pessoa está prestes a despertar. Como o sonho tem a ver com a vida inconsciente, segundo os conceitos da psicanálise freudiana, é durante o sono que ela se manifesta. Freud, em Interpretação dos sonhos, por meio de suas interpretações, defendeu essa teoria, indo de encontro ao que pregava a ciência, para quem os sonhos eram tidos como o lixo do pensamento. "Freud se opôs desde o inicio à ciência de sua época, que via o sonho como uma desordem proveniente de processos somáticos, e dessa forma se aliou à tradição antiga que via um sentido nos sonhos, como acontece até hoje (FRAYZE-PEREIRA, 1999). Nessa tradição, havia um método de interpretar o sonho como um todo, o que servia para explicar sonhos mais ordenados, ou criados de forma artificial. O sonho de José no Egito, que substituía as sete vacas magras por sete anos de fome e as sete vacas gordas por sete anos de fartura é um exemplo disso. Nestor explica que outro método adotado pela psicanálise de Freud é o de decifrar os sonhos decompondo-os em partes e utilizando uma espécie de chave de leitura, criando um tipo de código. Sonhar com carta e funeral, por exemplo, significaria transtorno e noivado. O psicanalista afirma que Freud se aproximava mais desse segundo método, mas com a ressalva de que levava em consideração a história do sonhador e suas peculiaridades, bem como as sutilezas da linguagem utilizada (FRAYZE-PEREIRA, 1009). Para Freud, o inconsciente era como a parte de baixo de um iceberg, sendo o consciente o lado visível. A psicanálise serve justamente para a 'apropriação' dessa parte de baixo. Quando a pessoa sabe o que é produzido no inconsciente, pode ter a chance de mudá-lo. É importante lembrar que somos mais influenciados por nosso inconsciente do que imaginamos. Para Freud (1932), a doutrina dos sonhos é o que mais diferencia a sua nova ciência, uma possibilidade de se fazer uma nova leitura de conhecimentos que outrora estiveram apenas ligados às crenças populares e ao misticismo. Para Lacan (1998), esse texto freudiano serve como referência que permite distinguir o lugar que ocupa um analista durante o percurso de uma análise. A seu ver, deve-se reconduzir a psicanálise à fala e à linguagem, sendo a tarefa do psicanalista mostrar que esses conceitos só adquirem sentido quando orientados numa estrutura de linguagem. Mas o que Lacan teria visto nesse texto inaugural que lhe permitiu avançar na delimitação de uma interpretação distinta de um esclarecimento do sentido, a ponto de afirmar que esse direcionamento da interpretação a afasta do princípio proposto por Freud? Toma-se a palavra de Freud a fim de esclarecer a proposta lacaniana quanto à interpretação. Freud (1976) vê a interpretação dos sonhos como a via régia para conhecer as leis do inconsciente. O sonho não é equivalente ao inconsciente, contudo sua interpretação possibilita o advir de uma lógica que lhe é própria e que pode ser atribuída a todo falante. Essa lógica não se institui como um avesso da consciência. As leis que a regem possuem um estatuto diferenciado e agregam efeito de sentido, o qual não é apreendido de forma direta. Lacan (*Seminário 4*) pensa esse efeito de sentido principalmente como efeito de metáfora, na medida em que no sonho as coisas não se apresentam diretamente, mas em relação de substituição:

> "O método de interpretação dos sonhos que pratico já difere em um aspecto importante do popular, histórico e legendário método de interpretação por meio do simbolismo, aproximando-se do segundo método, ou método de "decifração". Como este, ele emprega a interpretação *en détail* e não *en masse*; como este, considera os sonhos desde o início, como tendo um caráter múltiplo, como sendo conglomerados de formações psíquicas" (FREUD, 1976, p. 125).

Também:

> "Os casos mais bem-sucedidos são aqueles em que se avança, por assim dizer, sem qualquer intuito em vista, em que se permite ser tomado de surpresa por qualquer nova reviravolta neles, e sempre os enfrenta com liberalidade sem quaisquer pressuposições. A conduta correta para um analista reside em oscilar, em evitar especulação ou meditação sobre os casos, enquanto eles estão em análise, e em submeter o material obtido a um processo sintético de pensamento após a análise ter sido concluída" (FREUD, 1976, p. 153).

A interpretação dos sonhos como a via régia para conhecer as leis do inconsciente. O sonho não é equivalente ao inconsciente, contudo sua interpretação possibilita o advir de uma lógica que lhe é própria e que pode ser atribuída a todo falante. Esta compreensão sobre os sonhos requer, em primeiro lugar, as associações daquele que sonhou. Seus significados' envolvem algo que está entre as coisas mais incríveis que o ser humano é capaz de fazer. E como todos sonham, mas ninguém consegue dominar totalmente o que acontece no sonho, o tema fascina a humanidade há milhares de anos. Teorias e formas de interpretar o significado dos sonhos existem aos montes, justamente porque não se trata de uma ciência exata. O que acontece enquanto dormimos é muito pessoal e está profundamente ligado com nossas experiências enquanto acordados; pois os sonhos surgem em momentos específicos durante o nosso sono. Eles são mais vívidos e frequentes durante a fase REM (*Rapid Eye Movement*),[22] quando os olhos fechados se movimentam rapidamente. Nesse momento da noite, os neurônios estão quase tão ativos quanto quando estamos acordados. Se despertamos nessa fase do sono, as chances de lembrarmos claramente o que estávamos sonhando são maiores. Portanto, a linguagem promove transformações e regem simbolismos e significados; condições lavradas no inconsciente. Neste sentido, a linguagem é metáfora promovente de interpretação dos desejos recalcados ou não recalcados. Estas lições expõem o que constitui os dois grandes pilares da teoria de Jacques Lacan, o inconsciente e o gozo, bem como os conceitos deles derivados: significante, sujeito do inconsciente e sujeito

---

[22] Acessado em 18/04/2024: https://www.sleepfoundation.org/

do objeto. A linguagem aplicada ao desejo está relacionada à economia de nossa experiência (LACAN, 1959, p.252). Daí a impressão de arejamento que se tem sempre que se vai aos textos originais, fala dos textos que se constituem e se reconstituem ocorrentes na própria estrutura que se encontra nas dificuldades, que a função do desejo, tal como articulada. Esse desejo apresenta assim certas arestas, um certo ponto de obstáculo, e é precisamente nisso que ocorre que a experiência freudiana complicada à direção dada ao homem de sua própria integração:

> "Na experiência sugere que a noção e a finalidade do bem lhes sejam problemáticas. Que bem exatamente perseguem vocês no que se refere à paixão? Essa pergunta está sempre na ordem do dia de nosso comportamento. A cada instante temos de saber qual deve ser nossa relação efetiva com o desejo de fazer bem, o desejo de curar. Temos de contar com ele como algo suscetível de desencaminhar-nos, e, em muitos casos, instantaneamente. Diria mais, poder-se-ia de maneira paradoxal, ou até mesmo decisiva, designar nosso desejo como um não-desejo de curar. Essa expressão não tem outro sentido senão o de nos alertar contra as vias vulgares do bem, tal como elas se oferecem a nós tão facilmente em seu pendor, contra a falcatrua benéfica do querer o bem-do-sujeito" (LACAN, 1959, p.67).

O desejo é causado por uma falta que não faz sentido. Lacan chama essa falta que não se subjetiva de objeto, que ele escreve com uma letra. O objeto designa a falta de nomeação, por parte do significante, do ser do sujeito, ou seja, daquilo que não se sujeita à sua representação pelos recursos do Outro; isso significa que o desejo é causado por uma falta que não faz sentido. Nota-se que é objeto o desejo é objeto de si mesmo; tudo aquilo que vem satisfazer a um impulso, muitas vezes inconsciente. Lacan diz que o desejo pelo desejo é paradoxal; esta expressão oferece a interpretação, também, o desejo de não desejo. Tomando este ponto de partida, Lacan mostra que a linguagem manifesta uma demanda, para além do objeto intencionado e significado; levando em conta a realidade do inconsciente, através da enunciação nos seus tropeços, é possível a dedução de uma falta, indicando o movimento do desejo e a manifestação de uma estrutura psíquica. O desejo aparece como um elemento essencial da experiência humana, que emerge na linguagem e só por ela, revelando-se inconsciente, e só podendo ser contornado num processo interminável. Para formalizar tal fenômeno, Lacan (1959) propôs que se pensasse como referência do desejo o desejo do Outro (grande outro), para diferenciá-lo do outro (pequeno), o objeto percebido e intencionado. Neste momento conceitual, a enunciação que aparece na relação de fala, comanda e produz os efeitos inconscientes, os tropeços na relação de linguagem. Há aí o pressuposto de que esse Outro, como lugar dos significantes, possa dar uma resposta à investigação analítica. A psicanálise estaria propondo uma investigação do sentido da linguagem inconsciente. Seria a recuperação da verdade subjetiva, anteriormente investigada pela introspecção, agora, produzida pelo método da Associação Livre e com o manejo da

Transferência. Assim sendo, a linguagem é uma metafórica; o recalque pode ser traduzido como metáfora:

> "Aprendemos com a psicanálise que a essência do processo de recalque não está em pôr fim, em destruir a ideia que representa uma pulsão, mas em evitar que se torne consciente. Quando isso acontece, dizemos que a ideia se encontra em estado 'inconsciente', e podemos apresentar boas provas para mostrar que, inclusive quando inconsciente, ela pode produzir efeitos, incluindo até mesmo alguns que finalmente atingem a consciência" (FREUD, 1996, p. 171).

Estas são as possibilidades teóricas considerativas quanto à fundação do inconsciente e a consequente constituição do psiquismo humano. E é somente a partir da perspectiva adotada que todo o raciocínio teórico e clínico que a psicanálise enseja pode se dar. Assim, destaca-se que a hipótese do inconsciente é condição para a psicanálise. Tudo de que trata a disciplina está fundado sobre os pilares da existência do sistema inconsciente. A questão aqui levantada se refere à possibilidade de articulação entre o recalque originário, instaurador da divisão consciente/inconsciente, e a marca empreendida pelo traço como localizador desse atravessamento do ser promovido pelo recalque originário. Assim, considerando que Lacan (1969-70), o sujeito na psicanálise é representado entre significantes e possibilita sua primeira entrada no campo simbólico para que a cadeia, ou se desencadeia; ou seja, o significante se articule de modo a representá-lo, percorrendo a linha de pensamento da qual se considera o recalque originário como primeira operação de fundação do psiquismo. É neste sentido que articulá-lo ao Traço Unário se faz possível, na medida em que este atravessa o ser puramente biológico marcando-o irremediavelmente pelo simbólico, recalcando sua condição de puro real para torná-lo ser de linguagem (LACAN, 1998).

1.1.1.1.1. A psicanálise e os discursos religiosos

O atual cenário político mundial, no qual política, religião e ciências do campo da saúde, embora ainda de maneira tímida, andam de mãos dadas, sobretudo, é um exemplo de algo antecipado por Jacques Lacan (1974); que ter dito que a religião não triunfará apenas sobre a psicanálise, triunfará em todas outras áreas de conhecimento tal como as ciências humanas, ciências exatas, biotecnológicas e como as da tecnologia da informação. É difícil imaginar o quão poderosa são as dimensiones da a religião:

> "se a psicanálise não triunfar sobre a religião, é porque a religião é inquebrantável. A psicanálise não triunfará: sobreviverá ou não; assim, ela não triunfará apenas sobre a psicanálise, triunfará sobre muitas outras coisas. É inclusive impossível imaginar quão poderosa é a religião" (LACAN, 2005, p. 65).

Isto significa que para Lacan o triunfo da religião está intimamente concantenado as dimensões da subjetividade e. portanto, ela é originado e desenvolvida pelos processos mentais do homem; ou seja são aquelas estruturas relacionados aos constructos do consciente e do insconceinte dos seres humanos. Freud conceitua inconsciência como que:

> "papel sobra, em nossa apresentação, para a consciência, antes toda poderosa e que tudo ocultava? Nenhum outro que o de um órgão sensorial para a percepção de qualidades psíquicas. Considero a percepção pela consciência como a função própria de um sistema particular, ao qual convém a abreviação de consciênte". (FREUD, 2019, p.583)

Ainda sobre a consciência Freud menciona ela

> "tem para nós o sentido de um órgão sensorial para a apreensão de qualidades psíquicas, é excitável, no estado de vigília, a partir de dois lugares. A partir da periferia do aparelho global, do sistema da percepção, em primeira linha; e em seguida, a partir das excitações de prazer e desprazer. Mas, a consciência tornou-se também um órgão sensorial para uma parte de nossos processos do pensamento. Há duas superfícies sensoriais, uma do perceber, a outra voltada para os processos de pensamento pré-conscientes" (FREUD, 2019a, 2019b, p.547).

Denota dizer que, tornar-se consciente, para uma representação, significa, portanto, ser percebida por este sistema onde as excitações se produzem de maneira fugaz e sem deixar traço. Entre as representações do pré-consciente, só algumas são escolhidas pela atenção, a cada momento, para tornarem-se conscientes. Observa-se que a prática psicanalítica vai exercer uma grande influência sobre esta escolha, ao insistir sobre a verbalização e a exploração das idéias incidentes (associações livres), ao apontar os lapsos, ao sublinhar as reticências, as interrupções, a repetição de certos significantes, etc., induzindo assim o paciente a seguir cadeias associativas que normalmente não seguiria (MELTZER, 984; FRAYZE-PEREIRA, 1999; MÁRCIA, 2006). Sendo assim, no consultório do psicanalista, diversas representações pré-conscientes, que ordinariamente não teriam chegado à consciência, se tornarão conscientes. E este exercício se generaliza a momentos fora do consultório, em que o paciente, em sua vida cotidiana, será levado a tomar consciência de representações de seu pré-consciente que, sem esta influência, teriam permanecido não conscientes. Para tal Freud conceitua inconsciente que:

> "suposição psicanalítica da atividade mental inconsciente nos aparece como a extensão da correção trazida por Kant à nossa concepção da percepção externa. Assim como Kant nos advertiu a não deixar passar despercebido o condicionamento subjetivo de nossa percepção e a não considerar nossa percepção como idêntica ao que é percebido mas não é conhecível, da mesma forma a psicanálise nos alerta a não por a percepção pela consciência no lugar do processo psíquico inconsciente que é seu objeto. Como o físico, o psíquico também não tem necessidade,

com efeito, de ser como nos aparece". (FREUD,2019, p.130).

Para Lacan (1982), no inconsciente estão as pulsões, que são duas forças complementares, pulsão de vida e de morte. As pulsões são forças que estimulam o corpo a liberar energia mental, Freud os dividiu em duas categorias: os instintos de vida que se referem à autopreservação, esta forma de energia manifesta é chamada de libido; e instinto de morte que é uma força destrutiva, e pode ser dirigida para dentro. O consciente é a parte da mente que estamos cientes, porém Freud se interessou mais pelo inconsciente, que é uma área menos explorada e exposta. Estes conceitos são significativos por possibilitar entendimento e processos mentais dos seres humanos, como por exemplo, por se processa a religião na cérebro; ou seja, as função da subjetividade humana são as várias facetas da religião. A contribuição teórica mais especial de Freud é a de que o comportamento é governado por processos inconscientes e não somente pelos processos conscientes. Freud explica a libido como uma pulsão sexual instintiva existente desde o nascimento, e esta é a força motivadora do comportamento. A psicanálise é uma teoria que possui como característica inicial o determinismo psíquico, sua função é explicar que nada ocorre por acaso, ou seja, não há descontinuidade na vida mental. Cada evento mental tem explicação consciente ou inconsciente, mas eles ocorrem tão espontaneamente, que Freud os descreve ligando um evento consciente a outro. Com isso, percebe-se a religião como algo inerente ao ser humano; é da ordem do indestrutível; é estrutural, aparece como repetição, insiste e resiste. Diferente de Sigmund Freud, que acreditava no domínio do saber científico positivista sobre a religião, Lacan afirma que a religião dará "um sentido a todas as reviravoltas introduzidas pela ciência. E, no que se refere ao sentido, eles, os líderes religiosos, conhecem um bocado. São capazes de dar um sentido a qualquer coisa. Um sentido à vida humana, por exemplo. São formados no significado que a pessoa tem dela. Conquanto a religião é legitima para os estudos sobre a psicanálise:

> "Na construção do sujeito: A religião terá o papel principal: ela (a religião) encontrará um, a correspondência de tudo com tudo. É inclusive na sua função. Verifica-se que as tensões do cotidiano como: Angústias, sofrimentos, tensões e desejos, a religião faz que esses sentimentos adquiram o sentido ao indivíduo, triunfando assim, na construção desse sujeito" (LACAN, 2005, p. 65).

Lacan reconhece a legitimidade do saber religioso. É um saber entre tantos outros: enquanto analistas, pensamos que não há saber algum que não se erga sobre um fundo de ignorância. É isso que nos permite admitir como tais muitos outros saberes além do saber cientificamente fundado. Assim sendo, a psicanálise e a religião nascem da mesma demanda: uma resposta à angústia, mais precisamente a angústia da morte – angústia que marca a condição humana. Para lidar com essa angústia, a religião e a psicanálise percorrem caminhos diferentes. Os discursos religiosos fundamentalistas são da ordem da completude e da moral. Nada pode escapar ao sentido. Buscam apaziguar os seres angustiados. Sua missão é "curar os homens para não perceberem o que não funciona" (LACAN,1986p.66). A psicanálise tem outro viés. Não trabalha com discursos ordenadores da realidade. Não há generalizações possíveis. É da ordem da incompletude e da ética. Sabe que há demandas existenciais que não cabem nas palavras. O conceito de Real em Lacan[23] tem raízes em Sören Kierkegaard, teólogo cristão e filósofo dinamarquês, que percebeu algo na existência que escapa ao pensamento lógico, racional e que não permite uma síntese (diferente da tríade tese-antítese-síntese de Hegel). Retoma o mito de Adão e Eva. Os vê como seres angustiados, que não tinham consciência da existência do bem e do mal. Eles se angustiavam diante da ignorância, da inocência. Uma angústia diante do vazio, do nada, das escolhas. Não era angústia por não poder fazer nada. Era a angústia por não

---

[23] Segundo Lacan (1985), se há vários reais, na medida em que esse real é abordado a partir de vários pontos, a realidade é que, como vou tentar mostrar, é do mesmo real que se trata, ainda que aqui não serei exaustivo, dada a frequência das referências ao real. Evidentemente, conhecer esses reais, mas aquele que, na esteira das apresentações já feitas durante esses dias, desempenha o papel mais decisivo, é *o real da alucinação*. Ele é privilegiado por distinguir bem o real da realidade, porque a voz ouvida não é imaginada - tomem isso no sentido literal, não é imaginário, mas real -, e não podemos entrar no manejo da transferência com um sujeito psicótico, se não captarmos essa diferença fundamental e sem a qual, aliás, teremos as maiores dificuldades em compreender o que Lacan diz sobre o real no sujeito neurótico. Esse real alucinatório surge desde o primeiro seminário, com relação à alucinação do dedo cortado do Homem dos lobos. Vocês conhecem a fórmula: o que é foracluído do simbólico reaparece no real.

saber o que fazer. Angústia diante do que não se nomina (nomearam tudo), menos o inominável, o resto, o que sobra, a variância. Os discursos religiosos (ALVES, 1999) fundamentalistas têm conquistado mais visibilidade. São frutos de teologias em que há uma negação da angústia. Tudo pode ser nomeado e ordenado pelas palavras. Busca-se o tempo todo tamponar o Real. Rompem com os discursos religiosos cientificista e intelectualizados. A "verdade" está em uma única fonte: nas Escrituras Sagradas. Afirmam o "direito" dos fiéis ao paraíso aqui e agora. Sem angústia. Não precisam mais "sofrer". O sacrifício de Cristo "desculpabilizou" todos. O castigo dado a Adão e Eva não precisa mais ser aplicado. Perdeu o prazo de validade. É uma experiência religiosa mediada por um "contrato", que transforma o fiel em "sócio" de Deus. Ao pagar o tributo, ele exige e cobra a sua cota de bênçãos diárias. Trata-se de uma nova dinâmica libidinal para lidar com Deus e com a realidade. Distancia-se de uma religiosidade marcada pelas proibições. Já não se enquadra numa neurose obsessiva de massa, marcada pela culpa, típica das religiões tradicionais. Está mais próxima de uma histeria. Nessa nova economia libidinal, o fiel cobra de Deus o que lhe foi tirado: sua perda (o paraíso). Assume uma posição reivindicatória, alguém me tomou algo. Insatisfeito, busca o que lhe é "devido". Uma insatisfação estrutural, sempre está faltando alguma coisa. Vive-se no ciclo "satisfação-insatisfação". O pai (Deus) dessa relação histérica, causador da neurose e do sofrimento inicial, é substituído pelo Diabo (ALVES,1999). Este se torna o maior (e único) responsável por todas as desgraças que acometem os fiéis. Tanto a salvação (o bem) como a perdição (o mal) são causadas por agentes externos. Isso leva os fiéis a cobrarem de quem está lhe devendo, Deus, e a "guerrear" com quem lhe tirou o paraíso, o Diabo, o inimigo a ser eliminado. Qualquer sintoma, novo ou velho, tem uma única fonte: o Diabo, entidade espiritual que também se manifesta em pessoas, instituições, obras de arte, livros e outras produções artísticas. Há uma simplificação da realidade cotidiana e; isso é retorno à magia pré-moderna e, também, ao considerar o fato de que tudo se resolve por meio de palavras de ordem (FRED, 2019a). A fé fica restrita à dimensão emocional, e o importante é "sentir" Deus. Palavras como doação e sacrifício não fazem parte do repertório dessa experiência religiosa hedonista e narcísica. Em um caminho oposto, a psicanálise lacaniana não tem receitas, fórmulas mágicas para 'desangustiar' o ser humano. A angústia é um corte impossível de ser suturado. O desafio é saber conviver com ela e chegar à singularidade da verdade mentirosa (LACAN, 1960). Como afirma Lavam, cada ser humano "deve costurar a sua própria camisa", ou, nas palavras de Alves (1999), "fora do sofrimento prêt-à-porter, cada um inventa a sua singularidade; sendo isso serve para os que creem e para os que não creem. Portanto, é muito deselegante entender ou não considerar que para aperfeiçoar a relação é essencial a interpolação epistemológica consoante a inter-relação entre psicanálise, a prática da psicoterapia com os discursos religiosos. Bem como faz-se essencial ressaltar as informações se resvalem a partir da consciência que nela pode está alguns elemento neurofisilógico, psiquiátrico e, também, devidos os aspectos influenciados por fenômenos psíquicos, que está formatada ou está em processo de formatação (FREUD, 1893). Sendo assim, a subjetividade é fator constitutivo da inconsciente, como mencionou Freud (2019a, 2019b); e divido as maiores dificuldade de estudo inconsciente com sua subjetiva sempre em pauta.

1.1.2. Subjetividade e patologia

O eixo "subjetivação pela doença"[24] mostra como os indivíduos se constituíram após o diagnóstico psiquiátrico. Antes de conhecerem sua patologia, há um longo processo de medicalização, social e individual, que se consolida no recebimento do diagnóstico. Nesse momento, os usuários entrevistados se identificam com a

---

[24] Como exemplo é a depressão é atualmente um dos assuntos mais difundidos na sociedade. Trata-se de um quadro clínico que acomete milhões de pessoas no mundo inteiro todos os anos e seu diagnóstico é cada vez mais frequente. Nessa perspectiva, ela é tratada como um problema do campo médico e sua etiologia estaria associada à uma desordem neuroquímica. A psicanálise propõe outra alternativa que vai além da perspectiva biomédica. Nesse sentido, nos amparamos no ensino de Lacan e realizamos uma articulação precisa entre a tristeza e o desejo. Dessa maneira os estados depressivos seriam na verdade uma consequência da desorientação do sujeito em relação ao seu desejo. Essa direção se mostra precisa, pois nos fornece elementos para pensarmos o diagnóstico diferencial de melancolia e os estados depressivos que se apresentam sob esse quadro. Trata-se de uma situação em que ocorre o apagamento do desejo do sujeito em função da sua identificação com o objeto perdido. Essa perspectiva também nos permite pensar a depressão neurótica e situá-la como um recuo do sujeito diante do seu desejo que é suscitado pelo Outro. Por fim, a psicanálise nos mostra que a depressão enquanto entidade clínica não existe. Nessas coordenadas, os estados depressivos traduzem sempre uma posição do sujeito diante do objeto, que deve sempre ser analisada a partir da lógica pulsional.

doença mental e se confortam com a explicação de seus sintomas. Como exemplo, a seguir, a titulo didático, isso pode ser verificado nas falas que se seguem, quando lhes foi questionado se consentiam com o diagnóstico dado pelo médico: segundo depoimento de uma pessoa com desequilíbrio relata que que faz tratamento pediátrico em uma clínica psiquiátrica na cudade de Montes Claro - MG, ela argui:

> "concordo com o profissional, detentor do conhecimento científico, o diagnóstico, ele fez eu me levantar de novo. Sinto-me mais calma, mais tranquila; Sempre fui ansiosa, desde os 16 anos eu tinha idealização suicida. Era uma coisa que passava pela minha cabeça, mas eu não associava a idealização suicida com alguma patologia; Sim, eu tô concordando com ele. Eu tenho que concordar, né?".

Percebe-se, nos excertos, que os sujeitos incorporam e aceitam o diagnóstico recebido. A classificação produz efeitos nas maneiras de viver e emerge em conexão com os processos sociais e com o contexto em que se situam esses indivíduos. Aí se percebe a maleabilidade da subjetividade que se constrói a partir da classificação atribuída (FOUCAULT, 1984). Complementando a discussão, observa-se nos seguintes fragmentos como alguns participantes se sentiram ou se perceberam após o conhecimento do diagnóstico. O paciente em observação in natura durante anos continua arguindo que,

> "agora eu consigo me controlar, agora eu tenho uma motivação para não cair de novo na depressão. Transtorno eu tenho, às vezes eu estou alegre, às vezes chorosa, mas graças a Deus agora eu estou tranquila; Graças a Deus agora eu me sinto feliz; Me sinto mais calma, mais tranquila; Sou bem mais tranquila, né? As falas remetem à ideia da "tragédia" da subjetividade contemporânea, caracterizada em quatro atos".

Os atos iniciam com o paciente que sente um mal-estar e sai à procura de um profissional para ser ouvido/assistido. A sequência prossegue com a queixa sendo decodificada em alguma categoria nosológica. O terceiro ato acontece quando, após o exame dos sintomas, o paciente é diagnosticado e medicado, para voltar a seu estado normal, sadio. Infelizmente, o sujeito não se dá conta do jogo de poder ao qual está submetido. Ele não se reconhece mais, não sabe o que quer e acaba sendo

> "escravizado pelo objeto de desejo, pelas imagens associadas aos produtos que interpelam suas emoções e seu imaginário e não consegue ver nem a dominação a que está submetido, nem o que é realmente" (ALVES, 1999, 59).

Neste sentido, o médico ao constatar que si, o paciente não se reconhece como alguém "normal" e confia que tenha uma resposta. O médico, ao classificar os sintomas, exerce sobre o paciente um controle disciplinar de orientação. O paciente, por sua vez, julga não ter o poder do conhecimento e que está cansado de se sentir "estranho". Pela percepção que tem de si e de seu contexto social, acata o saber do profissional, submetendo-se ao tratamento medicamentoso e acreditando que a medicação restabelecerá a "normalidade" perdida e a esperança da resolução de seus problemas que, geralmente, revelam uma condição de dificuldades e sofrimento. No processo, o paciente deixa de pertencer a si próprio, sua vida passa a ser administrada pelas regras que lhe são ditadas pelo outro, apenas reproduzindo um comportamento que acredita ser compatível com seu diagnóstico. Do mesmo modo, o paciente ressignifica seus valores e a si mesmo de acordo com o diagnóstico e a medicação prescrita. Os relatos demonstram a relação de alguns participantes com o processo medicamentoso que, por vezes, remonta a longos anos de suas vidas. Esses excertos demonstram que, a partir do uso da medicação, os indivíduos naturalmente sentem-se melhor dos sintomas de sua patologia. Observa-se, na íntegra das entrevistas, que quase não aparecem questões críticas ou mesmo explanações a respeito do uso de medicamentos ou mesmo sobre seus efeitos colaterais. Poderíamos inferir que, ao encontrar o médico e ao receber o tratamento medicamentoso, os sujeitos estão diante de um conhecimento verdadeiro e adequado a seu "problema".[25]

---

[25] Depoimento de um paciente com transtorno mental da Cidade de Montes Claro. Seu nome não aparece por motivos de reserva a identidade dela.

2.1. A pulverização da subjetividade na modernidade

Este capítulo é relativo à psicanálise de Lacan como instrumento para os estudos investigativos aplicados à pulverização da subjetividade na modernidade. Tratado impacto da realidade epistemológica dessas áreas científicas aplicados nas relações humanas no tange as dimensões comportamentais e expressas na cultura religiosa. Neste caminho, também, faz-se uma reflexão no tange a contribuição da psicanálise para a relação indivíduo e sociedade com vista para a ciência da religião; seguidos de uma interpretação congruente à psicanálise para o fenômeno religioso; este enquanto arcabouço da Ciência.

2.1.1. Na realidade epistemológica e na psicoterapêutica

A psicanálise possui instrumentos epistemológico e metateórico relevantes para a operacionalização das ciências da mente tanto âmbito aniversário quanto extra universitário, com intensidade profissional do profissional clínicas, empresas, igrejas, turismo religioso, palestras auditorias e orientações para discursos políticos partidários, propagada e mídia dos meios de comunicação, ara a áreas institucionais de estado, como acessórias ao Instituto Brasileiro de Geografia e Estatística,[26]

---

[26] Acessado em 04/11/2024: h ttps://www.gov.br/mdh/pt-br/navegue-por-temas/observatorio-nacional-da-familia/fatos-e-numeros/5.SADEMENTAL28.12.22.pdf. Este apresenta que de

Ministério da Educação,[27] do Turismo, da Reforma

acordo com dados do Instituto Brasileiro de Geografia e Estatística (IBGE), comparando-se os anos de 2013 e 2019, houve no Brasil significativo aumento do número de indivíduos que reportaram diagnóstico de depressão por profissional de saúde mental. Em 2019, 10,2% das pessoas com 18 anos ou mais de idade referiram ter recebido tal diagnóstico, o equivalente a aproximadamente 16,3 milhões de pessoas. O percentual apresentou um aumento de 34% em relação a 2013, quando havia 7,6% de pessoas em situação equivalente (Gráfico 1). Desagregando os dados por sexo, verificou-se que independentemente do ano em análise mulheres referiram diagnóstico de depressão com aproximadamente 2,8 vezes mais frequência do que os homens. Outrossim, comparando-se os anos de 2013 e 2019, a proporção dos que reportaram diagnóstico de depressão aumentou ligeiramente mais entre as mulheres (35%) do que entre os homens (31%) (Gráfico 1). Em 2019, os idosos entre 60 e 64 anos representavam a faixa etária proporcionalmente mais afetada: 13,2% tinham sido diagnosticados com depressão. Já o menor percentual, de 5,9%, foi observado entre jovens adultos de 18 a 29 anos de idade (Gráfico 2). Contudo, no período analisado, a maior variação na proporção de pessoas que relataram ter sido diagnosticadas com depressão foi verificada entre os adultos de 18 a 29 anos (51% de aumento), seguidos dos idosos de 75 anos ou mais 48% de aumento".

[27] O ministério da Educação remete a ideia de que a relação da Psicanálise com a Educação tem seus primórdios com Sigmund Freud, que observou pontos em comum entre ambas, ou mesmo de discordância, entre as especificidades dos campos de conhecimento aqui mencionados. Freud demonstrou seu interesse pelas conexões que a Psicanálise e a Educação poderiam vir a construir entre si, a importância das ligações possíveis, fornecendo, também, algumas ideias de como elas poderiam ocorrer. Vale ressaltar que quando se faz referência à Psicanálise não se trata somente dos conceitos freudianos como também de alguns conceitos de Jaques Lacan, que embora seja um pensador influenciado por Freud, muito contribuiu para a Psicanálise, inferindo pontos de originalidade em relação a seu mestre. É óbvio que a Psicanálise não se limita aos saberes formulados por esses dois autores somente e a existência de outros

Agrário e para a Pasta das Relações exteriores. Assim sendo, a importância da psicanálise reside na sua capacidade de fornecer uma fundamentos teóricos profundos relativo à mente humana e aos problemas emocionais. Segundo a teoria psicanalítica de Lacan, os problemas mentais e emocionais são causados por conflitos inconscientes entre diferentes partes da personalidade (no *Seminário 4*). Quanto a importância da psicanálise para os dias atuais, no geral, pode-se dizer que os principais benefícios da psicanálise são: aliviar o sofrimento psíquico, proporcionar uma vida mais consciente e responsável, ressignificar traumas e sentimentos, promover o amadurecimento emocional, o autoconhecimento e elaborar teoria da relação psicanálise e religião (RIBEIRO, 2014). Com suas ferramentas epistêmica a psique instrumentaliza--se a ciência ao provocar impacto na sociedade, nas relações sociais, como as experiências religiosas recheada de subjetividade. Outro aspecto da psicanálise é quanto a subjetividade, conflito:

---

deve ser igualmente considerada. Serão tomados como base, para os objetivos a que se propõe o artigo, basicamente Freud e outros teóricos da Psicanálise. A Educação e a Psicanálise percorrem um complexo caminho, entrelaçando seus saberes sobre o desenvolvimento do ser humano. Esse entrelaçar permitiu o levantamento de questões relacionadas ao funcionamento psíquico do ser humano, à relação de transferência aluno-professor, ao prazer em aprender (questão do desejo), à terapêutica da Educação, à linguagem etc. Assim, a Psicanálise, como corpo teórico, e a Educação, como discurso social, imbricaram-se em um processo de mudanças que afetou tanto uma quanto outra no que tange suas áreas de atuação (REBEIRO, 2014, p.24).

"questionamento da "objetividade" supõe presumir que toda teoria é abordada partir de um lugar e que isso supõe aceitar a existência de um "viés". Por isso, é preciso admitir que o panorama observável depende do ponto de vista do observador, e renunciar então às pretensões de totalidade de "universalidade" do observado. A assunção dessa perspectiva pode levar a reconhecer a implicação do lugar a partir do qual se trabalha e se pensa. No entanto, essa tomada de partido supõe uma ótica que leve em conta o atravessamento inevitável do conflito social e a contradição histórica em toda empreitada de conhecimento. A única "objetividade" esperável seria aquela que não esconde seus valores, mas assume consciente e explicitamente os pressupostos que a sustentam" (FLORES, 2001, p17).

A subjetividade é inerente ao objeto de pesquisa sobre religião. A psicanálise é inserida como instrumento e veículo de compreensão e analítica epistêmica e clínica para tentar explicar as motivações que levam o homem a criar um mundo simbólico religioso, ao longo dos séculos. A religião, como reguladora, faz um paralelo com a Lei, agindo como um regulador da sociedade, contém e inibe o desejo. A religião atravessa as mais diversas épocas e culturas sendo, ainda na cena moderna, instituição reguladora da moralidade e dos costumes. O desafio do longo e difícil processo de humanização é, em primeiro lugar, o de conter a força primitiva do desejo. Isso significa que o desejo individual encontra limite num outro desejo individual. O domínio de si, técnica construída para otimizar a realização de desejo (no sentido de realizar sobre eles um trabalho de atenuação), se configura na primeira empresa do primitivo, na instituição da civilidade. Esse homem é impelido a dominar uma demanda pulsional complexa, que move poderosa e violentamente o psiquismo. Essa complexidade compreende, antes de qualquer coisa, uma ambivalência pulsional, que se configura num polo agressivo-sexual e em outro egóico-social. O mundo da religião acompanhou, como não poderia deixar de ser, o mundo da cultura. Não há mais linhas divisórias fixas e as marcas identitárias já não contam como antigamente. A religião deixou de ser uma herança e passou a ser, cada vez mais, uma opção de um sujeito autônomo. Não é mais possível falar de uma religião matriz ou de uma religião oficial. Hoje convivem inúmeras denominações religiosas, inclusive dividindo espaço com a possibilidade de não se ter religião. Num mundo em constante trânsito entre as denominações, como afirmar qual a mais verdadeira. Será sempre aquela em que o indivíduo se encontra num dado momento. Visto de tantas perspectivas quantas forem possíveis, o discurso sobre a religião perdeu seu porta voz. Assim, as teorias do conflito explicam as estruturas sociais, interações, rivalidades, que, então, podem resultar em violência. Ou seja, conflitos caracterizam-se pelos desentendimentos entre as pessoas do mesmo meio social, que, em tese, têm interesses contrapostos, fazendo com que se enfrentem. Após a abordagem tradicional da Sociologia sobre a teoria do conflito, diversas outras teorias se propuseram para explicar como funciona os conflitos sociais, nas mais variadas áreas do conhecimento. Como, por exemplo: sociologia, criminologia, economia, psicologia, dentre outras; sobretudo, os conflitos possuem em sua definição, precipuamente, uma disputa ou desentendimento entre pessoas, em meio a incompatibilidade e diferenças em suas necessidades e interesses. O que, em sua maioria, envolve questões subjetivas, de natureza eminentemente psicológica. Diante das incompatibilidades entre as pessoas, sob o aspecto subjetivo, há repercussões de ordem psicológica, em sentimentos e emoções. Em resultado, para atender às suas necessidades pessoais, podem gerar alterações do comportamento que, consequentemente, resultam em conflitos. As necessidades humanas que não são atendidas, bem como qualquer violação aos Direitos Humanos, é fonte inesgotável de conflitos. Ainda, mostra que essas alterações podem também afetar a pessoa fisicamente:

> "Existem inúmeras necessidades humanas, como as necessidades fundamentais das pessoas são classificadas sob seguintes aspectos: subsistência, proteção, afeto, compreensão, participação, recreação (diversão, lazer, ociosidade), criação, identidade e liberdade. Junto a essas duas dimensões mencionadas acima, subjetividade e conflito religioso, está a dimensão da objetividade. A objetividade se encontra intimamente ligada ao aspecto social do método científico, ao fato de que a ciência e a objetividade científica não resultam (nem podem resultar) dos esforços de um homem de ciência individual por ser 'objetivo', mas da

cooperação de muitos homens de ciência". (FLORES, 2021, p. 17).

Esse critério, que separa a objetividade das pretensões de "imparcialidade" (aspiração que implicaria desumanizar o observador ou concebê-lo como "dessocializado") para aproximá-la de uma sorte de resultado estatístico surgido da integração de muitos pontos de vista diferentes (e tão mais aproximado quanto mais se acerque a amostra ao que é pedido pelo enunciado dos "grandes números"), abre as portas para o debate da atribuição de "objetividade" à sociedade e à história. Sob essa ótica já não se busca manter afastada a subjetividade do pesquisador, pretensão ilusória e inútil, mas incorporar outras subjetividades equivalentes. Sociedade e história constroem, assim, uma "objetividade" que deve incluir os conflitos e questiona uma pretensa "imparcialidade" por uma "parcialidade múltipla" que daria conta exata das relações de força em cada momento. Sobre o tema da objetividade, coloca-se para a psicanálise um problema relevante: não pode contentar-se com uma mera repetição dos slogans genéricos que se aplicam em outras ciências, por "duras" que sejam e por mais que ostentem prestígio. A necessidade de circunscrever o objeto, afastando tanto quanto possível as perturbações que as

> "projeções individuais" produzem, de saber como objetivar a relação com o objeto de modo tal que o discurso sobre o objeto não seja uma simples projeção de uma relação inconsciente com o objeto" (FLORES, 2021, p. 18).

E que

> "essa tarefa exige uma análise profunda das relações e implicações entre sujeito (pesquisador, analista) e objeto (fenômeno, paciente), e de ambos com o marco de referências imediato da observação (teoria, enquadre) e, ainda mais além, com o contexto histórico social, determinante último das condições de existência e desenvolvimento de cada um desses elementos" (FLORES, 2021, p. 18).

Este enunciado relaciona sujeito, objeto e observação como fundamentos para análise dos sujeitos sociais:

> "O sujeito da psicanálise é o sujeito do desejo, delineado por Freud através da noção de inconsciente, marcado e movido pela falta, distinto do ser biológico e do sujeito da consciência filosófica" (TEREZAN, 2011, p.529).

Objeto está correlacionado a pulsão; pois segundo Freud (1905/1996) define o conceito de pulsão que denomina

> "como o representante psíquico de uma energia que leva ao movimento, ou ainda "uma espécie de demanda por ação que seria feita ao psiquismo cuja fonte seria o processo excitatório em um órgão" (NELSON, 2001, p.39).

Na psicanálise observação significa que,

"fazendo ver, tem o objetivo de tornar constante a presença do objeto, isto é, torná-lo objetivo. A primazia do "ver" na pesquisa científica se traduz como o controle metodológico do método da pesquisa científica" (ROSA, 2010, p.185).

Isso significa que a pesquisa requer rigor metodológico, epistemológico e transparência, capaz de filtrar inferências no processo de conhecimento. Essa exigência implica a maneira particular de relacionar-se com o objeto de conhecimento que é característica da psicanálise, maneira que se apoia justamente, pela via da análise da transferência e da contratransferência, no papel assumidos pelos vínculos sujeito-objeto e analista paciente, na produção de conhecimento e na transformação da realidade subjetiva. Quanto à implicação do contexto históricosocial na produção do conhecimento, quer provenha das condições "objetivas" da investigação, quer das que nesta se implicam por intermédio dos agentes, é constitutiva de toda prática social e extensiva a qualquer produto ou conhecimento, além de representar, em última instância, nada mais, nada menos, que o meio pelo qual estes resultam incluídos na história. Mantém-se de pé o fato de que ao controle objetivo só se chega pela via do controle social visualizado nas experiências sociais.

2.1.2. Subjetividade na relação indivíduo e sociedade

Esta sessão trata da psicanálise vista na relação indivíduo e sociedade.. Isto justifica porque as teorias psicológicas têm tratado a temática da subjetividade na sua externalidade, ancorada em uma compreensão dicotômica da relação indivíduo e sociedade. A visão predominante que tem se configurado na trajetória da psicologia privilegia uma concepção naturalizada de indivíduo, sedimentando e legitimando um determinado tipo de procedimento racional que se alastra e se consolida no seu campo. O indivído sedimentado quer dizer que ele

"cumprir esse objetivo, o artigo está dividido em duas partes. A primeira apresenta uma breve discussão sobre as relações entre natureza humana e Estado político, por meio das noções de liberdade e igualdade, conflito e ordem sociopolítica, egoísmo e empatia, naturalidade e artificialidade, dentre outras, procurando mostrar como a partir delas derivam as relações entre indivíduo e sociedade em sua fase germinal. Aqui enfatizando as principais ideias de Thomas Hobbes e Jean-Jacques Rousseau. Ainda nesta parte, haverá uma seção intermediária em que a natureza humana não será mais o ponto de partida analítico, mas uma imaginação social. Isso será feito a partir de dois autores — David Hume e Alexis Tocqueville —, que apesar de ainda apresentarem continuidades com o pensamento dos autores das duas primeiras seções, não compartilhavam com algumas de suas ideias. A segunda parte será voltada para o debate da relação entre indivíduo e sociedade, sobretudo tentando apontar, de forma mais implícita do que explícita, como as reflexões desses autores estavam em diálogos, não só entre si, mas também com as reflexões dos autores da primeira parte. A primeira seção dessa parte irá expor algumas ideias de Karl Marx, sobretudo como esse autor concebe a relação entre indivíduo e sociedade por meio das relações materiais de produção e reprodução da vida humana; e ainda em diálogo com a primeira parte, como ele concebe um possível ordenamento sociopolítico. A segunda seção será voltada para alguns pensamentos de Emile Durkheim, tentando aproximar suas inspirações e críticas aos autores da primeira parte. E, por último, a ênfase será em Max Weber, sobretudo como esse autor recupera a noção de ação racional. Espera-se que ao final dessa breve revisão bibliográfica, seja possível identificar as continuidades e descontinuidades nos pensamentos expostos desses autores, e assim perceber como as noções de indivíduo e sociedade podem ter sido influenciadas pelas continuidades e descontinuidades do debate inerente à antropologia filosófica nas ciências sociais".[28]

---

[28] Acessado em 20/10/2024:
https://periodicos.ufpb.br/ojs2/index.php/caos/article/view/51982/307 27

O processo de naturalização do indivíduo corresponde o processo de naturalização da sociedade, concebida como realidade distinta, quando não oposta, externa e independente dele. Como resultado desse procedimento, o conceito de sociedade remete a um todo e o de indivíduo a uma parte, ambos abstratos. Nesse sentido, é possível afirmar que a predominância de uma concepção de indivíduo e sociedade em oposição, aprisionados em campos diversos e antagônicos, acaba por converter em abstrações realidades que, na sua essência, estabelecem relações concretas que não se excluem e carregam em si componentes de tensão e conflito que as constituem num único movimento: é nessa lógica que entra a psicanalise e a ciência da religião aparelhando epistemologicamente a psicologia:

> "um procedimento para a investigação de processos mentais que são quase inacessíveis por qualquer outro modo; um método (baseado nessa investigação) para o tratamento de distúrbios neuróticos; e uma coleção de informações psicológicas obtidas ao longo destas linhas, e que gradualmente se acumula numa nova disciplina científica" (FREUD, 1996 p.253).

Assim, a psicanálise não é unicamente um procedimento terapêutico; ela é, também (ou, para ser mais exato, ela é tornada, pouco a pouco) uma ciência, aquela do psiquismo, aquela dos processos inconscientes que se desenrolam não apenas no indivíduo isolado, mas também nos grupos, nas instituições, nas produções do espírito. Ela é a ciência que fundamenta muitas áreas do conhecimento, sobretudo a ciência da religião por trabalhar, como por exemplo, com as experiências religiosas, com as linguagens religiosas, expressões religiosas, com a subjetividade e objetividade embricadamente. Assim sendo, a

> "psicanálise aplicada" fora do tratamento suscita apreensões e, em geral, rejeição. Jacques Lacan é bastante firme a este respeito. Ele escreve: "A psicanálise não se aplica, no sentido próprio, senão como tratamento e, portanto, a um sujeito que fala e que escuta" (LACAN apud JULIEN, 1990, p.55).

Apesar de tais reservas ou reprovações, a psicanálise anexou, pouco a pouco, novos campos do saber, de tal modo que certos autores a concebem como podendo dar nascimento a uma nova ciência da religião". neste contexto:

> "O sublime acaso da genialidade talvez não explique, por si só, que tenha sido em Viena, centro, na época, de um Estado que era o meltingpot das mais diversas formas familiares, desde as mais arcaicas até as mais evoluídas, desde os derradeiros grupos agnósticos de camponeses eslavos até as mais reduzidas formas do lar pequeno-burguês e as mais decadentes formas do casal instável, passando pelos patriarcalismos feudais e mercantis, que um filho do patriarcado judaico imaginou o complexo de Édipo" (LACAN, 1938, p.67).

Todavia, o interesse de Freud e de Lacan pela análise do campo social não é suficiente para resolver os problemas epistemológicos colocados pela aplicação de uma ciência do sujeito individual às ciências do coletivo (sociologia, pedagogia, mitologia), de uma ciência da realidade psíquica (cujos motores são o desejo e a fantasia e cujo domínio é aquele do imaginário e do simbólico) às ciências da realidade histórica, que estão centradas sobre os grupos e movimentos sociais que definem conscientemente projetos, defendem causas, empreendem lutas e constroem instituições. Esta tensão entre dois tipos de ciências levou psicanalistas e sociólogos a desconfiarem da psicanálise aplicada e a distinguir, na obra freudiana, uma parte científica (sua obra de desbravador e de decifrador da psique) de uma obra puramente especulativa, na qual Freud se deixaria levar pelos demônios de sua juventude imaginativa (o que acontece a muitos homens sexagenários), afastando-se de seu domínio, enunciando aos princípios metodológicos e abandonando-se a um discurso geral sobre o laço social, a civilização, a horda, a massa, bastante banal porque não se apoiava em nenhuma investigação precisa. Discurso em contradição com aquele de um psicanalista no curso do tratamento, que escuta com atenção a palavra de um cliente singular e que estabelece, com este, relações específicas. Assim, torna-se claro que o indivíduo não existe fora do campo social. O sujeito humano é um sujeito social. Não são senão os outros (em particular, os pais ou os primeiros educadores) que podem reconhecê-lo enquanto totalidade, da qual eles falam, e que acede a seu primeiro regozijo de existir no momento do "Estágio do espelho" (LACAN, 1998) e como portador de desejos que podem assegurar-lhe seu lugar na dinâmica social, lugar que ele deverá investir. É neste contexto que a religião sempre foi objeto de estudo de diversas áreas do conhecimento, principalmente da própria ciência da religião e posteriormente da própria psicanálise. Nos tempos hipermodernos em que vivemos, o pensamento sobre a Religião vive um curioso paradoxo. Se por um lado há uma certa indisposição em se falar sobre religião por parte da maioria das pessoas, cada vez mais se vê um ressurgimento da questão religiosa na sociedade. Ao mesmo tempo em que a Religião é tomada como assunto da esfera privada de cada pessoa, mas a Religião toma conta e espaço deem eventos públicos. Esse paradoxo evidencia para nós a força que a Religião ainda possui em nossa sociedade. Por religião entenderemos que se trata antes de tudo de uma forma da vida humana. A religião é uma interpretação de uma vivência humana que pertence aos bens culturais produzidos pelo homem. Por religião entendemos um encontro vivencial do homem com a realidade sagrada, ou seja, a religião se vincula a uma relação que o homem estabelece com o sagrado que a qual culmina em uma atitude no mundo que não se encerra apenas sobre um sujeito fechado sobre si, mas se reflete em uma tendência para além de si. Mas se é possível ao ser humano algum tipo de experiência religiosa, ela deverá ocorrer num plano que integre os três modos de presença da realidade à consciência, porque, se não for assim, a experiência não será humana. Falar de experiência religiosa é falar de relação ao sagrado como objeto de amor e de reverência. Religião é relação ao sagrado, que pode ser chamado Deus, e que comporta necessariamente um aspecto social. Essa relação pessoal e social é também integral, posto que é toda a pessoa e, também, toda a comunidade que estão implicados na experiência religiosa. Dito de outro modo, existe experiência religiosa autêntica quando a pessoa se capta em relação ao sagrado, Deus, sem excluir-se ao mundo e aos outros. Não há verdadeira experiência religiosa que não conduza a uma presença ao mundo e ao outro. Qualquer religião que fosse usada para tirar o ser humano do seu lugar no mundo seria um atentado à liberdade humana. Se há uma possibilidade de realizar a relação com o sagrado, com Deus, ela deve acontecer no aqui e agora da liberdade situada no mundo e com os outros. A experiência humana que tem créditos para se apresentar como autêntica experiência religiosa pode ser definida como "experiência do sentido". segundo Kant (1999), a experiência religiosa, como estamos comentando se se torna a experiência humana por excelência uma vez que é a experiência de um sentido radical. No entanto esse sentido radical não abre mão da contingência, mas a entende como que vinculada a um sentido último da realidade. Ao nosso ver, tal sentido último irá se colocará para o homem como uma grande aposta, uma tentativa também última de postular um sentido para o mundo. Na medida em que não renuncia à sua humanidade, ele é capaz de se compreender em um universo de sentidos que são criados por ele mesmo, mas que não dão conta de responder à carência de sentido último que habita tal sujeito. Por isso é que a Religião, mesmo que remeta a uma experiência de vinculação ao sagrado, sempre se constitui uma linguagem, ou seja, é sempre uma experiência humana. A linguagem é aquilo que faz a separação entre os homens e os animais, é a partir dela que se pode criar novos mundos, abrir se para algo que transcende a vida meramente biológica do ser humano. Em última instância, a linguagem humana só pode ser compreendida num horizonte de sentido da cultura humana, e é nesse sentido que a própria religião se vincula a uma linguagem. Se por um lado a fonte da religião são os problemas da vida cotidiana, a indagação pelo "para quê" de sua existência passageira neste mundo, o "por quê" do sofrimento, por outro lado é a revelação de um poder que transcende o próprio humano. É como se o homem não encontrasse um sentido nas coisas transitórias e, para isso, precisasse crer em um sentido que o transcende. A questão do sentido emerge nas experiências de felicidade, na experiência de confiança, de amor, amizade, mas também nas experiências da morte, da dor, nas vivências negativas, ou seja, a questão do sentido se coloca quando a experiência do mistério e da finitude da vida inquieta e abala o sujeito. A religião então surge não apenas de dentro do sujeito, mas possui uma dimensão externa. A religião afirma que nela própria, na religião, se encontra o Sagrado, o Absoluto, ela visa dizer a esperança do sujeito que quer viver em um mundo que faça sentido para ele, mas em que ele mesmo não consegue dar tal sentido à sua existência. A Religião, nesse sentido, atesta não um desejo de onipotência do sujeito, mas sim a consciência de sua impotência em dar um sentido último à sua realidade, enquanto objeto da linguagem. Na linguagem comum, a palavra "experiência" designa pelo menos dois tipos de conteúdo. Ela pode ser concebida como busca de uma verdade e, nesse caso, será dirigida para a descoberta, para a prova e para a verificação. Experiência é, então, o conjunto de empreendimentos que visam à captação e à formulação de uma verdade nova por meio de uma pesquisa organizada em vista de um fim. A trajetória que vai da pesquisa à posse da verdade é a experiência. Mas a palavra designa também o acolhimento e, ao mesmo tempo, a captação de uma realidade, isto é, a tomada de consciência de algo dado em mim. Nesse caso, ela não é dirigida para a descoberta, para a prova e para a verificação, ela não é a busca de uma verdade, mas a vivência de uma realidade. Ela, então, não será o caminho que vai da pesquisa à verdade, mas será a própria posse de uma realidade dada, definindo-se pelo ato ou conjunto de atos que captam a realidade como presença. A experiência será, então, uma estrutura vivida, uma atividade de contato e até mesmo de comunhão. Se aceitar a definição de experiência, que contempla os dois sentidos anteriores, como "a face do pensamento que se volta para a presença do objeto", podemos dizer que toda experiência se articula nos polos do sujeito e do objeto: o objeto enquanto aparece, enquanto se apresenta; o sujeito enquanto consciência que o penetra e se penetra da sua presença. Daí decorre que a toda experiência corresponde uma linguagem de acordo com o modo da presença ao pensamento: existem coisas, existem outros e existe eu mesmo presentes ao meu pensamento. O ato de voltar-se do pensamento para as coisas, para os outros e para si mesmo pode ocorrer tanto no plano empírico como no plano experimental. No plano empírico, isto é, imediato, temos o relacionamento ingênuo do sujeito consigo mesmo e com o mundo ao seu redor. No plano experimental, temos o sujeito manejando e coordenando os elementos de uma experiência para construir o universo da ciência. Nesse caso, trata-se de um relacionamento crítico com as leis de necessidade pelas quais os fenômenos se impõem ao sujeito. Contudo, existe outro plano no qual a experiência é tomada na sua totalidade pessoal. É o plano no qual ocorre o relacionamento do sujeito com o outro, que a ele se apresenta como interpelação e convocação da sua liberdade ao acolhimento desse outro, também como liberdade. Aqui, ao contrário dos dois primeiros planos, a liberdade é determinante, uma vez que só por ela o ser humano pode abrir-se para acolher o outro como sujeito livre, tecendo com ele o mundo da história e da cultura. Somente nesse plano o ser humano encontra a plenitude do seu lugar, pois aqui ele se situa no horizonte de um sentido que não é particular. O ser humano pode abandonar-se no dia-a-dia a uma série de condicionamentos naturais e culturais sem perder-se neles porque está aberto a algo que vai além deles. Ele pode fazer ciência porque capta o universal no particular, expressando-o coerentemente na linguagem das relações de necessidade. Mas, se é possível ao ser humano algum tipo de experiência religiosa, ela deverá ocorrer num plano que integre os três modos de presença da realidade à consciência, porque, se não for assim, a experiência não será humana. Falar de experiência religiosa é falar de relação ao sagrado como objeto de amor e de reverência. religião é relação ao sagrado, que pode ser chamado Deus, e que comporta necessariamente um aspecto social. Essa relação pessoal e social é também integral, posto que é toda a pessoa e, também, toda a comunidade que estão implicados na experiência religiosa. Dito de outro modo, existe experiência religiosa autêntica quando a pessoa se capta em relação ao sagrado, Deus, sem excluir-se ao mundo e aos outros. Não há verdadeira experiência religiosa que não conduza a uma presença ao mundo e ao outro. Qualquer religião que fosse usada para tirar o ser humano do seu lugar no mundo seria um atentado à liberdade humana. Se há uma possibilidade de realizar a relação com o sagrado, com Deus, ela deve acontecer no aqui e agora da liberdade situada no mundo e com os outros. A experiência humana que tem créditos para se apresentar como autêntica experiência religiosa pode ser definida como a "experiência do sentido", que não se esgota numa das dimensões particulares da existência humana, mas ocupa o espaço total no qual elas se desdobram. Provemo-nos aqui no campo delicado das questões limite, campo no qual toda conceptualização corre o risco de fracassar se pretender mais do que pode alcançar. Contudo, toda experiência humana deve poder ser traduzida em linguagem se quiser permanecer humana, isto é, se quiser permanecer no campo de significações e de sentido, próprio do ser humano. A experiência religiosa é a experiência humana por excelência justamente porque é a experiência de um sentido radical. É claro que essa afirmação só parecerá sensata para quem não recusar uma significação positiva à mais radical das experiências humanas, que é a experiência da contingência. E o caminho que leva da experiência da contingência radical à experiência do Sentido radical deverá ser, negativamente falando, o caminho da recusa à absolutização de todo e qualquer sentido particular, por mais importante que seja, e, positivamente falando, o caminho da afirmação livre de um Sentido último sem o qual toda a realidade seria insensata. Toda experiência humana está marcada, desde a origem, pelo sentido e só é humana porque está carregada de sentido. O ser humano surge no mundo como uma síntese de dois movimentos: o da intenção, pelo qual abre se ao horizonte infinito do ser, referindo-se, ao mesmo tempo, ao universal e ao aqui e agora; e o movimento da expressão, pelo qual intencionada objetos exprimindo-os para si e situando-os no plano da consciência, que é o plano das significações. E, dado que o ser humano sempre se encontra inserido numa comunidade de sujeitos, a expressão do objeto para si é também a sua expressão para o outro.

2.1.3. Subjetividade na expressão religiosa

Conforme Silva (2017), O fenômeno religioso, sem dúvida alguma, pode ser considerado um dos elementos mais complexos da investigação científica. Visto que,

> "o Fenômeno Religioso é explicitamente verificado em todas as épocas e lugares, as pessoas necessitam de um ser superior, para servir-lhes de consolo diante dos embates do mundo que muitas vezes deixam-nas aflitas e sem direção, naquele momento em que tudo parece não ter sentido, no exato momento em que a razão já não explica mais a nossa realidade, gemina a fé, a crença e a esperança num amanhã glorioso circundado pelo gosto da vitória. A religião solidifica nossa crença, amadurece nossa relação com o transcendente, nos leva a uma realidade

metafísica para *posteriori* compreendermos nossa realidade física e humanamente limitada. Somos limitados! Mas, nossas ações tornam-se ilimitadas quando deixamos frutos de nossa existência, quando as pessoas captam em nos valores, e, agregam esses valores dando novo sentido ao seu existir. Nossos valores serão sempre renovados com o contato religioso, quando se adere a uma religião não pode ser uma decisão precipitada, mas uma convicção a ser seguida, uma vez que as maiores de todas as religiões (Cristianismo) (Judaísmo) (Protestantismo) se solidificam baseados no valor da dignidade humana! Assim devemos conduzir nossa vida respeitando em primeiro lugar nossa vida e fazer dela um testemunho vivo da presença do sagrado".[29]

Isso acontece porque na área da fenomenologia humana ele se manifesta simultaneamente como sendo pertencente a diversos campos, quais sejam, experiencial, filosófico, teológico, antropológico, sociológico e psicológico. Por isso, pode-se afirmar que ele se apresenta, dada a sua complexidade, como sendo algo de importância fundamental para a compreensão do ser humano. É, portanto, um elemento que confere ao homem um significado marcante e decisivo na construção de sua subjetividade. Destaca-se, partindo da afirmação acima reproduzida, alguns aspectos de estimada importância para o estudo da religião enquanto fenômeno

---

[29] Acessado em 21/10/2024:
https://meuartigo.brasilescola.uol.com.br/religiao/o-fenomeno-religioso.htm

antropológico. Ela é portadora e, ao mesmo tempo, doadora de sentido para a existência humana, de modo especial naqueles momentos que se apresentam como verdadeiramente determinantes, nos quais toda a solidez parece se diluir e toda referência é vislumbrada na sua mais completa fragilidade. Quando as respostas não parecem oferecer nenhuma segurança, o elemento religioso surge como algo a que se "amparar", desafiando toda e qualquer experiência de desamparo, ainda que seja mesmo aquele desamparo que denominamos "original". Devido a sua importância e pertinência na vida do ser humano, o fenômeno religioso também foi objeto de estudo da área psicanalítica. Qualquer processo cultural é o resultado do saber e do poder do ser humano em controlar a natureza e dela extrair bens (FREUD, 1974). A cultura deve incluir, por outro lado, os regulamentos necessários para ajustar as relações entre os homens na distribuição dos bens disponíveis. É justamente em relação à repartição dos bens que o processo cultural esbarra em dificuldades. Isto porque as relações humanas são regidas pela quantidade de satisfação pulsional que os bens disponíveis propiciam e oferecem. Acrescente-se a isso o lembrete de Freud de que um homem pode vir, ele próprio, a funcionar como bem em relação a outro homem na medida em que pode ser explorado, seja na sua capacidade de trabalho, seja, até mesmo, como objeto sexual. Assim, lembra que "não há discurso, e não apenas o analítico, que não seja do gozo, pelo menos quando dele se espera o trabalho da verdade" (LACAN, 1992, p.74). Nisso, o discurso do mestre é exemplar e nele se denuncia a espoliação do gozo, a redução do próprio trabalhador a ser apenas valor. O mais-de-gozar passa a se inscrever simplesmente: "como valor a registar ou deduzir da totalidade do que se acumula, o que se acumula de uma natureza essencialmente transformada" (LACAN, 1992, p.76). Pode-se dizer que o empunho à produção desenfreada de bens a serem consumidos gera na cultura esse peso morto, traduzido por um mais-de-gozar que já não circula. Ora, a manutenção dessa maquinaria exige a exploração do trabalho escravo. Nesse sentido, a figura inaugural do mestre e senhor encontra sua verdade no trabalho do outro, daquele que só se sabe por ter perdido seu corpo, "esse mesmo corpo em que se sustenta, por ter querido preservá-lo em seu acesso ao gozo" (LACAN, 1992, p.83). Isso significa a força do discurso religioso: Sabe-se que foi devido à fraqueza e desamparo do ser humano diante das forças impiedosas da natureza que se criou a cultura, cujo objetivo inicial foi proteger o homem dos perigos naturais. Porém, na medida em que as tentativas de controle da natureza se mostraram falhas, foi preciso forjar a ilusão de uma Providência benevolente, que velava por todos. Desse estado de coisas nasceu o poder das ideias religiosas, sistemas de crenças que, acordes com os desejos do homem, passaram a fornecer a ilusão de proteção e segurança. A ilusão religiosa (FREUD, 1930), ao se inscrever no campo do desejo, coloca-se fora, ou mesmo, acima, da jurisdição da razão. Ela não é passível de ser provada ou refutada pela razão. Nesse sentido, difere do trabalho científico sobre a natureza, o qual se depara continuamente com o erro e exige ser verificado. Tal trabalho esbarra em duas limitações: por um lado, nosso aparelho psíquico não é fidedigno pois, detrás dos predicados do objeto que se apresenta diretamente à nossa percepção, algo escapa e permanece incognoscível. Por mais que tentemos aumentar a eficiência de nossos órgãos sensoriais mediante auxílios artificiais, algo permanece inabordável em relação àquilo que "se poderia supor ser o estado real das coisas" (FREUD, 1975, p.225). Assim, resta à ciência se contentar em inferir processos, em si inapreensível, e traduzi-los para a linguagem acessível pela via de nossas percepções. Por outro lado, não poucas são as pessoas que encontram sua única consolação nas doutrinas religiosas e só suportam a vida com o seu auxílio. Mesmo que a ciência progredisse ao máximo, ela não bastaria para o homem. Este "possui necessidades imperiosas de outro tipo, que jamais poderiam ser satisfeitas pela frígida ciência" (FREUD, 1974, p.48). Ao ser perguntado sobre a eficácia da religião, Lacan (2005) responde que esta triunfará não apenas sobre a psicanálise, mas sobre muitas outras coisas. Isto porque, diante da expansão do real, a religião, diz ele, terá razões de sobra para apaziguar os corações. E o fará a partir daquilo em que é competente, a sua capacidade de atribuir sentido a tudo, especialmente à vida humana. Completa Lacan (2005). "A religião vai dar um sentido às experiências mais curiosas, aquelas pelas quais os próprios cientistas começam a sentir uma ponta de angústia. A religião vai encontrar para isso sentidos truculentos. É só ver o andar da carruagem, como eles estão se atualizando" (LACAN, 2005, p.66). Portanto, a Psicanálise e o fenômeno religioso é a pontos para a construção de diálogos e resolução de problemas da vida humana. Diante da importância 86que estas duas áreas representam para o sujeito contemporâneo, encontrado numa condição de fragmentação interna e externa por se perceber imerso num mundo em situação de constantes e profundas transformações, buscaremos indicar possíveis caminhos que favoreçam o intercâmbio de ideias, possibilitando, desta forma uma contribuição ao ser humano na construção de sua subjetividade (SILVA, 2017). O fenômeno religioso, sem dúvida alguma, pode ser considerado um dos elementos mais complexos da investigação científica. Isso acontece porque na área da fenomenologia humana ele se manifesta simultaneamente como sendo pertencente a diversos campos, quais sejam, experiencial, filosófico, teológico, antropológico, sociológico e psicológico, entre outros. Por isso, podemos afirmar que ele se apresenta, dada a sua complexidade, como sendo algo de importância fundamental para a compreensão do ser humano. É, portanto, um elemento que confere ao homem um significado marcante e decisivo na construção de sua subjetividade: Há um consenso entre cientistas sociais, filósofos e psicólogos sociais de que a religião é uma importante instância de significação e ordenação da vida, de seus reveses e sofrimentos. Sendo que a religião

> "é elemento constitutivo da subjetividade e doador de significado ao sofrimento, defendo que ela deva ser considerada um objeto privilegiado na interlocução com a saúde e os transtornos mentais" (DALGARANDO, 2008, p. 16).

Destaca-se, partindo da afirmação acima reproduzida, alguns aspectos de estimada importância para o estudo da religião enquanto fenômeno antropológico. Ela é portadora e, ao mesmo tempo, doadora de sentido para a existência humana, de modo especial naqueles momentos que se apresentam como verdadeiramente determinantes, nos quais toda a solidez parece se diluir e toda referência é vislumbrada na sua mais completa fragilidade. Quando as respostas não parecem oferecer nenhuma segurança, o elemento religioso surge como algo a que se "amparar", desafiando toda e qualquer experiência de desamparo, ainda que seja mesmo aquele desamparo que denominamos "original".[30] Devido a sua importância e pertinência na vida do ser humano, o fenômeno religioso também foi objeto de estudo da área psicanalítica. Embora, frequentemente, seja difundida a concepção de total ruptura e antagonismo entre estes dois campos de estudo, podemos identificar a possibilidade de se estabelecer um diálogo fecundo entre os mesmos que favoreça um aprofundamento da compreensão do homem nas suas mais variadas dimensões.

2.2. A práxis da religião na infância: olhar da ciência da psicanalise

[30] Segundo Freud (192), as experiências de sofrimento, potencializadas em momentos críticos, convocam o sujeito a perceber-se num lugar desconfortável, onde a insegurança e a ausência de previsibilidade balançam sua estrutura, colocando em questão todas as amarrações que o sustentavam até vivência de desamparo, em toda e qualquer situação de sofrimento, sinaliza as bases instáveis a partir das quais a experiência humana inicia-se. Através dela, adquire-se uma forma de saber que só pelo sofrimento faz-se possível descreve que "todo sofrimento contém uma demanda de reconhecimento", nesse sentido, é preciso reconhecer a fragilidade integrada à própria existência, a fim de que o sujeito não seja engolido pelas experiências de sofrimento.

Neste capítulo elencam-se interpretações concernentes à religião na infância segundo o olhar da psicanálise (FREUD, 1920, 1986, 2019b) enquanto, também, instrumento, para suas pesquisas referente ao objeto, religião no contexto geral. Conquanto, sumariamente, a psicanálise conhecida como ciência do comportamento, busca compreender e esclarecer o processo mental e emocional do ser humano, explorando as mais diversas formas de comportamento e modos de interpretar o mundo ao seu redor. Assim, a religião é um fenômeno cultural complexo que engloba: crenças, práticas, rituais e valores morais. No que tange ao debate entre psicanálise e religião, cabe trazer à discussão as importantes contribuições da crítica freudiana, que são base de averiguação científica para a psicologia. Para Freud, os atos obsessivos presentes nas práticas religiosas, apontavam para uma analogia bastante profunda entre neurose e religião, em outras palavras, de certa forma esses atos obsessivos oferecia à neurose um caráter religioso e à religião um caráter neurótico. A crítica da psicanálise à religião, especificamente ao fundamentalismo religioso, discutindo sobre os elementos históricos e epistêmicos em torno dos debates e embates entre ciência e cristianismo. Ressalta-se que um dos fatos mais apavorantes do século XX, foi o erguimento de uma religiosidade militante conhecida como fundamentalismo. Nascido entre as grandes tradições religiosas, esse acontecimento se apresenta como uma reação contra o meio da cultura secular e científica, surgida no Ocidente e, depois, difundida para outras partes do mundo. O debate entre psicanálise e religião, cabe trazer à discussão as importantes contribuições da crítica freudiana, que são base de averiguação científica para estas áreas de conhecimento. Para Freud, os atos obsessivos presentes nas práticas religiosas, apontavam para uma analogia bastante profunda entre neurose e religião, em outras palavras, de certa forma esses atos obsessivos oferecia à neurose um caráter religioso e à religião uma possibilidade caráter neurótico. Portanto, embora a obra de Freud tenha contribuído para a compreensão das influências religiosas na formação da personalidade e nos processos mentais, é necessário considerar uma variedade de perspectivas e abordagens teóricas para uma compreensão mais abrangente desse tema. Considerando que essa é uma análise complexa, que envolve aspectos diversos das experiências humanas, as quais podem ser compreendidas sobre prismas diferentes, Freud clarifica que a psicanálise, utiliza-se de dos seus conceitos de transferência, inconsciente e interpretação para entender e criticar a experiência religiosa humana, argumentando que o sujeito tende a ajustar suas vivências e experiências em consonância com suas crenças e estrutura de personalidade. Logo os fenômenos místicos podem ser abordados do ponto de vista da clínica psicanalítica para com a subjetividade humana. Neste contexto freudiano, a *práxis* da ciência da religião vista na psicanálise possui um olhar epistemológico e empírico da religião na infância, entre outro a abordagem do ensino religioso deste público. Para Freud, a religião faz parte do contexto das crenças do ser humano e, como tal, atravessa os contextos da saúde no seu termo científico, influenciando, diretamente ou não, na saúde mental. O psicanalista Sigmund Freud traz em suas pesquisas um olhar crítico para a transcendência. Assim sendo, pode-se afirmar que a contribuição da psicanálise é de grande relevância para a crítica ao fenômeno religioso e a transcendência, pois, ocupa-se da análise da expressividade do fundamentalismo religioso na sociedade pós-moderna, ancoradas nas linhas de pensamentos freudiana e atualizações contemporâneas. Pode-se concluir que a análise da crítica freudiana, revela-se relevante no campo da psicanálise contemporânea, oferecendo uma compreensão mais profunda das influências religiosas na saúde mental e no bem-estar mental das pessoas. Essa perspectiva crítica permite uma reflexão aprofundada sobre os efeitos da religião na formação da personalidade, destacando a importância de uma abordagem equilibrada e saudável da religiosidade. A expressão religião é a expressão do convívio e de um nova ou retomada vivência. É neste passo que o ensino religioso na infância traz mais benefícios do que se possa imagina. Possibilitam valores, rumo de vida; como valores, ética, cultura e amor ao próximo são alguns dos aprendizados que auxiliarão a criança a compreender seu papel na sociedade como ser humano e cidadão. A religião por ser uma realidade social trabalha a formação do indivíduo ainda na infância. É considerado um aprendizado para a vida, levantar e resolver questões relacionadas à ética, moral e, também, ao comportamento que envolve a sociedade. Além disso, ele abre espaço para que as crianças aprendam mais sobre paz, justiça, empatia e a importância do amor ao próximo. Isso significa que, além do aprendizado intelectual com matérias voltadas ao processo natural escolar, como matemática, português, inglês, entre outras, o aluno aprenderá sobre a importância de valores essenciais para a sociedade, como a bondade, o respeito, a coletividade e tantos outros que, com o tempo e a correria do dia a dia, estão se perdendo. A ideia de momento religiosa e lealdade são tomados por Smith (2018)[31] como fundamentos das reflexões sobre educação enquadrado nos fundamentos religiosos da infância. A história de Smith é semelhante à de muitas meninas, hoje mulheres, espalhadas por todo o mundo. Essa experiência pode ser colocada ao lado de histórias de opressão e violência, como as de Adália, Tulipa, Magnólia, Margarida, Rosa Flor, enfim, todas as mulheres que, generosamente, partilharam pedacinhos de vida com a pesquisa que embalsa este texto. Nesses fragmentos percebe-se semelhanças entre diferentes países, culturas, realidades: crianças que vivem dentro de um contexto fundamentalista extremista, a relação com um líder carismático, mentiroso patológico, abusivo e narcisista e sua posição definida para sacrificar mulheres e crianças. Apesar de a temática da violência contra criança em contextos fundamentalistas extremistas vir sendo colocada em debate há algum tempo em outros países, parece ser invisível aos pesquisadores brasileiros,[32] e a comunidade acadêmica parece não considerar importante discutir uma questão ainda quase tabu. Em razão de o depoimento, de certo modo, trazer um pedacinho de cada história compartilhada no período da pesquisa, sua inclusão neste texto traz um enorme significado, já que, a escuta da narrativa de Smith se articula à que empreendemos às narrativas das

---

[31] Acessado em 30/05/2021:
https://somosamadas.wordpress.com/type/video/
[32] Acessado em 10/10/2024: https://institutodeneurociencias.com.br

biografadas. Suas declarações expõem o quanto a patologia de um líder religioso não se mantém nele, mas afeta todo um grupo. Isso explica porque pessoas boas acabam fazendo coisas terríveis, conforme:

> "Mal entrei no quarto e meu pai já estava lá. Sentado à mesa esperando que eu me sentasse para me comunicar sobre mais uma surra explicada como um sermão. Lembro-me de sua expressão: altiva, calma, com certo tom de frieza nos olhos. Meu pai. Ele havia criado uma forma cruel de "educar" uma menina e parecia desfrutar dela. A presença dele no "quarto da surra" não deixava dúvidas de que se tratava de uma forma planejada de agressão. Em pouco tempo, encontrava-me nua, da cintura para baixo, tremendo toda, embora ele mantivesse tão firmes as mãos. De um lado as varas (porque não bastava uma em cada sessão de tortura), do outro a bíblia aberta no livro de Provérbios: "Não retires a vara do teu filho" (depoimento de um entrevistado durante uma aula de ensino religiosa numa determinada escola Municipal em Bocaiúva - MG)".

Tal depoimento demonstra como as palavras de Smith falam, exatamente, de situações que meninas brasileiras, hoje mulheres, viveram. As tantas proibições impostas a elas, uma vez infringidas, geraram castigos, cujas cicatrizes estão impregnadas em suas almas. Smith nasceu e vive nos Estados Unidos (EUA), no entanto, fala de algo que não recebeu importância até há bem pouco tempo na educação brasileira: a importação de práticas religiosas para o Brasil. Tais práticas demonstram, como afirma Fatou Sow (2018, p.18), por que e como a religião e a cultura podem ser fontes e lugares de expressão para fundamentalismos, particularmente em relação à política. Nesse sentido, o que nos conta Smith provoca, e pode ser analisado sob diversos ângulos. O estilo cômico da autora é, particularmente, uma grande chave para tratar de algo tão duro como a opressão fundamentalista a crianças, especialmente meninas. A sátira de Smith contextualiza a vida das participantes da pesquisa, mulheres que nasceram entre as décadas de 1970 e 1980 em cidades brasileiras do Sul, Leste e Centro-Oeste, que, possivelmente, gostariam de abraçar Smith como uma delas. A religião é um mecanismo que está presente na transição da fase infantil para a adulta. As abordagens científicas que relacionam religião e infância não são abundantes. Localizamos alguns estudos que se concentram numa interface entre religião e infância, embora não se restrinjam à ciência da religião/psicanálise; sendo que os estudos sobre crianças e religião se concentram em uma abordagem quantitativa e altamente psicológica. Percepções e conceitos religiosos não são baseados em dados sensoriais diretos, mas são formados a partir de outras percepções e conceitos de experiência. Os místicos, que afirmam terem sensações divinas diretas, são exceções, mas como eles são casos extremamente raros, ainda mais raros na adolescência e praticamente desconhecidos na infância, nós não precisamos explorar a sua significância. Algumas pesquisas apostam, no entanto, na validade de estudos sobre religião que tenham como foco as crianças. A educação espiritual, afirmam que as crianças têm experiências religiosas mais intensas que os adultos porque naturalmente os seres humanos são equipados com uma consciência religiosa que vai sendo esquecida com o passar dos anos. Por sua vez, a experiência religiosa, denominada "a visão original", é uma experiência ordinária que ocorre de primeira mão e, por isso, de maneira mais completa na infância. Como na experiência mística, o sujeito sente que foi abalado por um poder maior que ele próprio. Portanto, não há dúvida que Freud dá importância que se deve dar quanto a relação íntima entre a criança e a religião; visto porque a infância faz parte da história da psicanálise como uma de suas marcas indeléveis. Cenas e lembranças referentes aos primeiros anos de vida dos pacientes estão presentes nos escritos freudianos desde os seus primórdios. O que marca da elaboração teórica em torno deste período da vida humana e, consequentemente, o modo próprio como os psicanalistas ouvem os relatos de seus pacientes em relação aos seus primeiros anos de vida. Em linhas gerais, talvez possamos dizer que a principal característica da compreensão psicanalítica em relação à infância consiste no interesse de resgatar na fala dos pacientes, não sua própria constituição como, também, seu modo de relembrar o passado. É exatamente este duplo movimento que o infantil estabelece, ao mesmo tempo em que constitui, ele próprio oferece modos de interpretação dessa constituição. É importante lembrar que essa compreensão do infantil tem uma ressonância fundamental no trabalho analítico. À medida que esta noção era lapidada, a prática analítica ia assumindo contornos diversos, passando gradualmente pelos terrenos da hipnose, da sugestão e da associação livre. Na medida em que Freud distanciava-se dos fatos em direção à interpretação que o próprio sujeito lhe atribuía, ele caminhava em direção à valorização da associação livre como técnica fundamental da psicanálise. Nesse percurso das transformações do método psicanalítico, o infantil assume uma posição central. Outro aspecto relevante consiste no fato de que o infantil não conceitual que contorna a idéia de infância e de infantil na psicanálise sempre esteve, de algum modo, presente nos trabalhos construções teóricas (FREUD, 1910, 2019). Este autor já havia a compreensão de que na reconstrução dos primeiros anos de vida feita em análise estão contempladas tanto as recordações de infância proferidas ao analista como a infância esquecida. Não era apenas aquilo que o paciente recordava que Freud considerava relevante na com preensão dos sintomas, mas também e, sobretudo, a infância Mesmo quando se voltava à reconstituição dos fatos de infância relatados por seus pacientes, o que mantinha Freud ocupado com a infância era algo da ordem do recalcado. O infantil recalcado, muito mais que um relato sobre a infância, foi, desde sempre, o seu verdadeiro interesse. Porém, para o próprio Freud, a sustentação metapsicológica da compreensão dos primeiros anos de vida exigiu um permanente trabalho de elaboração. O modo de tomar o infantil na constituição do psiquismo, na formação dos sintomas ou no trabalho de análise não se apresenta placidamente em seus escritos. Ele oscilou, constantemente, em um movimento pendular entre as experiências da infância e o material recalcado. Revendo os escritos freudianos, percebemos que não é exata mente uma precisa delimitação conceitual das noções de infância e de infantil que caracterizará o modo como Freud fez uso das mesmas para explicar a importância dos primeiros anos de vida na constituição psíquica. Assim, com o intuito de desvendarmos as questões que fomentaram o deslizamento da infância ao infantil nos primórdios da psicanálise, pesquisamos, por meio de alguns textos da obra freudiana, o percurso realizado por Freud nessa elaboração. Nesse caminho, percebemos que existem momentos em que essa construção teórica assume contornos mais precisos. Ressalta mos, em especial, o momento em que a fantasia passa a ocupar um lugar teórico relevante na compreensão da constituição do psiquismo. Esse lugar consiste em atribuir à realidade psíquica um valor de determinação antes atribuído apenas à realidade material. Será nesse momento de valoração da realidade psíquica, que Freud (1910, 1960) realiza uma mudança na compreensão teórica do modo como os primeiros anos de vida participam do processo de constituição psíquica. A fantasia é reposicionada na metapsicologia e assume um lugar de destaque na compreensão e na reconstrução do infantil em análise. A partir de então, a consideração da fantasia enquanto verdade psíquica confere ao infantil um estatuto que se estende para faculdade de compreensão coloca-se exatamente nesse ponto, pois no psiquismo nos primórdios da constituição psíquica. Os sons, os cheiros, as sensações táteis compõem as marcas mnêmicas primordiais e estende-se para além delas. Assim, pensar o infantil como um conceito psicanalítico passa pela compreensão de uma infância que desliza da simples cronologia e das experiências passíveis de narração à realidade psíquica, e da fantasia como um elemento irrevogável da constituição do psiquismo. Desse modo, na psicanálise, a infância cronológica não pode ser confundida com o infantil reconstruído no discurso do analisando no contexto da relação transferencial. Como um conceito metapsicológico, o infantil não se dá a ver, mas se faz presente no discurso e no modo como o analisando se põe em análise. de conhecimento distinto da psicologia e das outras ciências. É nesse campo metapsicológico que inscrevemos a compreensão psicanalítica do infantil. Na psicanálise, infância e infantil estão remetidos a estruturas conceituais diversas. Enquanto a infância refere-se a um tempo da realidade histórica, o infantil é atemporal e está reme tido a conceitos como pulsão, recalque e inconsciente. Assim, se o infantil na psicanálise é constituído em referência aos conceitos metapsicologia em seu afastamento e diferenciação ao tempo da infância, embora que irrevogavelmente referido à mesma. O infantil diz do modo peculiar de tomar a infância no trabalho de análise, ou seja, como marca mnêmica recalcada, referente aos primeiros anos de vida. A propósito da preservação de seus fundamentos, podemos Podemos dizer que a construção a posteriori do infantil em análise não abandona propriamente a realidade histórica vivida pela criança. A questão transferencial na criança passa pela concepção do conceito de superou, que segundo Freud (1933/2010), ainda não se encontra constituído. Para o autor, o surge no a posteriori do naufrágio edípico. A criança no início da vida, devido a sua condição de desamparo em que necessita de cuidados para sua sobrevivência, investe seu impulso libidinal no objeto que ela julga que a mantém viva numa condição de maternagem.[33] Esse objeto de amor da criança, a mãe, ocupa um lugar central na vida do infante até que ela constate a presença de um terceiro, o pai. Esse comporta aos olhos da criança o alvo a quem ela investe sentimentos de conteúdo ambivalente. Para a criança, o pai funciona como obstáculo para que ela tenha acesso a esse objeto de amor, que é a mãe. Tal romance familiar é o que consideramos como o Complexo de Édipo. O Complexo edípico, no entanto, declina quando a criança recalca os sentimentos edípicos dirigidos à mãe e coloca seu pai num lugar afetivo e de identificação para ela. A entrada e o declínio edípico dão-se de forma diversa no menino e na menina, como Freud (1925/2011b) esclarece em seu texto Algumas consequências psíquicas da distinção anatômica entre os sexos, texto considerado o seu quarto ensaio sobre a teoria da sexualidade. O que leva o menino ao Complexo de Édipo é sua investigação sobre a origem dos bebés e o que leva a menina ao Édipo é a constatação da presença do pênsis no menino e ausência em si desse membro. O declínio do Édipo da menina ocorre também de maneira diferente. Freud enumera três maneiras de a menina enfrentar o sentimento de inveja do pênis que ela desenvolve. Primeiramente, de acordo com Freud (1925/2011b), a menina constata a ausência do pênis e quer tê-lo. Numa dessas formas de enfrentar a inveja do pênis, ela constata que o possui e dá curso à busca pela feminilidade. Outra forma seria a menina não aceitar tão facilmente que não possui o pênis e manter a esperança de algum dia consegui-lo. Dessa forma, ela passa a se parecer com um

---

[33] Acessado em 20/10/2024: https://revistaft.com.br/a-religiao-na-perspectiva-psicanalitica/

homem e diante dessa percepção, comporta-se de forma estranha e inexplicável, como descreve Freud (1925/2011b). E ainda, numa terceira forma, a menina rejeitaria a ideia de que não possui um pênis e viveria com a convicção como se tivesse um, agindo como se fosse um homem. O autor esclarece que esse comportamento em uma criança não é raro, nem muito perigoso, mas em um adulto significaria o começo de uma psicose. Freud (1925/2011b) considera que o fim do Édipo da menina não ocorre como no menino. De acordo com o autor, falta um mobilizador para que naufrague o Complexo de Édipo da menina. O Édipo na menina vai sendo progressivamente abandonado ou sendo elaborado a partir do recalque, ou ainda apresenta influência na vida psíquica da mulher. Freud (1923/2011) chama a atenção para o final edípico, em que ocorreria uma internalização da identificação do menino com o pai e da menina com a mãe. O autor considera as situações ambivalentes que podem surgir das escolhas objetais e identificações, que devido à rivalidade com genitor de mesmo sexo, possam levar à bissexualidade marcando assim, as disposições sexuais. Mediante o contexto edípico na menina, Freud (1925/2011b) afirma que o superou nas mulheres é caracterizado como menos exigente do que nos homens em termos da ética, senso de justiça. Entre as características ticas do superou feminino, também estaria a dificuldade em enfrentar as adversidades da vida. Além disso, a mulher teria sua capacidade de avaliação e julgamento influenciada por sentimentos de afinidade ou antipatia. Freud (1925/2011b), no entanto, retifica que o caráter masculino não deve ser encarado como correspondente ao ideal, pois devemos considerar o aspecto da disposição para a bissexualidade e herança cruzada. Nelas, são aglomeradas tanto características masculinas quanto femininas, de maneira que tanto o caráter masculino quanto o feminino, em estado puro, não passam de constructos teóricos de conteúdo incerto. Uma pontuação importante é apresentada por Freud (1923/2011) ao fim do Complexo de Édipo. Nela, temos como resultado a formação do que o autor chama de um precipitado no eu, que se compõe desse emaranhado de identificações as quais se opõem aos outros conteúdos do eu e tomam a consistência de um ideal do eu ou superego. O superego, desse modo, consiste em um resíduo de escolhas inconscientes primitivas, bem como é composto por uma constituição que reage energicamente essas escolhas. Ao mesmo tempo em que o superou comporta um imperativo "você deveria ser assim", essa instância psíquica também comporta um imperativo "você não pode ser assim". Freud (1923/2011) ressalta que a ação do supereu dá-se de forma mais repressora quanto mais intenso foi o Complexo de Édipo. Também, comporta o caráter do pai, reforçado por alguns elementos da ordem social, como a influência da autoridade do ensino religioso, a educação escolar e a leitura. Com isso, resulta-se em uma precipitação sobre o eu na forma de consciência ou sentimento inconsciente de culpa. Freud (1925/2011b) declara que os resultados que obtemos do Complexo de Édipo são o abandono do incesto e a instituição da consciência e da moralidade, efeitos considerados uma vitória da civilização sobre o indivíduo. Se tomarmos o superou como constituído por uma internalização do que ficou do romance edípico, temos um mecanismo utilizado pelo sujeito para resgatar o material infantil tão frequente no discurso dos pacientes em uma análise e ausente em crianças que ainda não trazem constituído o ideal do eu. Na relação transferencial da criança, portanto, há um predomínio dos sentimentos ambivalentes que o infante alimenta em relação aos pais, correspondentes à travessia do romance edípico e, consequentemente, em análise, a criança tende a transferir ao analista esses sentimentos. Além disso, a criança busca respostas para seus enigmas sobre a origem dos bebês e a morte, saber que ela supõe transferencialmente que o analista detenha. Hans[34] manifesta de acordo com Freud (1909/2015), a mesma pre ocupação diante do enigma da vida, em que investiga a chegada da irmã dentro de "grandes caixas" e, em como se preocupa, se abaixo do lugar onde ele estava na calçada, haveria um homem enterrado ou se isso apenas se daria nos cemitérios. Notamos como esse processo se dá na análise de Hans. De acordo com a análise que Freud (1909/2015) faz do caso, observamos como Hans estabelece o contato com o Professor Freud por meio de seu pai, que afirma que aquele professor saberia dizer algo sobre a "bobagem", como era chamada por Hans a sua fobia. No encontro entre Freud e Hans, o psicanalista comunica ao menino os motivos de angústia que vinha apresentando relacionada a cavalos e que isso acontecia, porque ele temia o pai por causa do amor que sentia pela mãe. Ao término da consulta, Hans pergunta a seu pai se

---

[34] Acessado em 15/10/2024: https://ippbrasil.com/o-caso-do-pequeno-hans-relacao-entre-fobia-e-sexualidade-infantil/ e, também, em:
https://appoa.org.br/correio/edicao/340/hans_e_a_mancha_contribuic oes_ao_conceito_de_objeto_na_psicanalise/1396

o professor falava com Deus, pois parece que já sabia tudo previamente. Esse foi o único encontro entre Hans e Freud enquanto a criança apresentava a fobia, mas o menino aparentemente mostrava-se transferido com Freud, pois algumas vezes pedia ao pai que per guntasse ao professor sobre as coisas que se passavam com ele. Constatamos, portanto, que Hans foi capaz de estabelecer um vínculo transferencial com Freud por intermédio de seu pai, que alimenta uma transferência em relação ao professor. Em outro momento, Hans relata a seu pai o temor que tinha de subir numa carroça e ela partir. Quando o pai questiona sobre o motivo do medo dele, ele diz que não sabe, mas talvez o professor saiba. Na prática de nossa clínica, averiguamos essa transferência ambivalente em momentos em que a criança compara, verbalmente, o analista à sua mãe ou a seu pai, "você parece com minha mãe". Ou, no discurso dos pais quando dizem: "No caminho para o consultório, ela vinha me apressando, dizendo que não poderia se atrasar para a sessão e, ao chegar aqui, diz que não quer entrar". Esse discurso é da mãe ao se referir ao comportamento da filha de 5 anos. É importante ressaltar que Freud não trabalhou em sua clínica com crianças e, apesar de apresentar tantos exemplos e considerações sobre as crianças em sua obra, ele não se dedicou a encontrar meios na clínica para contornar os problemas que ele apontou no atendimento de crianças, como a questão transferencial e dificuldade com a regra fundamental da associação livre. Podemos considerar que os pressupostos estabelecidos por Freud sobre a criança não apresentavam por parte do autor uma afirmação de um constructo que poderia ser aplicado à clínica com crianças. Mas, muitos desses pressupostos podem ser tomados como legítimas contribuições que auxiliaram os analistas de crianças a construírem uma prática no atendimento clínico, como suas observações sobre o ato do brincar. A leitura é uma boa ferramenta para conversar com as crianças sobre religião. Papais e mamães podem optar por livros que trazem a ideia de Deus como uma força universal que não se restringe à uma religião específica. Esse é o caso do livro "Vamos Conversar Sobre Deus", de Angels Comella. A obra fala muito sobre a presença divina em tudo e em todos e tem muitas ilustrações. Porém, é importante também trazer obras que explicam sobre o sistema de crenças de outras religiões e sobre o ateísmo. As religiões de matriz africana, por exemplo, são alvos constantes de agressões e preconceitos. Como pontuamos, isso originou o Dia Nacional de Combate à Intolerância Religiosa. Por isso, é importante ensinar às crianças o respeito às diversas crenças, considerando nenhum, um ou diversos deuses. Aliás, as crianças têm maior capacidade de compreender e respeitar a pluralidade do que os adultos. Diante deste panorama, Alexandre de Paula e Silva,[35] menciona que A religião faz parte do contexto das crenças do ser humano e, como tal, atravessa os contextos da saúde no seu termo científico, influenciando, diretamente ou não, na saúde mental. A partir das principais descobertas,[36] pode-se afirmar que a contribuição da psicanálise é de grande relevância para a crítica ao fenômeno religioso e a transcendência, pois, ocupa-se da análise da

---

[35] Acessado em 20/10/2024: https://revistaft.com.br/a-religiao-na-perspectiva-psicanalitica/
[36] Acessado em 20/10/2024: https://revistaft.com.br/a-religiao-na-perspectiva-psicanalitica/

expressividade do fundamentalismo religioso na sociedade pós-moderna, ancoradas nas linhas de pensamentos freudiana e atualizações contemporâneas. Pode-se concluir que a análise da crítica freudiana, revela-se relevante no campo da psicologia contemporânea, oferecendo uma compreensão mais profunda das influências religiosas na saúde mental e no bem-estar psicológico das pessoas. Essa perspectiva crítica permite uma reflexão aprofundada sobre os efeitos da religião na formação da personalidade, destacando a importância de uma abordagem equilibrada e saudável da religiosidade. Assim, a religião e a espiritualidade trazem como estruturas vários significados que conferem sentido à existência humana, e, por conseguinte, às experiências de sofrimento, caracterizando-as como parte da realidade e cultura humana, constituindo-se assim, um dos aspectos da subjetividade do homem. Desta maneira, uma das principais contribuições de Freud foi: a compreensão de que a religião aparece como uma forma de proteção contra os sentimentos de impotência e abandono enfrentados pelo ser humano, com destaque para a projeção da figura paterna, que é colocada como uma resposta para as questões existenciais, proporcionando uma sensação de segurança e bem-estar emocional. No entanto, é importante considerar os possíveis efeitos negativos, ou também positivamente,[37] da religião na

---

[37] Várias investigações mostram que a participação religiosa está relacionada com efeitos benéficos para pessoas que estão em recuperação de doenças físicas e mentais, inclusive a psicologia aborda questões especiais em detrimento as correlações positivas entre convicção religiosa e prática, saúde mental e física. Portanto, historicamente, as relações entre religião e saúde foram assuntos de interesse no passado e atualmente tornou-se

saúde mental, como a perpetuação de crenças irracionais ou dogmas que podem levar à culpa excessiva, intolerância ou sentimentos de exclusão.

crescentemente visível nas reuniões sociais, de comportamento, e ciências da saúde. Dentre as várias questões a serem consideradas, o presente trabalho apresenta uma breve discussão sobre as relações entre a saúde e a religiosidade no processo de cura e tratamento de doenças. Várias investigações mostram que a participação religiosa está relacionada com efeitos benéficos para pessoas que estão em recuperação de doenças físicas e mentais, inclusive a psicoterapêutica aborda questões especiais em detrimento as correlações positivas entre convicção religiosa e prática, saúde mental, física e longevidade. Por outro lado, a religião também pode ser associada a resultados negativos de usos impróprios de serviços de saúde como fanatismo, asceticismo, mortificações e tradicionalismo opressivo. O potencial para efeitos positivos e negativos de espiritualismo em saúde combinado com os altos níveis de compromisso com a espiritualidade evidencia a necessidade de pesquisas futuras. Independente dos possíveis mecanismos, se os indivíduos recebem lucros provindos da saúde pela religião; esses deveriam ser motivados, respeitando às convicções individuais de cada um.

Capitulo 3
3.1. A subjetividade religiosa e qualidade de vida

Inicialmente, neste quito capítulo está discussões acerca da importância das ciências para a psicoterapia e suas aplicações técnicas-instrumentais nas operacionalizações clínicas analíticas relativas aos estudos sobre os comportamentos dos seres humanas particularmente e, para com suas relações. Para tratar sobre isto aborda-se temáticas como o espírito científico dessas ciências e, os comprometimentos com estudo sobre religião, experiência das linguagens religiosas.

3.1.1. Para com espírito do conhecimento

A abordagem no que tange a religião como um dos objetos de trabalho da psicanalise é uma análise histórico-comparativa de questões metateóricas da psicanálise, que desde a década de 1870, quando surge como empreendimento academismo, vem enfrentando um problema fundamental, cuja resposta justifica sua existência epistemológicas é religião. Consequentemente, de que forma podemos estudar esse objeto para dele derivar do conhecimento e prover explicações cientificamente válidas. Assim sendo, defende-se que uma resposta a este problema é obrigatória para a ciência que toma religião como objeto exclusivo de estudo ou para ciência de utiliza a religião como estudo ou trabalho.

Assim, enquanto área do conhecimento, esta disciplina precisa dizer o que é religião de um ponto de vista científico (BACHELARD, 1996). Além disso, a definição desse conceito precisa não só existir, mas sobretudo ser ssumida academicamente pela disciplina, pois é a partir dele, como demonstraremos ao longo desta sessão, que a referente subjetividade e religião às vistas da estrutura epistemológica da psicanálise. Considera-se que renunciar a este "imperativo categórico"[38] pode significar

---

[38] Sgundo Kante (1991; 2013), o imperativo categórico é um conceito da filosofia desenvolvido pelo filósofo Immanuel Kant, que defende que todo ser humano deve agir de acordo com princípios morais. O imperativo categórico tem como cerne do seu conceito o senso de moral e o dever como princípio. Kant buscou criar uma espécie de fórmula (como as da física) que pudesse orientar todas as ações. Assim, uma ação seria moral somente se passasse no crivo do imperativo categórico. Toda e qualquer ação deve ser avaliada em si mesma, não sendo relevante a história anterior ou o contexto em que a ação seria realizada. Também não faria sentido projetar os efeitos da ação, se seriam benéficos ou não. Para Kant, é importante que a conduta de quem exerce a ação tenha uma preocupação moral intrínseca, que independa de punição ou vantagem, de qualquer tipo de prejuízo ou lucro. O imperativo categórico defende que os indivíduos deveriam agir conforme aquilo que gostariam de ver como lei universal, ou seja, só deveria agir da maneira que gostaria que todos (sem exceção) agissem. Por conta desse conceito de lei, o imperativo categórico também era designado de imperativo universal. O conceito de imperativo categórico tem uma grande importância no ideal de vida harmoniosa em sociedade, pois defende que todas as pessoas se comportem de forma ética e moral e ajam sem prejudicar ou tirar proveito do próximo. A novidade trazida por Kant é que a moral está fundamentada no senso de dever, e não na religião ou no medo de uma sanção, ou punição. O respeito ao imperativo categórico, poderia educar a vontade para só desejar o que se deve fazer. Isso tornaria os crimes impossíveis de serem cometidos, as leis desnecessárias e conduziria a humanidade a uma paz perpétua.

a continuidade de um modelo teórico-metodológico anárquico, estabelecido de qualquer forma por definições de outras disciplinas que abordam "religião" a partir de seus próprios objetos e marcos teóricos. Metodologicamente, parti-se de uma extensa revisão bibliográfica sobre a questão central, seguida de uma discussão mais técnica em relação ao próprio termo religião, após a qual realizamos uma análise epistêmica. Demarcações são inevitáveis, sobretudo quando estamos considerando um objeto cuja definição passe a orientar todo um programa científico de pesquisa (BACHELARD, 1996). Embora a ideia de limitação esteja implicada necessariamente numa definição, do ponto de vista científico, isto não é algo negativo, muito pelo contrário. Por exemplo,

> "aceitar a ideia de uma diversidade de definições, poderia significar admitir como sendo religiões coisas como arte, futebol, nacionalismo, veganismo, ambientalismo e até ateísmo" (BACHELARD, 1996, p.87).

Por isso, em algum momento,

> "os estudiosos serão solicitados a dar suas opiniões sobre o tema, visto que de tempos em tempos, administradores e tribunais também exigem definições de religião. Então, para estas situações, qual seria a resposta da disciplina que se coloca como a ciência deste objeto? O que teria a ciência a dizer nesses casos de uma forma geral, e em tantos outros de forma específica, em

diversas áreas da existência humana? Teria esta ciência um *locus* epistemológico próprio ou dependeria de categorias estabelecidas por outras disciplinas? Embora a defesa por auto (própria) nomia (diretriz) pareça uma obviedade, sua concretização deve enfrentar em seu ponto de partida a questão definicional necessariamente, não sendo sem razão todo o debate realizado em torno dessa questão metateórica central (BACHELARD, 1996, p.87).

Não podemos e não devemos depender de outras disciplinas para resolver esse problema. A ciência pode e deve definir conceitualmente seu objeto, estabelecendo a partir daí uma epistemologia própria, com a qual possa elaborar proposições teóricas cientificamente consistentes e relevantes para a sociedade. Parti-se da constatação de que este problema é fundamental para disciplina e da afirmação de que deve ser enfrentado em primeiro lugar, apresentamos a seguir a estrutura de nosso trabalho. Em seu capítulo de abertura, consideramos pelo menos três posições relacionadas com este desafio: definir religião não é necessário ou possível; definir religião é relativo e; definir religião é necessário. O problema conceitual e suposto comprometimento semântico inerente à sua raiz histórica na direção de uma explícita proposta de substituição (FIGUEIREDO, 2022) Segundo este autor, "o amálgama de piedade interna e instituição externa" em um certo estágio de seu desenvolvimento dinâmico, "foi intelectualmente reificado sob os termos 'religião' e 'religiões'" (FIGUEIREDO, 2022, p.92). Sua proposta alternativa era a de que aquilo que os seres humanos tenderam a conceber como "religião" e sobretudo como "uma religião", poderia

> "ser concebido de forma mais recompensadora e verdadeira em termos de dois fatores diferentes em espécie e ambos dinâmicos: uma 'tradição cumulativa' histórica e a fé pessoal de homens e mulheres" (FIGUEIREDO, 2022, p.93).

Além disso, no plano linguístico, o autor sugere que a palavra "religião", por ter vários significados, deveria ser deixada de lado, em parte em função de sua "desnorteante ambiguidade", e em parte porque "a maioria de seus significados tradicionais são, uma vez minuciosamente examinados, ilegítimos". Smith[39] admite o uso apenas de um significado que se pode atribuir razoavelmente ao termo que é o de 'religiosidade', embora ainda prefira para essa "abstração genérica". Neste sentido, conforme

---

[39] Emmy van Deurzen (1998) diz que o, o rol psicanalítico em Smith, ao confrontar o tabu do envolvimento da história pessoal e das emoções do psicoterapeuta no processo terapêutico. Ao mostrar que os terapeutas eles podem recorrer a toda a riqueza da sua própria experiência para serem mentores verdadeiramente credíveis e inspiradores para os seus clientes. Paradoxos e dilemas da vida humana? tais como solidão versus integração social, segurança versus aventura e confiança versus humildade - são discutidos de forma clara e direta, e relacionados com um amplo espetro de questões que os psicoterapeutas e os seus clientes fariam bem em colocar a si próprios. Ao longo do livro, a autora revela as suas lutas pessoais com as mesmas dificuldades que os seus clientes procuram compreender e resolver. Este processo de revelação, e o facto de tecer casos e problemas vívidos de clientes juntamente com questões filosóficas mais gerais, fazem deste um livro prático e inspirador que demonstra a realidade e a paixão da psicoterapia.

Porfírio (2022), a relação religião e fatores genéticos encontra registros que datam desde 1900, buscavam compreender a relação entre a hereditariedade e o ambiente na vida das crianças, mas além deste, o autor afirma que não há muito a respeito. A Psicologia da Religião e da Espiritualidade consiste na divisão nº 36 da APA (Associação Americana de Psicologia),[40] possui como objeto de estudo o comportamento religioso. Por se tratar de uma área de pesquisa no campo da psicologia, não busca realizar discussões teológicas ou metafísicas sobre os sistemas religiosas, mas é guiada por um caminho de preocupação com as formas de lidar com o Religioso que aparece, sempre guiada pelos princípios éticos da profissão. genética, busca-se compreender que tipos de fatores biológicos estão presentes e como eles podem influenciar a psique humana, em busca de uma melhor compreensão sobre a importância que a influência de diferentes religiões e sistemas de crença possuem para o comportamento humano. Assim, o objetivo do trabalho é apresentar possíveis relações entre o comportamento religioso com fatores genéticos, como objetivos específicos busca refletir sobre a importância da interação genética versos ambiente na dimensão da saúde pessoal e da sustentabilidade. Portanto, ao buscar caminhos científicos de compreensão do fenômeno religioso explora-se a possibilidade de pesquisa e inovação que a genética oferece. A genética pode ser realizada a partir de três níveis de análise, que ocorreu a partir da descoberta da estrutura do DNA, de forma que permitiu o estudo sobre replicação, expressão e mutação de genes. E por fim, pelo nível das populações, buscando encontrar

---

[40] Acessado em 18/10/2024: https://www.apa.org

diferenças entre paralelos nos genes, fatores que causam as distinções entre as pessoas, de forma geral, estudando a constituição genética dos membros de uma população. As correlações encontradas pelos autores para gêmeos monozigóticos foram maiores do que para os gêmeos dizigóticos, para todos os fenótipos. Encontraram que as correlações monozigóticas de gêmeos[41] relacionado com a religiosidade; atual ou retrospectiva e, comportamento antissocial são muito maiores do que as mesmas correlações para gêmeos dizigóticos, o que sugere que a covariância entre o comportamento antissocial e religiosidade ocorre devido a influências genéticas compartilhadas. Para o comportamento altruísta, as correlações são muito mais semelhantes, embora as correlações monozigóticas entre comportamento altruísta e religiosidade entre os gêmeos sejam ligeiramente maiores do que as correlações dizigóticos. Significa mencionar que isso sugere que, junto com uma correlação genética, também pode haver covariância ambiental compartilhada entre altruísmo e religiosidade. Os estudos que buscam correlacionar a genética e o fenômeno religioso são exploratórios, visto que para uma ciência avançar sobre um terreno, alguns pioneiros precisam estar dispostos a percorrer esse caminho e ir apontando direções e possibilidades. Demais fatores genéticos

---

[41] Quando um óvulo é fecundado por um só espermatozoide e se divide em duas linhas de células completas, ele dá origem aos gêmeos idênticos, ou monozigóticos, ou ainda univitelinos. Sempre são do mesmo sexo. Os gêmeos idênticos têm o mesmo DNA ou genoma. Conquanto, as relações entre o comportamento religioso e crenças religiosas com fatores genéticos e também buscou refletir sobre a importância da interação genes x ambiente na dimensão da saúde pessoal e da sustentabilidade.

podem estar envolvidos nessa complexa relação, como exemplo, as interações entre genes, meio e dados de hereditariedade. Para que o progresso científico no estudo da área cresça cada vez mais, é fundamental que princípios éticos guiem a construção do conhecimento, tendo em vista que assim, instrumentos, metodologias e análises foram possíveis de serem utilizados. Sendo assim, mesmo usando o adjetivo religioso enquanto rejeita o substantivo religião, Smith defende que viver religiosamente é um atributo das pessoas, que não surge porque essas pessoas participam de uma entidade chamada religião, mas porque participam naquilo que chamei de transcendência. Neste ponto, entra a substituição do termo religião e genética, posto que para Smith

> "seria mais realista e proveitoso abandonar a hipótese de que religião é uma 'coisa' que tem seus limites inerentes e está à espera de ser mapeada". Isto porque "não apenas inexistem religiões como entidades biosocioteológicas contrapostas, tampouco existe religião como uma essência definível" (FIGUEIREDO, 2022, p 15).

Mas qual seria alternativa para evitar estes termos, isto é, como apreender os variados fatos do universo do discurso religioso? Aqui temos propriamente a proposta de substituição: a sugestão é que se fale de duas realidades diferentes chamadas por Smith de fé e de tradições cumulativas, como as faces internas e externas da vida religiosa da humanidade, em que a primeira seria "a relação de um indivíduo, ou de muitos indivíduos, com o transcendente divino" (FIGUEIREDO, 2022, p 17), significando nesse sentido uma experiência religiosa, enquanto a segunda seria a área histórica nas quais está fé se manifesta. Essa mesma ideia de substituição, embora tecnicamente diferente, ao buscar no conceito de "semelhanças familiares" uma aplicação produtiva não apenas à categoria religião e às famílias denominadas religiões, mas também a elementos que os estudiosos atribuem de várias formas a religião e religiões (por exemplo, teísmo, conceitos de alma, rituais e ritualizações). Religião seria uma categoria folclórica ocidental que estudiosos ocidentais contemporâneos se apropriaram para definir ou caracterizá-la de forma academicamente refinada e aprofundada. Conquanto, a relação que entre as ciências tem elaborado estudos significativos entre a relação ciência e religião são validas para a psicanálise. O estudo está situado na perspectiva da tradição monoteísta, pois se considera que nela está a reflexão é mais extensa que nas outras tradições, tanto do ponto de vista histórico quanto do atual, pois foi suas relações sociais, fortemente influenciada e construída sobre as bases da tradição monoteísta, que a ciência se firmou e se desenvolveu de forma significativa para se permitir transformar o mundo todo, de maneira cada vez mais acelerada, por meio das inovações tecnológicas derivadas do pensamento científico. Segundo Sanches (2012), as relações entre religião e ciência podem ser compreendidas a partir de quatro posições que são assumidas pelas pessoas: o *conflito*, ocorre entre as pessoas com os pontos de vista extremados. De um lado os literalistas bíblicos que acreditam que as teorias evolucionistas estão em conflito direto com a fé religiosa.

Mas também estão os cientistas ateus, afirmando que as provas científicas da evolução alegam incompatibilidade com qualquer forma de teísmo. A mídia se utiliza dessas posições para acirrar as discussões, acreditando que é o que lhe rende notícias, pois cada lado trata o outro como inimigo e, quando acontecem os debates, estes são calorosos. A *independência*, os que assumem esta posição alegam que não deve haver conflito, mas sim coexistência em separado, já que religião e ciência, sendo estranhas, devem ser mantidas a distância uma da outra. A ciência, por lidar somente com fatos objetivos, investiga como as coisas funcionam. A religião se preocupa com os valores de vida e o sentido último da pessoa humana. As linguagens são diferentes para religião e para ciência e suas funções são completamente diferentes no que se refere ao ser humano. O *diálogo*, aqui se muda o sentido dos vetores e, ao invés de independência por meio do distanciamento, ocorre uma aproximação quando se procura identificar onde existem semelhanças entre os métodos empregados nas duas áreas. Modelos conceituais comuns e analogias são usadas principalmente para explicar o que não se pode ver: o infinitamente pequeno e o infinitamente grande. O diálogo mais produtivo acontece nas questões-limite de fronteira que a ciência não consegue explicar e então recorre à religião ou às analogias, utilizando conceitos científicos que a religião emprega para mostrar as relações de Deus com a humanidade. A *integração*, esta é a posição mais amigável entre as duas disciplinas, quando pode ocorrer uma verdadeira parceria entre religião e ciência de um modo sistemático e abrangente. Neste posicionamento sobressai, por exemplo, que a religião vem buscando indícios sugestivos da existência de Deus ou que na visão de certos cientistas, para acontecerem condições necessárias à existência da vida e do Universo, tal qual houve a necessidade de um ajuste fino nas constantes astronômicas, o chamado Princípio Antrópico, consequência de um planejamento intencional. Outra consideração importante para a integração, levantada por autores religiosos, seria a necessidade de uma reformulação de certas crenças, à luz da ciência. Para valorizar a integração, podem-se utilizar abordagens interessantes, como a teologia da natureza, diferenciada da teologia natural e aquela que pessoalmente é mais simpática para Barbour (1990), que é a filosofia de processo. Ian Barbour (1990) simplifica um pouco e reduz a quatro as poposições que os estudiosos do assunto têm assumido na relação entre religião e ciência, a saber: conflito, independência, diálogo e integração.tem-se afirmado que a nossa sociedade precisa aceitar e valorizar o diferente. Diante da diversidade cultural, defendemos que uma cultura precisa aprender com a outra (abertura), saber que os esquemas culturais escondem relações de poder (crítica), permitir que na cultura do outro existam coisas que não entendemos direito (respeito), que, portanto, não podemos deixar nossa cultura ser engolida pela outra (não submissão). O conjunto desta postura: abertura, crítica, respeito e não submissão, se torna uma boa medida para que possamos dialogar com a diversidade. Gostaríamos de aplicar este modelo ao diálogo entre religião e ciência. Religião e ciência, portanto, passam a ser vistas como partes de uma diversidade cognitiva. O ser humano conhece o mundo por muitos caminhos, tais como: arte, filosofia, ciência, religião, sabedoria e outros. O conhecimento que a sabedoria possibilita não se reduz aos métodos da ciência, nem à crença religiosa, nem à inspiração das artes. Enfim, cada tipo de conhecimento é diverso do outro, e é com este conceito de diversidade cognitiva que gostaríamos de analisar a relação religião e ciência. O ponto de partida para o diálogo entre religião e ciência é a necessária abertura de um conhecimento para o outro. Isto significa que para estudar a dimensão de inter-relações infinitas, que é a ciência, e a dimensão do sentido do existir ou do infinito envolvimento, que é a religião. A busca pela unidade do existir e a realidade última é um elemento no interesse religioso, como é no filosófico.A única diferença é que a abordagem religiosa é mais abrangente; ela não vai reconhecer a realidade última, vai se unir com ela. Assim, para que com a sua filosofia do processo defende a aproximação entre religião e ciência, religião é a visão de algo que está além, atrás e dentro do fluxo transitório das coisas imediatas; algo que é real e ao mesmo tempo esperando para ser realizado; algo que é uma possibilidade remota e ao mesmo tempo o maior dos fatos presentes; algo que dá sentido para tudo que passa e mesmo assim escapa da apreensão; algo cuja posse é o bem final e ao mesmo tempo além de todo alcance. Uma postura crítica se desenvolve quando se percebe que: cada uma das grandes religiões surgiu dentro de um determinado contexto sócio-histórico-cultural. E, assim, cada uma das grandes religiões corre o risco de defender a sua visão de ser humano como a única possível ou como a única visão cor reta. Se isto for levado ao extremo, então, tem-se exatamente a base do fundamentalismo religioso, ou seja, a identificação de uma deter minada mensagem religiosa, com a visão cultural da sociedade onde esta mensagem religiosa aconteceu. Também a ciência, por sua vez, está inserida numa complexidade própria, principalmente porque também está articulada com a realidade cultural e histórica de sociedades específicas. Por algum tempo se acreditou que a ciência era sempre a mesma, independentemente de quem a observava. Diante deste contexto, outra característica da relação dessas duas áreas cientificas, ciência da religião e psicanálise é a formação do princípio cientifico:

> "o fascínio da ideia de substância, será preciso procurar-lhe o princípio até no inconsciente, no qual se formam as preferências indestrutíveis. A ideia de substância é tão clara, tão simples, tão pouco discutida, que deve apoiares numa experiência bem mais íntima que qualquer outra" (BACHELAD, 1996, p.162).

De fato, a convicção primeira do realismo não é discutida, como nem chega a ser ensinada. De forma que o realismo pode, com razão, ser considerado a única filosofia inata, o que não nos parece vantagem. Para aquilatá-lo, é preciso ultrapassar o plano intelectual e compreender que a substância de um objeto é aceita como um bem pessoal:

> "Apossa-se da substancia primeira espiritualmente como se toma posse de uma vantagem evidente é seguir a argumentação de um realista; imediatamente ele está em vantagem sobre o adversário porque tem, acha ele, o real do seu lado" (BACHELAD, 1996, p.163).

Segundo Passos (2020), as ortodoxias epistemológicas das diversas ciências resultam de processos complexos que envolvem práticas teóricas e metodológicas distintas, tais como, empréstimos, transposições, traduções, composições e criações próprias de "cunho científico", ancoradas em processos políticos de legitimação e institucionalização. O que aparentemente se mostra completo, coerente e acabado, habilitando-se como ciência, resulta, na verdade, de processos mais complexos e epistemologicamente "impuros", de quadros metodológicos marcados por diversidades e, até mesmo, de possíveis divergências, entre teorias e métodos que se encontram nos exercícios concretos de investigação. Em outros termos, nenhuma ciência nasce pronta com um estatuto definido, mas emerge gradualmente, na medida em que se define como objeto, teorias e métodos, dentro de um entorno mais amplo que perfaz as ciências de um modo geral: as ciências geram ciências em um processo de especialização e de composição que avança para domínios mais delimitados, seja pela regra da especialização, e já pela regra da composição e do sincretismo metodológico que desenha novas áreas e novas disciplinas e teorias da religião.

3.1.2. Comprometimento com estudo sobre religião

A partir da reflexão acima, abordar-se-á, a seguir, sobre o comprometimento da psicanálise, como ciência terapêutica, para com as análises sobre as experiências religiosas. Toma-se como referência o segundo capítulo, a teoria nuclear: comprometimento religioso, do livro Uma teoria da religião de Stark e Brindringe (2008). Este capitulo traz para a discussão Durkheim (2021) ao tratas das formas elementares da vida religiosa, como propriedade básica da religião nos espectros etnográficos:

> "A religião não apareceu pela primeira vez em uma catedral ou em sociedade avançadas. Há evidencias claras de que os humanos já possuíam religião na pré-história, que ela se desenvolveu pela primeira vez quando as pessoas andavam em pequenos grupos em busca da sobrevivência" (STARK e BRINDRINGE, 2008, p.35).

Isso significa que, "os aspectos fundamentais da religião devem ser necessidades e atividades humanas muito básicas" (STARK e BRINDRINGE, 2008, p.35). observa-se que a religião de origem humana através das suas relações sociais e suas relações com a natureza; elas são expressões culturais de atitudes e linguagens as quais manifestam vários comportamentos do homem tanto conscientemente quanto inconscientemente, por tal ela possibilita manifestações recalques e traumas. Essa é uma das principais características de a religião é subjetiva objetiva e objetiva subjetiva. Conquanto, conforme Durkhaein (2021) o campo religioso é atingido pelas grandes transformações sociais, como parte da modernidade líquida, criando-se uma religiosidade subjetiva, individualista e difusa, muitas vezes, desligada das instituições religiosas. É um fenômeno próprio da nossa época, aonde os valores perenes e sólidos são cada vez mais relativizados, transitórios, subjetivos, emotivos.

As pessoas escolhem a religião, sem depender da "tradição" ou instituição. O sagrado se apresenta como migratório provocando um nomadismo místico. Isto é, o indivíduo, batizado no catolicismo, muitas vezes pode atravessar por um mundo plural religioso. Há um tempo, não muito distante, os descrentes, sem amor a Deus e sem religião, eram raros. Todos eram educados para ver e ouvir as coisas do mundo religioso e a conversa cotidiana confirmava que este é um universo encantado que esconde e revela um poder espiritual. A exigência de um sentido para a vida trazia às religiões certa identidade e lhes dava vida. Durante muitos séculos a religião esteve na vida cotidiana e no centro da existência humana. Os sinais religiosos ditavam o ritmo do tempo. As festas religiosas regulavam os ciclos da vida dos indivíduos e da coletividade O ano estava determinado pelos tempos litúrgicos, com suas festividades e comemorações sagradas, o dia obedecia ao ritmo marcado pelas sucessivas horas sagradas, o toque do "Angelus", o chamado à missa, ao rosário, ao serviço religioso. O relógio paroquial instalado no alto da torre da Igreja com seus toques era o indicar do tempo sagrado e profano. A religiosidade popular repousava no fundamento da religião cosmológica do Deus transparente no cosmos. Na atualidade, a religião popular parece ser a manifestação de Deus nas emoções, na subjetividade individual. O mundo religioso era um mundo encantado. Apesar de o encanto ter sido quebrado, a religião não desapareceu. Entretanto, houve um processo de mudança chamado de secularização, na qual as instituições religiosas não foram mais referência religiosa, os indivíduos apresentaram diferentes atitudes e relações com o transcendente, com a ideia de Deus. As crenças passaram a não ser mais herdadas e transmitidas de uma geração para outra. Em muitos casos a religião como instituição deixou de dar aos indivíduos e grupos o conjunto de referências, normas, valores e símbolos que deram sentido à vida e a existência. Como consequência, vivemos uma época de subjetivismo, pluralismo e trânsito religioso, acentuado pela modernidade líquida; passou o tempo em que as instituições religiosas, podiam propor à sociedade um conjunto de exigências relativas à fé e aos comportamentos, esperando uma aceitação social imediata. Nas sociedades contemporâneas, os indivíduos decidem livremente a respeito do tipo de religião a se adotar, ou escolhem ficar sem religião; o que as organizações religiosas oferecem tem que ser atrativo para os potenciais consumidores. Assim a religião sofre o impacto dessa nova mentalidade da sociedade líquida. Ela deixa de ser dominada pela tradição para se tornar objeto de escolhas e gosto do indivíduo. A sociedade líquida moderna (BAUMAN, 2021) também induz as transformações religiosas, isto é, fazer a opção por uma igreja ou religião nunca foi tão fácil, de modo que as religião tornou pulverizada[42] e flutuante[43] ao mesmo

---

[42] Entendo como religião pulverizada demonstra expressão à saciedade a que se reduziram determinadas referências historicamente tradicionais. E nem tão antigas. Nos dias atuais e na esteira daquele autor, um olhar atento para o mundo do trabalho formal e informal, por uma parte, e para a complexidade das migrações, por outra, talvez nos leve a pensar numa "sociedade multifacetada". Emblemas vivos disso são, por exemplo, as organizações de expressões religiosas praticamente no mundo inteiros, bem como outros grupos, forças e associações do género. Com efeito, pulverizadas, fragmentadas e extremamente fragilizadas,

tempo. Melhor ainda, deixar uma igreja ou religião e adaptar outra, ir e vir ou abandonar tudo, parecem ser movimentos constantes de uma "religiosidade líquida". Nunca ao longo da história houve tanta mobilidade religiosa, de maneira especial dentro do pentecostalismo. A modernidade líquida produziu um tipo de mentalidade secular que toca na base das identidades e sistemas de sentido individuais. Tanto o movimento de adesão a uma religião quanto o de abandono são acalentados por essa mentalidade na qual o que prevalece é a relativização do papel soberano da religião na vida de cada indivíduo. A pessoa sente-se à vontade para assistir a um culto evangélico, participar de uma cerimônia budista ou de um ritual afro-brasileiro sem constrangimento e, posteriormente, participar de uma missa. O sentimento de "bem estar" "tocar o coração", produzir um apelo de tipo

---

não poucas organizações se batem com um individualismo e um tomismo exacerbados à máxima potência. Mais do que a família, a comunidade e o partido, tropeçamos hoje com indivíduos autônomos e átomos de uma sociedade que progressivamente e, a pessoa, não se reduz a escombros.

[43] Entendo vivemos mediante religiões flutuantes; pois, em nossos dias, no entanto, constatamos a existência de religiões flutuantes por se regerem pelas leis do mercado da globalização e da sociedade de consumo. Seus membros são cristãos professos, mas imaturos, improdutivos, sem compromissos, sem raízes e consumistas. Os votos que fazem na profissão de fé e batismo são formais e vazios. Migram com facilidade de uma igreja para outra. Estão sempre à procura de bênção. Para elas, hoje é como "super-mercado" com opções variadas de consumo. Vão sempre onde recebem mais. Jamais entendem o culto como oferta a Deus, mas como oportunidade de receber benefícios. Se gerarem filhos espirituais, não assumem a paternidade, mas transferem essa responsabilidade. São chorões e murmuradores conforme conveniências.

emocional, parecem determinar a escolha do grupo religioso, e ainda a aproximação com Deus, são as principais motivações para mudar de religião. A opção religiosa está relacionada com experiência sentimental, individual e subjetiva, desligada da comunidade e da realidade. O importante é se sentir bem no grupo religioso. Para Stark e Bainbridge (2008), os diferentes dados mostram que há situações em que não existe identificação com a religião que se professava e acaba mudando ou abandonando tudo. Cada vez mais as pessoas procuram a religião para atender a necessidades de consumo pessoal. Muda-se de religião de acordo com o estado de ânimo. As motivações para a desfiliação e trânsito religioso são de ordem pessoal. A tradição e doutrina perdem o peso na escolha. Sentem-se livres para abraçar a religião com a qual mais se identificam sem o temor de romper com a tradição herdada. A religião passou a ser um bem privado. Motivações pragmáticas existenciais estão na base da escolha da religião, como a necessidade de resolver problemas pessoais, tais como desemprego, doença, desavenças familiares entre outros, estão presentes na opção da igreja ou religião. A diversidade e pluralismo religioso permite a pessoa autônoma e moderna ter acesso a uma experiência religiosa individual, privada, subjetiva e líquida, inclusiva à mobilidade religiosa. O que hoje é de um jeito amanhã pode ser diferente. A religião no paradigma da modernidade é uma questão complexa, ambivalente, subjetiva, individualista. Nenhuma certeza pode ser imposta a ninguém. Cada um faz sua crença e sua religião de acordo com suas necessidades imediatas. O valor último ou padrão aferidor é a própria pessoa. Essa é uma busca pelas propriedades fundamentais da religião verificando princípios acerca de como são os seres humanos e como eles se integram. Lógica que vai de encontro com a epstemologia e a prática clínica da psicanálise; pela necessidade se analisar o que provoca a religião nos seres humanos; em razão de que "os revestimentos culturais e sociais da religião são adornos somente enquanto se procura o elementar" (STARK e BAINDRIDGE, 2008, p.35). O estudo destes autores sobre a teoria da religião da ciência da religião para a psicanálise; porque certos tipos particulares de povos são religiosos de forma distinta. A influência da religião nas dimensões emocionais dos seres humano e mediante um recalque como a religião se manifesta. Assim, a religião causa recalques, como os recalques morais se manifestam. Estas questões são inerentes a qualquer pessoa religiosa. Mesmo realizando uma análise suficientemente abstrata, como é o caso da psicanálise, informações com fim psicoterapêutica e análises dos fatores escondidos na mente inconsciente não escapam d operacionalização da psicanálise sob fundamento da expressão humana. Os estudos de teoria da religião sob a lógica da ciência da religião possibilitam o

> "quão longe podemos chegar ir com este simples modelo, e quais macroestruturas complexas surgem conforme nossa cadeia dedutiva" (STARK e BAINDRIDGE, 2008, p.36)

Isto é, sempre procurar tirar o máximo do mínimo: a investigação da ciência da religião vale para a psicanálise pela fato dos estudos daquela ciência consistir em um conjunto ordenado de informações mentais religiosas; inspirada em axiomas: premissa considerada necessariamente evidente e verdadeira, fundamento de uma demonstração, porém ela mesma indemonstrável, originada, segundo a tradição racionalista, de princípios inatos da consciência ou, segundo os empiristas, de generalizações da observação empírica. O princípio aristotélico da contradição de nada pode ser e não ser simultaneamente foi considerado desde a Antiguidade um axioma fundamental da filosofia. Os axiomas aproximam do mundo real observeis dos elementos constitutivos das relações sociais. A ciência da religião da ação humana. No plano religioso, "as pessoas fazem escolhas da mesma maneira que fazem outras escolhas, pesando custos e benefícios" (Stark e Bainbridge, 2008, p. 265). Na busca por benefícios, os seres humanos "querem religião" por ser a única fonte plausível de certas recompensas, incluindo aquelas indisponíveis aqui e agora para todos, como a tão desejada vida após a morte, para as quais, a seu ver, há uma "demanda geral e inexaurível. Nessa formulação, tal demanda parece independer da ação dos produtores religiosos e dos contextos históricos e culturais, o que, além de sociologicamente problemático, torna a secularização, em teoria, impossível. Pressuposto de que a "condição humana nos confere uma necessidade permanente" de recompensas sobrenaturais, questionando a existência de uma religiosidade intrínseca aos seres humanos. Para obter recompensas religiosas, os indivíduos procuram utilizar e manipular o sobrenatural, efetuando relações de troca com os deuses. As trocas com deuses poderosos, atentos às necessidades dos devotos e capazes de prover recompensas extramundanas, tendem a gerar custos mais levados e relacionamento exclusivo de longo prazo. As organizações religiosas, portanto, serão capazes de requerer compromissos exclusivos e longos à medida que oferecerem recompensas extramundanas. Nesse ponto, Stark e Bainbridge (2008) sustenta a distinção sociológica clássica entre religião e magia, observando que a primeira, por centrar-se numa relação de troca com os deuses e na oferta de recompensas extramundanas de longo prazo, tende a gerar compromissos estáveis, duradouros e institucionalmente organizados, enquanto a última, baseada na coação e manipulação de forças sobrenaturais e na oferta de recompensas pontuais, imediatistas e mundanas, tende a formar clientela. As trocas que envolvem custos e compromissos de longo prazo com vistas à obtenção de recompensas extramundanas, como a salvação paradisíaca, implicam risco, já que estas não podem ser efetivamente demonstradas. Sendo pois, "como confiar, então, em sua veracidade? Problema universal da religião" (Stark e Bainbridge, 2008, p. 282), a confiança é gerada pela interação com os (e socialização dos) membros do grupo religioso, que depositam fé nessas recompensas e, assim, as legitimam internamente. De modo que a pregação, o discipulado, os rituais, as orações, as experiências místicas, os milagres atribuídos às forças divinas e, sobretudo, os testemunhos de bênçãos recebidas, compartilhados coletivamente, são responsáveis por tornar confiáveis tais promessas extramundanas. Stark e Bainbridge (2008) reconhecem que o raciocínio humano é um tanto não sistemático e intuitivo, e que a maximização frequentemente é apenas parcial, mas acentua que seus postulados simples e formais sobre a condição e a racionalidade humanas têm a vantagem de permitir a formulação de modelos matemáticos e explicações de alto nível. Baseado no conceito de racionalidade subjetiva de John Ferejohn e Raymond Boudon, Stark e Bainbridge (2008) definem racionalidade da seguinte forma:

> "Dentro de seus limites de informação e compreensão, restringidos pelas opções disponíveis, guiados por suas preferências e gostos, os seres humanos tentam fazer escolhas racionais". Fazer uma escolha racional significa sempre "tentar maximizar". A "intenção" do agente de maximizar "é tudo"" (STARK e BAINBRIDGE, 2008, p. 266),

não importando se ele carece de informação ou se age apoiado em cálculos errados. O conceito de racionalidade subjetiva, portanto, não permite considerar irracional uma ação baseada na ignorância. Pressupõe que os indivíduos agem de acordo com o que percebem ser de seu auto-interesse, mesmo nas situações em que não detêm o conhecimento necessário para avaliar em que ele consiste, o que, nesse caso, implica presumir sua percepção maximizadora do auto-interesse. Desse modo, a noção de racionalidade dos teóricos do novo paradigma não supõe objetivamente uma ação maximizadora, antes postula uma atávica intenção de todo agente de maximizar suas escolhas, premissa que não tem como ser refutada de forma empírica. Na prática, "a subjetividade contida nessa racionalidade torna-a radicalmente distinta da noção de racionalidade da teoria econômica, que considera racional somente a ação em que o agente emprega meios apropriados aos fins perseguidos e persegue fins mutuamente coerentes. Embora admita que a cultura, as normas e a socialização constrangem a ação dos indivíduos" (STARK e BAINDRINGE, 2008, p. 266).

Significa que isto omite dos axiomas sobre a conduta racional a ação orientada por valores, importantíssima na análise weberiana da religião. A noção de racionalidade proposta por Stark familiariza-se com o tipo de ação com relação a fins, que orienta a ação econômica, analisada e considerada por Weber adversária da ação religiosa. A familiaridade apontada entre ambas as racionalidades se limita, a meu ver, a seu caráter instrumental e à exclusão de normas e valores, porém a religiosa difere da racionalidade objetiva presente na teoria econômica. Mas a semelhança é suficiente para Sharot questionar a propriedade do uso, na análise sociológica da religião, de um conceito de racionalidade dotado de significado próximo ao de zweckrational. Haja vista que, na teoria weberiana, é a ação mágica que se aproxima da zweckrational, por ser orientada para o mundo e para fins imediatos e materiais, ao passo que a ação religiosa nas religiões de salvação, em contraste, tende a ser orientada para fins extramundanos e valores éticos (wertrational), tipo de orientação que leva muitos agentes a perseguir crenças e valores independentemente dos custos envolvidos. Como observa Richard Swedberg, segundo

Weber, nas religiões mais avançadas, os benefícios religiosos tendem a ser do outro mundo e não econômicos, e a atividade religiosa em si não é mais vista exclusivamente em termos de fins e meios, como nas religiões primitivas. À medida que a noção de racionalidade religiosa do novo paradigma define como racionais apenas as ações que tentam maximizar benefícios com o menor custo ou que estão a serviço do auto-interesse dos agentes, qualquer ação que não se encaixe nessa definição estrita se torna automaticamente não-racional e, portanto, excluída de sua abordagem. Com isso, descarta-se, em grande medida, o papel dos fatores afetivos, simbólicos e emocionais no desenvolvimento de identidades coletivas. Entretanto, dada a tendência de Stark e discípulos de hipertrofiar a racionalidade instrumental dos agentes, as ações baseadas na restrição do auto-interesse pela moral, como o altruísmo, tendem a ser reduzidas a um comportamento egoísta. Assim, o altruísmo só se torna passível de compreensão nessa perspectiva quando se transforma em seu oposto e perde seu sentido, passando a visar à auto-satisfação. O problema é que a racionalidade normativa, baseada na conformidade a valores e ideais morais, não pode ser reduzida empírica e conceitualmente à racionalidade instrumental. Disso resulta que esconsiderar a ação orientada por valores significa optar por restringir a capacidade de a sociologia compreender o comportamento religioso. Ao considerá-la, contudo, resta evitar o erro de deduzir, automaticamente, comportamentos de valores religiosos. O lado positivo da perspectiva de considerar racionais escolhas e comportamentos religiosos consiste, de um lado, em "enfatizar mais o papel da agência humana nos processos religiosos", ao menos no que concerne à escolha da religião e, de outro, em desfazer-se de um sem-número de concepções preconceituosas, que os consideram, de saída, opiáceos, irracionais, patológicos, produtos da ignorância, de lavagem cerebral e de crises sociais:

3.1.3. Subjetividade e linguagens

O primeiro ponto sobre a abordagem sobre as linguagens religiosas. Ao contrario que disse Croatto (2001), nem sempre a pessoa tem que ter experiência religiosa para entender e analisar as expressões das linguagens religiosas. Hoje em dia, devido os meios de comunicação midiática, redes sociais, sistemas de informações e volumosas quantidade de publicações acadêmicas disponíveis na internet possibilitam que o interessado por está ou aquela religião entre em contato com experiências das linguagens religiosas; neste as tecnologias religiosas ganharam outro fôlego diferente da posição de Croatto. Mesmo que a experiência religiosa seja uma experiência humana, os espaços tecnológicos de informação vêm atendendo demandas como esta, uma que os meio de tecnologia e sistema de informação possibilita a pessoa entrar em contato com contexto histórico e cultural: é a nova forma de exercer atividades empíricas. Embora sabe-se que a experiencia humana é uma vivência relacional. Mas até que ponto o acesso a informações através de tecnologias não é também uma experiencia? Até que ponto os meios de comunicação não sejam possibilidade para relações e adquirir experiências? Nesta sociedade liquida, como disse Zygmunt Bauman, vivemos momentos de grandes transformações e experiencias sociais culturais. Diante deste panorama de *vivência relacional*, Croatto (2001) elenca alguns tópicos relacionada a experiência humana: o homem relaciona com o mundo, com o indivíduo, com os grupos humanos. Estas características de vida influenciam na socialização e, cada vez mais, está dimensão construí o ser humano e, ao mesmo tempo, o ser humano as constroem; isso significa o homem em relação, ocasionado experiencias religiosas. São características sociais em suas relações de vida humana que influencia a socialização. Estes elementos apresentados através da ciência da religião, dos seus fundamentos epistemológicos, as dimensões teóricas e práticas das relações e experiências religiosas humanas; isso se faz relevante para a psicanalise nos quesitos epistemológicos e clínicos; pois a religião desempenha um papel fundamental na formação da identidade e na busca de sentido na vida. Ele argumentava que a religião é uma forma de lidar com o desejo humano e com o desconhecido. Lacan a considera um campo indestrutível do humano, onde persistem as "verdades eternas", ou seja, de estrutura. É aí que situamos aquilo que retorna como repetição, que resiste e insiste, levando-nos a dizer: a religião é de estrutura; as quais podem, seguramente, ser objeto de traumas e recalques. Diante disto tudo, com segurança é dizemos que o ser humano oscila constantemente entre o subjetivo, intersubjetivo e objetivo racionalmente. Como menciona Croatto (2001, p.42), o ser humano não é um ser pleno, busca metas, melhor saúde, melhor condições de vida, sempre procura novos caminhos, desejos. Portanto, o ser humano é substanciado por desejos que são orientados por valores e; estes valores estar relacionado às necessidades, consciência-de-Si, consciência-do-Outro (como menciona Hegel). Esta é a tríplice limitação de todos ser humano; devido as fragmentações da vida, dos projetos; finitude que mostra que a vida é cíclica; falta de sentido, uma vida vazia. "O ser humano, no entanto, tende à totalidade" (CROATTO, 2001, p.43); temática abordada pela fenomenologia da ciência da religião (como Hegel, Russel, Kant, Otto, Heidegger, Sater, MerleauPonty) necessária e de fundamental importância para busca interpretar o significado inconsciente de sonhos, pensamentos, palavras e ações. Para isso, um dos métodos dessa terapia é a livre associação, no qual o paciente fala o que lhe vem à mente com a menor racionalização possível, trazendo os pensamentos e memórias inconscientes à tona, conforme a psicanálise. São questões de tenção dialéticas entre o objeto e realização: objeto, pensado aqui, perspectiva da ciência da religião que é religião, suas tensões e; concatenadamente relacionado com a concepção de objeto na psicanalise; isto é, objeto como uma pulsão. O conceito de pulsão permite-nos, portanto, compreender os fenômenos psíquicos pulsionais como aqueles que representam, no sentido de estar no lugar de outra coisa. Isto é, a pulsão seria a representante dos estímulos corporais no psiquismo: representação psíquica de uma energia que leva ao movimento, ou ainda uma espécie de demanda por ação que seria feita ao psiquismo cuja fonte seria o processo excitatório em um órgão. O segundo ponto sobre a abordagem sobre as linguagens religiosas: a psicanálise tem a linguagem como ferramenta de

108trabalho tanto epistemologicamente quanto clinicamente. A religião é uma linguagem; logo, a experiência religiosa é uma experiencial das linguagens dos fenômenos religiosos. Para Croatto (2001), a vivência religiosa insere-se na experiência religiosa: "a experiência religiosa se dá na experiencial geral; elas poder ser diferenciadas, mas não separadas" (TILICHI apud CROATO, 2001, p.44). Isso significa que a vidência religiosa é igualmente relacional; isto é, a experiência religiosa é limitada pela realidade. Isto justificada a argumentação inicial sobre as experiências das linguagens religiosas: as mídias tecnológicas de informação, escancaram o domínio que essas mídias exercem no cotidiano da sociedade, como experiencias religiosas, influenciando na forma em que pensamos, agimos e vivemos. Jogando luz sobre os bastidores das grandes empresas de tecnologia, expõe a necessidade de se atentar para a gratuidade dos aplicativos de redes sociais, uma vez que, como disse o ex-designer do *Google, Tristan Harris*: "se você não está pagando pelo produto, então você é o produto". Dentre os inúmeros pontos apresentados e discutidos está o monitoramento constante exercido pelas redes sociais e suas provocadas relações sociais, já que fornecemos dados pessoais às plataformas a todo momento. De acordo com o nosso comportamento nas redes, o algoritmo trabalha para que apareçam no nosso *feed* apenas opiniões e conteúdo que nos interessam, criando-se assim uma realidade personalizada, a chamada *bolha de informação*. Conquanto, sendo Croatto (2001) as necessidades humanas são físicas, psíquicas e sócio culturais. Neste sentido este autor ressalta que a criatividade humana, a parir das linguagens religiosas, estão relacionadas com o pensar fragmentada, pensar no finito duradouro e ter a falta de sentido das coisas, crise existencial. Portanto, o conhecer está relacionado à sabedoria, à técnica, e também uma parceria do conhecer. Também na experiência religiosa o conhecimento e a sabedoria têm grande relevância:

> "a experiência do ser é fundamental, como é a da vida em todas as suas formas. A "ordem" refere-se a inteligibilidade do mundo, à fundamental de suas duas partes: caos e a confusão, nos quais o ser humano não pode existir. Na experiencia religiosas, é um dado essencial, pois o caos deve ser vencido pelo ato cosmogônico, que não é simplesmente criação do mundo, mas especialmente, sua organização, faz com que um espaço inteligível e funcional" (CROATTO, 2001, p.47).

Diante deste panorama, o segundo ponto sobre a abordagem sobre as linguagens religiosas está relacionado com a descrição da simbologia. Pensar a ciência da religião e a psicanalise sem pensar os símbolos é como uma ciência "manca". Significa que o símbolo é uma linguagem da experiência religiosa, como expressão das manifestações religiosas. "O é a chave da linguagem inteira da experiência religiosa" (CROATT, 2001, p.81). O símbolo no contexto religioso tem sua representatividade e relevância. Ele pode exprimir algo, ou mesmo unir o grupo social em torno da divindade que o símbolo representa. Os símbolos ajudam a criar um corpo que exprime os valores morais da sociedade, os ensinamentos, criando um sentimento de solidariedade entre os seguidores religiosos, ou funcionando como uma forma de trazer um adepto mais perto de seu deus ou deuses. O símbolo fala e comunica por si. Mas, ao mesmo tempo em que comunica, ele esconde algo de misterioso. Os símbolos são irrenunciáveis na nossa vida. Eles têm uma linguagem própria de comunicar diferente da linguagem lógica e racional. O símbolo fala e comunica por si. Mas, ao mesmo tempo em que comunica, ele esconde algo de misterioso. Os símbolos são irrenunciáveis na nossa vida. Eles têm uma linguagem própria de comunicar diferente da linguagem lógica e racional. Isso significa que a experiência religiosa não pode ser vivida sem os símbolos, elas também não são vividas individualmente e isoladas, elas são essencialmente afetivas e participantes. Em um processo psicologia, a comunicação como forma e força da linguagem possui valor sacramental. Enquanto significa e realiza novamente, ressignificando, a presença das experiências das linguagens religiosas e dos símbolos: recria a experiência religioso, sendo que todos os processos sociais participam de suas características. Não é difícil responder que

> "as variações infinitas da expressão simbólica são uma evidencia do inesgotável das manifestações culturais religiosas dentro de um sistema simbólico" (CROATTO, 2001, P.83).

Segundo este autor (2001, p.84), nota-se que o homem cultural, a linguagem e a arte são sistemas simbólicos.

Através deles se encontram dois sentidos diferentes de símbolo: um, onde o símbolo apresenta uma função indicativa, apontando para o momento da cena traumática, denominado símbolo mnêmico ou, mais apropriadamente, símbolo mnêmico através de conversão por simultaneidade; outro, onde há uma relação conceitual entre signo e designado, chamado de conversão por simbolização. As exigências são satisfeitas quando se considera o símbolo como produto do processo primário. Em outras palavras, algo como escadas só pode funcionar como símbolo sexual a partir do momento em que a censura suprime o significado original, o ato sexual, recalcando-o para o inconsciente. A escada pode ser um símbolo do ato sexual, mas, por outro lado, o ato sexual não pode ser um símbolo da escada. Para que uma semelhança dê origem a um símbolo, é preciso que haja um momento onde a igualdade estabelecida: ato sexual; escada tenha sido recalcada e se tornado inconsciente. O analista deve interrogar-se sobre o momento em que isso ocorreu na história de desejo do sujeito - o que significa que não se abandonam as associações que ele produz em nome de uma suposta constante transindividual. Certamente são reconhecidos os fatores supraindividuais, as relações linguísticas, os paralelismos filogenéticos. Mas a mesma coisa ocorria na simbolização. Cecília não inventou a expressão "olhar perfurante", ela apenas a usou. Sempre esteve presente a crença freudiana de que, se o desejo é particular, a forma de expressá-lo é universal: o sujeito sempre trabalha com material fornecido pelo seu grupo social. Croatto (2001) apresenta uma breve história da noção de símbolo que se inicia na aurora da teoria freudiana. Aí se encontram dois sentidos diferentes de símbolo: um, onde o símbolo apresenta uma função indicativa, apontando para o momento da cena traumática, denominado símbolo mnêmico ou, mais apropriadamente, símbolo mnêmico através de conversão por simultaneidade; outro, onde há uma relação conceitual entre signo e designado, chamado de conversão por simbolização. No primeiro sentido, a relação entre o signo e o designado é uma relação arbitrária, contingente, determinada pela contemporaneidade das associações. O segundo sentido da noção de símbolo aparece na Interpretação dos sonhos; trata-se do "símbolo verdadeiro". Um exemplo trivial dele é ver escadas como figuras do ato sexual. Aqui também se revela uma tensão conceitual. Freud havia inovado a idéia de interpretação onírica quando colocara o papel de decifrador do sonho nas mãos do próprio sonhador, aliado à atenção flutuante do analista, procedimento que se funda necessariamente na crença de que o sonhador possui a chave para decifrar o seu sonho. Entretanto, a noção de símbolo verdadeiro supõe que exista um significado constante e independente de condições individuais. Portanto, a base subjetiva era reposta por uma crença na objetividade dos símbolos oníricos. Outro problema, intimamente ligado ao primeiro, era o de ver, nos símbolos oníricos, possíveis elementos para uma linguagem do inconsciente, o que criava as condições para transformar a metapsicologia em metafísica. Em Jung, por exemplo, os arquétipos são transformados em elementos invariantes e constitutivos do inconsciente. Nele, a interpretação sempre avança para um ponto terminal, enquanto em Freud, apesar de uma convergência necessária, ela é indefinidamente aberta, não havendo como desfazer, de forma completa, o trabalho de condensação. De qualquer maneira, Croatto vê no terceiro sentido da noção de símbolo uma etapa problemática, porém indispensável, na constituição da teoria psicanalítica. Para fugir a tais armadilhas, seria preciso. Os Símbolos são como "portais mágicos" que se abrem a uma comunicação muito especial e importante para o nosso desenvolvimento psíquico rumo à individuação. Eles promovem a união entre consciência e inconsciente. São como "portais mágicos" que nos levam além lá onde o visível e o invisível se encontram. As expressões simbólicas do nosso inconsciente fluem e falam sobre nossa totalidade psíquica revelando a realidade de nosso mundo interior. Talvez, nos lembrar que a vida pode ser percebida para além do que é literal e concreto, e que a imaginação e a criatividade permitem dar vida ao nosso mundo interno de fantasias, sonhos e imagens. E que estes preenchem de significados aspectos de nossa existência, que se assim não fosse, cairiam no vazio das coisas desprovidas de sentido. O símbolo nos convida a isso, voltar nosso olhar ao invisível com a sensibilidade que toca o sutil, aquilo que não é percetível num primeiro momento, mas que está presente no visível de forma misteriosa. Os símbolos como uma fonte infindável jorra conteúdos que nos permitem o encontro com um mundo desconhecido, de descobertas e mistérios, do qual fazemos parte. Esta é uma maneira de olhar para os símbolos, dentre as infinitas possibilidades criativas de buscar entendê-los. Enfim, o que importa mesmo é que os símbolos possuem estas qualidades, inspiram à transcendência, ao ir além, à unificação de opostos, aqueles próprios da atitude unilateral da consciência, que classifica as coisas como certas ou erradas, boas ou ruins, dores ou prazeres, alegrias ou tristezas, belezas ou horrores. A confrontação destes opostos resulta em algo novo, uma transformação, como uma nova atitude consciente diante da questão apresentada pela expressão simbólica. Portanto o que foi mencionado acima, além de fornecer a perspectiva, a área de conhecimento das ciências favorece as práticas do respeito, do diálogo e do ecumenismo entre as religiões. Contribui, desse modo, com uma educação de caráter transconfessional que poderá incidir na formação integral do ser humano. A religião, segundo Freud, ainda oferece três benefícios: ela lhes dá informações sobre a proveniência e a aparição do mundo, ela lhes assegura proteção e felicidade final nas vicissitudes da vida e ela dirige as suas opiniões e ações por meio de preceitos que sustenta com toda sua autoridade. Não existe oposição entre Psicologia e religiosidade, pelo contrário, a psicanálise é uma ciência que reconhece que a religiosidade e a fé estão presentes na cultura e participam na constituição da dimensão subjetiva de cada um de nós.sendo assim, a Resolução 7/2023 do CFP veda a utilização do título de psicólogo associado a vertentes religiosas e a associação de conceitos, métodos e técnicas da ciência psicológica a crenças religiosas. Também proíbe os profissionais de utilizar a religião como forma de publicidade e propaganda. As práticas religiosas podem ajudar a manter a saúde mental e prevenir doenças mentais, porque elas influenciam psicodinamicamente, auxiliando o indivíduo a lidar com a ansiedade, medos, frustrações, raiva, sentimentos de inferioridade, desânimo e isolamento.

Capítulo 4
4.1. Predileções da relação religião e psicanálise

Ao lado da religião como um sintoma neursociológico está os estudos referente a psicanálise; cuja origem remonta à extrema desvalia das pessoas, em seus momentos iniciais, em face das adversidades do mundo externo, em particular no contexto das relações parentais. Neste contexto está a presença da religião traduzida na ação do exercício da cidadania e do direito, sobretudo, entre as populações. Está aceção transcorre os três primeiros capítulo e, este capítulo é uma nota interpretativa sobre a temática abordada no presente presente. Portanto, a seguir está um discurso a tecnologia aplicada à relação entre religião e psicanálise e; depois está uma abordagem sobre a força religiosa subtrai o cansaço.

4.1.1. Tecnologia aplicada à relação entre religião psicanálise

A tecnologia, como por exemplo, a inteligência artificial, ajuda na colonização não só espacialmente, mas também todos os espaços de convivência; por isso não há como investigar a funda as linguagens das experiências religiosas sem considera-la, uma vez que ela aproxima as pessoas, ferramenta de uso para imprimir experiências religiosas; já que elas são instituídas de signos, símbolos, significados e significantes em relação, e as experiências religiosas são fundamentas das linguagens provocante de relações sócio tecnológicas; neste caso a semiótica tem muito a contribuir com a ciência da religião e com a psicanalise para com as análises e as expressos dos fenômenos religiosos flutuantes na socialidade.[44] outro fator a este relacionado é a colonização de inteligência artificia das nossas residências está nos espaços de convivências, como em nossas residências, como as máquinas de lavar roupas, louças, tv, internet, automóveis, computadores, fogão elétricos, geladeiras, sistema elétricos, sistemas hidráulicos, enfim, as residências são

---

[44] Entende-se que a religião flutuante é um fenômeno religioso no mundo secularizado, mais especificamente a relação entre as categorias de religioso implícita e difusa. A transformação superficial da religião e da moralidade no mundo moderno, partindo do pressuposto de que, para os filósofos iluministas, a religião deixaria de fazer parte da vida humana, vista como uma etapa da educação do homem. Ela é um elemento constituinte da condição humana, já que a natureza histórica do humano é resultado de um longo processo de evolução. Assim sendo, pela visão histórica do mundo, transmitida através da linguagem e pelos símbolos onde se radica o sagrado, ocorre a transformação do homem enquanto indivíduo e enquanto sujeito, estando a religião ligada às experiências do tempo e do espaço. Quando as experiências subjetivas são objetivadas, criam-se elementos que as representam. Tal operação para tornar o sacro em algo inteligível inclui processos de representação e de hierarquização. A passagem da transcendência à realidade ordinária poderá dar-se ligada a experiências quotidianas menores (relacionada a questões de espaço e tempo) ou à diversidade e relação com outros seres, ou ainda filiando-se a questões relativas ao sonho, à morte, à salvação e à esperança no Além Tais experiências transcendentais engendram reflexões sobre a moralidade e a vida religiosa. Com o passar do tempo, porém, elas sacralizam-se e tornam-se norma, operando a distinção entre os aspectos humanos da religião e sua prática histórica.

constituídas por inteligências. Ela está presentes nos espaços públicos, como máquinas bancarias, clínicas médicas, aparelhos hospitalares, transporte pública e na vida de qualquer pesquisa acadêmicos. Torna-se redundante, nos dias atuais, pensar o quanto a tecnologia favorece o processo educacional em todos os seus níveis de aprendizagem, desde a educação básica até a formação acadêmica. Isto, em função da familiaridade que todos, no cotidiano, convivem com tal fenômeno recente. O acesso a ela permite que as pessoas ampliem seus conceitos e estreitem sua relação física e virtual. Nesse sentido, o que se aprende em sala de aula, com especificidades de determinado assunto, pode facilmente ser estudado num âmbito maior, nas quais se fazem notar outros aspectos ou variáveis desse mesmo assunto. Isso quer dizer que a tecnologia passa a ser uma extensão da sala de aula na busca por mais conhecimento, já que podem ser propostos novos modos de aprender e ensinar. Podemos, então, tentar a síntese dos dois modos de comunicação: o presencial e o virtual, valorizando o melhor de cada um deles. Estar junto fisicamente é importante em determinados momentos fortes: conhecer-nos, criar elos de confiança, afeto, aprendizagem com o outro através do que tocamos, pelos sentidos. Por outro lado, conectados, podemos realizar trocas mais rápidas, cômodas e práticas. É nesta perspectiva que Moran (2010) compreende que a comunicação virtual nos possibilita interações inúmeras, indicadas por ele como oportunidade de ser realizada interação espaço temporais livres, adaptando-se a ritmos de aprendizagens diferentes, com maior liberdade de expressão por parte dos alunos. Hoje se reconhece que a ciência e a tecnologia se viabilizam por meio de um processo de construção do conhecimento e que esse processo flui na esfera da comunicação. Isto não é diferente quando consideramos a instituição igreja Católica, aqui retratada neste trabalho. Juntas, Igreja e novas tecnologias vieram facilitar a comunicação e a comunhão entre as pessoas, anseios profundos que sempre existiram no coração humano e que agora estão sendo colocadas a serviço de aprendizagens mais significativas. Nesse contexto, a evangelização, por sua vez, por estar também interligada nesse cenário, não deve ser vista como um processo estagnado, alheia a isso, ou como sendo um projeto ideológico à parte. Ela não só faz parte, como pode apresentar à educação caminhos para seguir aliada num projeto maior de formação dos sujeitos. Dessa maneira, a religião e a sociedade da informação são caracterizadas pelas variadas formas que se obtém informação em uma velocidade imensa, de maneira multimídia, fazendo leituras de links e criando significações. A informação, dessa maneira, se torna conhecimento quando se torna produtiva, integrada em uma visão ética e pessoal, transformando-a em sabedoria. A Crítica do O *Dilema das Redes* (2020), documentário lançado pela Netflix, dirigido por Jeff Orlowski, conta com a participação de ex-funcionários e executivos de empresas como Google, Facebook e Twitter que expõem os perigos causados pelas redes sociais. Eles escancaram o domínio que essas mídias exercem no cotidiano da sociedade, influenciando na forma em que pensamos, agimos e vivemos. Jogando luz sobre os bastidores das grandes empresas de tecnologia, o documentário expõe a necessidade de se atentar para a gratuidade dos aplicativos de redes sociais, uma vez que, como disse o ex-designer do Google, Tristan Harris: "se você não está pagando pelo produto, então você é o produto". Dentre os inúmeros pontos apresentados e discutidos pelo documentário está o monitoramento constante exercido pelas redes sociais, já que fornecemos dados pessoais às plataformas a todo momento. De acordo com o nosso comportamento nas redes, o algoritmo trabalha para que apareçam no nosso *feed* apenas opiniões e conteúdo que nos interessam, criando-se assim uma re1alidade personalizada, a chamada *bolha de informação*. Esse cenário reforça as convicções pessoais de cada um e leva a pessoa a entender seu ponto de vista como traço absoluto da verdade. Nos encontramos em um momento, marcado pelo que se chama de *pós-verdade*, no qual ficções e distorções factuais podem ganhar contornos de realidade. Partindo de um pressuposto lógico, moral e ético, fatos e verdades científicas deveriam apresentar mais penso nas deliberações coletivas do que percepções pessoais e crenças; porém o que ocorre, atualmente, é justamente o contrário. A realidade pouco importa e sim a percepções que se pode produzir a partir dela. Em suma, essa nova era tem como objetivo produzir discursos que contradizem a realidade criando, assim, teorias da conspiração e disseminando *fake news*. O *boom* da pós-verdade ocorreu durante as eleições norte americanas, em 2016, com a vitória de Donald Trump; a polarização política é claramente um dos produtos dessa era. Qualquer discurso, tese, pessoa ou ideia que vá contra o que certo grupo acredita, diz e faz, são taxados como oposição. É um paradoxo, ao mesmo tempo que as pessoas acreditam em tudo, também não acreditam em nada. Por isso, como nos informam Vera França e Paula

Simões (2016), os usos funcionalistas das mídias conformam um importante âmbito de estudo para o campo da Comunicação. Nessa perspectiva, encara-se a sociedade como um organismo. Nela a comunicação passa a compreendida a partir de suas funções dentro do meio social. Ainda, tentou-se compreender, numa chave behaviorista, a questão psicológica do consumo midiático, com enfoque na utilização do condicionamento dos comportamentos para reformar e melhorar a sociedade, de acordo com os interesses de uma classe específica. Em adição, é trabalhada a teoria da sociedade de massa, relacionada à teoria da agulha hipodérmica (SIMÃO, 2016). Nesse âmbito as respostas do público à mídia são analisadas de maneira generalizada, colocando-o como receptor passivo de conteúdo e possuidor de reações completamente uniformes. Tais estudos se situam logo no início do século XX, com o início da imprensa de massa, a criação do cinema, do rádio e da TV, e explicitam que o poder dos meios de comunicação e sua capacidade de influência no modo de vida da sociedade podem ser percebidos bem antes da popularização da internet. Atualmente, encaramos um novo nível, uma nova fórmula, com novos métodos de condicionamento de opiniões e comportamentos. Percebemos, na relação entre as redes sociais e os usuários, o uso da ferramenta behaviorista para criar e manter uma dependência, daí o termo usuário. Como citado no documentário analisado, somente duas indústrias utilizam tal termo ao tratar de seus clientes: a das drogas ilegais e a de softwares. Entretanto, assim como é apresentado pelo documentário *O Dilema das Redes*, um novo nível de manipulação surge sempre que um novo meio de comunicação se apresenta. Durante um debate na *Chicago AntiTrust Tech Conference* o professor Kevin Murphy, da Universidade de Chicago, argumenta que apesar das adaptações feitas na maneira de viciar e influenciar os usuários, esse é só o mais recente "novo nível" de uma manipulação há muito presente.

> "Eu diria que os métodos utilizados para brincar com a habilidade das pessoas de se viciarem ou serem influenciadas podem ser diferentes dessa vez, e provavelmente são. Eles foram diferentes quando os jornais chegaram e quando a imprensa surgiu, foram diferentes quando a televisão chegou e você tinha três grandes canais. Mas a ideia de que há um novo nível, e que este novo nível já aconteceu tantas vezes antes. O que quero dizer é que esse é só o novo nível mais recente a ser observado" (MURPHY, 2018, tradução nossa).

Seguindo a perspectiva de Mauro Wolf (1987)[45], as mensagens da mídia são adequadas e interagem de maneira diferente com os traços específicos da personalidade dos destinatários. Analisando em associação com o documentário, é possível entender melhor esta dinâmica. Com a personalização dos conteúdos nas redes sociais, são provocadas reações e desejos únicos. A linha de raciocínio construída para encantar e engajar os expectadores das mídias sociais digitais acaba seguindo o mesmo padrão econômico

---

[45] Acessado em 20/10/2024:
https://www.passeidireto.com/arquivo/79696755/mauro-wolf-teorias-da-comunicacao

cultural pré-definido das mídias tradicionais tratadas no texto de Wolf: Construídos propositadamente para um consumo descontraído, não comprometedor, cada um desses produtos reflete o modelo do mecanismo econômico que domina o tempo do trabalho e o tempo do lazer. Cada qual volta a propor a

> "lógica da dominação que não se poderia apontar como efeito de um simples fragmento, mas que é, pelo contrário, próprio de toda a indústria cultural e do papel que ela desempenha na sociedade industrial avançada "(WOLF, 1987, p. 37).

É evidente, no entanto, assim como confirma o autor, que à medida que as posições da indústria cultural se estabelecem e se enraízam, mas elas podem agir sobre as necessidades do consumidor, guiando e disciplinando suas atitudes, opiniões e, como expõe o documentário, o próprio clique. Em *O Dilema das Redes*, esta reflexão torna-se pertinente, mas vai além ao revelar que, hoje, o usuário se torna produto, e não somente consumidor: os clientes são as outras empresas que investem dinheiro nas redes sociais e pagam para ter todas as informações sobre o usuário. Não obstante, independentemente de ser considerado consumidor ou produto, o usuário permanece guiado e disciplinado pela combinação infalível do algoritmo com o design de interface e com o conteúdo estrategicamente elaborado, fazendo escolhas pautadas menos na consciência e mais na dependência emocional do ambiente virtual. Itânia Gomes (2005), em seu livro Efeitos e Recepção, também apresenta elementos importantes para essa reflexão. A autora destaca uma contribuição direta dos estudos da Sociologia e Psicologia para o campo da comunicação. Através dessas contribuições, Gomes destaca que as diferenças psicológicas individuais passaram a se colocar entre emissores e receptores. Os efeitos das mídias tornaram-se dependentes da eficácia da mensagem; a teoria da agulha hipodérmica se torna antiquada, uma vez que é incompatível com a realidade que o público alvo é inerte e passivo. Passa-se a compreender a capacidade de persuasão das mensagens segundo a personalidade do público, ou seja, cada grupo de pessoas reagirá à mesma mensagem de maneiras diferentes. Ainda nesse sentido, existem cinco princípios que categorizam as reações da audiência sobre os conteúdos expostos. O princípio da exposição seletiva afirma que a audiência não se expõe aos meios num estado de nudez psicológica; pelo contrário, ela apresenta predisposições já existentes enquanto o princípio da atenção seletiva relata como diferenças individuais resultam em diversos modelos de atenção ao conteúdo dos media. Os princípios da percepção e ação seletiva dizem respeito a diferenças em fatores cognitivos, culturais ou sociais que implicam diferentes processos perceptivos e distintas interpretações da realidade e uma ação individualizada mediante a exposição à determinada mensagem dos media. O que *O Dilema das Redes* evidencia é que as mídias sociais, atentas para as predisposições psicológicas dos internautas, tentam limitar e controlar, de alguma maneira, as possibilidades de recepção. Com a personalização dos dados, as redes sociais apresentam uma realidade paralela, irreal, que são personalizadas individualmente para que o usuário acredite que todas suas conexões são compartilham da mesma opinião. A modificação é tanta que traz o questionamento sobre o que é realmente verdade. Podemos perceber a grande influência exercida pelos meios de comunicação na formação sociedade moderna e em sua segmentação. Apesar da inquestionável força da internet e das adaptações feitas para deixar-nos ainda mais expostos a ela, passamos a compreender que esse é um aprimoramento de um modelo antigo. A atenção humana é a mercadoria vendida para o anunciante disposto a pagar o valor mais alto. O que estamos observando é um específico processo comunicativo que tem por objeto conteúdos relacionados com aquilo que chamamos convencionalmente religião ou é uma forma moderna de expressividade religiosa, que encontra exatamente em um sítio web seu estado nascente; pois, desde que a observação seja feita sobre novas formas de comunicar a religião via computador, com qual metodologia pode ser enfrentada sua análise, já que uma coisa é examinar com uma pluralidade de métodos (análise semiótica, icônica, do conteúdo, dos estilos retóricos, do eixo semântico opositivo e assim por diante) como um sítio foi construído e, também, quem o construiu e com quais finalidades (manifestas e/ou implícitas), outra coisa é entender quem tem acesso ao sítio, com quais expectativas, por quanto tempo, por quais finalidades (por pura informação ou por uma efetiva necessidade de "religião"); neste caso, é realmente árduo sondar em termos quantitativos o perfil sociocultural e socioeconômico dos usuários (mas esta palavra, como bem se compreende, torna-se genérica demais para classificar uma plateia vasta e anônima de consumidores de um bem religioso via computador), tanto que até agora nos limitamos a nos concentrar nos sítios que oferecem um espaço interativo (chat, fórum, facebook) e a estudar que tipo de comunicação e de relações por via eletrônica se estabelece com indivíduos dos quais, na verdade, conhecemos somente o que dizem digitando em seu teclado pessoal. Quanto mais se expandem e se diferenciam as formas de comunicação mediada pelo computador, como, por exemplo, com a difusão do youtube, tanto mais torna-se complexo preparar instrumentos de levantamento eficazes, capazes de atuar nas duas pontas do fenômeno: a sua qualidade provisória e variável no tempo (um sítio pode existir hoje e não mais amanhã), por um lado, e sua estrutural precariedade e vulnerabilidade no que diz respeito ao princípio de autoridade. Quem decide que um sítio deva se apresentar de uma determinada maneira não sabe, de fato, se ele será efetivamente utilizado de acordo com sua vontade inicial e o risco da dupla contingência é muito mais elevado em relação a religiões institucionais que estão presentes visivelmente na realidade social: ego não sabe se alter aceitará comunicar conforme o código que ego pensou no início e, vice-versa, alter não sabe se a forma com que interpreta o sentido veiculado via computador pode ser reconduzido ao esquema comunicativo de ego. A nossa proposta, portanto, é mostrar as problemáticas encontradas pelo pesquisador quando, ligando um computador e navegando em um oceano de sítios dedicados à religião/espiritualidade, logo percebe a necessidade de se dotar de teorias e métodos adequados para um objeto tão complexo como aquele das religiões em rede. Especificamente, tentaremos avaliar se, e até que ponto, a teoria dos sistemas pode constituir um bom viático heurístico na compreensão, no significado próprio que Max Weber dava a este termo, como arte de compreender, de reconduzir dentro de ideal-tipos de comunicação assistida pelo computador os esparsos e fragmentados elementos que a realidade (no nosso caso o virtual) apresenta em matéria de religião. E, além disso, fornecer indicações de método para futuras pesquisas no campo do virtual. Mencionaremos, por fim, como o recente debate que se desenvolveu na sociologia da religião sobre a relação entre religião e espiritualidade ajuda a compreender, exatamente algumas dinâmicas atuantes na relação entre o indivíduo e o sagrado. Para tal e embricada com todos essa explanação está a práxis da religião na infância enquanto olhar da ciência da religião/psicanalise. O ensino religiosocontribui essencialmente para a compreensão do mundo e da vida à luz da fé. Parte-se de que, além de outros fatores, para que aconteça o desenvolvimento integral da pessoa, pressupõe-se a existência da religião, e, para que esta aconteça, faz-se necessário o ensino religioso. Além disso, ele abre espaço para que os alunos aprendam mais sobre paz, justiça, empatia e a importância do amor ao próximo. Conviver em sociedade significa respeitar o próximo e as suas escolhas. Por isso, o ensino religioso é algo que faz com que a criança aprenda desde cedo os valores do respeito e da empatia, além de compreender que a religião nada mais é do que um caminho para o mesmo lugar: o amor. A tolerância religiosa no ambiente escolar tornou-se um dos maiores desafios para as escolas brasileiras. Não somente para as que dispõem efetivamente de ensino religioso em seu currículo, mas também para as demais, uma vez que disciplinas como História, Geografia e até

Biologia transitam pelo tema transversalmente. A religião permite conhecer o local onde as pessoas vivem seus valores em uma cultura. Ela é influenciada pela cultura, mas ela também influencia a cultura daqueles que vivem em seu entorno. A religião permite um conhecimento maior dos valores que envolvem uma dada sociedade, principalmente seus valores éticos. Podemos dizer que respeitar a diversidade religiosa é uma das atribuições de ser cidadão, valorizando assim, as contribuições que cada cultura religiosa teve ao longo da história. Por isso, é fundamental considerar as diferentes tradições religiosas nos conteúdos escolares. Para limitar as ações do preconceito religioso no ambiente escolar, a melhor maneira é a alternativa. Quebrar a barreira do silêncio, do restrito e conversar naturalmente sobre a diversidade da fé no território brasileiro. Saber reconhecer e respeitar a riqueza das diferenças sejam elas, na aparência, nos costumes, nas crenças, na cultura, deve ser uma grande experiência de encontro, de troca de conhecimento e jamais de discriminação ou intolerância. Para combater a intolerância religiosa, é preciso defender os direitos individuais, promover o acesso à informação, com conhecimento, discussões e debates, além de lutar por políticas públicas que estimulem a tolerância e a liberdade. Além de fornecer a perspectiva, a área de conhecimento da Ciência da Religião favorece as práticas do respeito, do diálogo e do ecumenismo entre as religiões. Contribui, desse modo, com uma educação de caráter transconfessional que poderá incidir na formação integral do ser humano: Historicamente, a ciência tem tido uma relação complexa com a religião; doutrinas religiosas por vezes influenciaram o desenvolvimento científico, enquanto o conhecimento científico tem surtido efeitos sobre crenças religiosas. A religião permite conhecer o local onde as pessoas vivem seus valores em uma cultura. Ela é influenciada pela cultura, mas ela também influencia a cultura daqueles que vivem em seu entorno. A religião permite um conhecimento maior dos valores que envolvem uma dada sociedade, principalmente seus valores éticos. A religião permite conhecer o local onde as pessoas vivem seus valores em uma cultura. Ela é influenciada pela cultura, mas ela também influencia a cultura daqueles que vivem em seu entorno. A religião permite um conhecimento maior dos valores que envolvem uma dada sociedade, principalmente seus valores éticos: são tarefas da ciência da religião com a psicanalise e; elas embricadas: Desde então, a psicanálise se tornou uma disciplina independente na psicologia e psiquiatria brasileiras. A importância da psicanálise no Brasil reside na sua capacidade de fornecer uma compreensão profunda da mente humana e dos problemas emocionais. Dentre muitos, podemos dizer que os principais benefícios da psicanálise são: aliviar o sofrimento psíquico, proporcionar uma vida mais consciente e responsável, ressignificar traumas e sentimentos, promover o amadurecimento emocional e o autoconhecimento. O psicanalista, então, tem como principal função nos ajudar a superar traumas, preocupações, medos e dores emocionais conforme a análise do inconsciente. Já um psicólogo aplica métodos para ajudar o paciente a quebrar ciclos de condutas prejudiciais através da construção de hábitos saudáveis. Autoconhecimento. O processo psicanalítico permite ao paciente entrar em contato com seus desejos e emoções. Assim, ao se deparar com experiências e sentimentos reprimidos, desenvolve-se o autoconhecimento e as formas de lidar com estes fatores. A psicanálise traz a ideia do inconsciente como a parte mais significativa dos processos mentais, influenciando todo o modo de viver dos sujeitos. Para Freud, o inconsciente é constituído de desejos e pulsões, que reprimidos podem gerar efeitos nocivos à saúde psíquica do sujeito (neuroses). A ciência da religião sugere que mesmo que os profissionais da saúde mental não sejam religiosos, deveriam compreender o tema e se ocupar do mesmo, já que este assunto atinge toda a população. Mesmo que se trate de uma irreligiosidade, isso também irá refletir na vida do ser humano. É um tema que não há como escapar. Faz parte da vida do ser humano ou ser ateu, ou ser crente, ou ser agnóstico, ou gnóstico. Por que não tentar dialogar com a questão? Se pensar em assuntos ligados ao gênero, raça, cor, etnias, sexualidade, enfim, apluralidade são temas que também não podemos deixar escapar neste momento da humanidade. Dessa forma, a religião também se encaixa aqui nesta proposta multidisciplinar.

4.1.2. A força religiosa subtrai o cansaço vista na subjetividade

Não tem como negar que uma reflexão frontispísia à psicanálise passa pelo estado de avaliar o consciente e o inconsonante no patamar subjetividade; objetivando entrar contato com as dimensões da subjetividade com a religião enquanto produto humano. Com está noção é interessante ouvir Isaías ao menciona que o senhor "dá esforço ao cansado, e multiplica as forças ao que não tem nenhum vigor" (Is 40, 29:31). O Senhor dará força ao seu filho; o Senhor abençoará o abençoará. É um significa que remete, não temas, porque Eu estou contigo; não te assombres, porque eu sou teu Deus; eu te fortaleço, e te ajudo, e te sustento com a desta da minha justiça. O profeta Isaías pronunciou um ai sobre Israel: "ai dos filhos rebeldes', diz o Senhor" (Is 30:1). Assim sendo, tende-se toma conselho, mas não de Mim, e, eles, executam planos, mas não os do Meu Espírito Isso significa que eles fazem seus próprios planos. Simplificando, Deus disse: Meu povo não me procura mais para orientação e conselho. Em vez disso, eles se apoiam no braço da carne. Toda vez que eles agem sem me procurar, pedindo ajuda ao mundo, eles empilham pecado sobre pecado. Eles abandonaram sua confiança no meu braço forte. O povo de Deus sabia muito bem que eles deviam confiar no Senhor em todas as situações, não importa quão insignificante. Os Salmos constantemente os lembraram: quão preciosa é a Tua benignidade, ó Deus. Portanto, os filhos dos homens colocam suas confianças sob a sombra das Tuas asas; porque a minha alma confia em Ti; e à sombra das tuas asas me refugiarei. Porque Tu tens sido minha ajuda, por isso à sombra das Tuas asas me alegrarei. Isaías declarou que Deus derrubaria todos os seus muros de auto proteção: "

"portanto, essa iniquidade será para você como uma brecha pronta para cair cuja quebra ocorre repentinamente, em um instante. E Ele a quebrará como a quebra do vaso do oleiro, que está quebrado em pedaços; Ele não poupará" (Is 30, 13:14).

Deus estava dizendo: ou quebrar em pedaços todas as coisas falsas em que você confiou. Seus planos vão entrar em colapso. Então Isaías revelou o coração compassivo de Deus para com seu povo. Ele insistiu a Judá disse: você não precisa mais viver em confusão. Você não precisa aguentar essa quebra repentina. Deus providenciou a nós uma saída. Pois assim diz o Senhor Deus, o Santo de Israel:

> "Ao voltar e descansar, você será salvo; em sossego e confiança será a sua força. Aqui está, em resumo, o segredo de Deus para a força espiritual: Quietude e confiança serão a sua força" (Is 30:1,).

A palavra para quietude em hebraico significa repouso, indicando calma, relaxamento, livre de toda ansiedade,[46] deitado com apoio por baixo. Multidões de crentes estão envolvidos em um frenesi de atividades, correndo loucamente para obter coisas. Mesmo no ministério, os servos de Deus estão cheios de preocupação e medo, procurando respostas em conferências, seminários, livros

---

[46] Na Bíblia está, "não andem ansiosos por coisa alguma, mas em tudo, pela oração e súplicas, e com ação de graças, apresentem seus pedidos a Deus. E a paz de Deus, que excede todo o entendimento, guardará o coração e a mente de vocês em Cristo Jesus. Finalmente, irmãos, tudo o que for verdadeiro, tudo o que for nobre, tudo o que for correto, tudo o que for puro, tudo o que for amável, tudo o que for de boa fama, se houver algo de excelente ou digno de louvor, pensem nessas coisas" (Fel, 4:6-8).

mais vendidos. Todo mundo quer orientação, soluções, algo para acalmar seu espírito, mas as procuram em todas as fontes, exceto no Senhor. Eles não percebem que Deus já falou uma palavra para eles através do profeta Isaías. Ele descreve o que a justiça de Deus deve realizar em nós:

> "A obra da justiça será paz, e o efeito da justiça será quietude e segurança para sempre. Se realmente estivermos caminhando em retidão, nossas vidas produzirão o fruto de um espírito calmo, quietude de coração e paz com Deus. Pedro fala da "beleza incorruptível de um espírito manso e quieto, que é muito precioso aos olhos de Deus" (1 Pe 3:4).

Tal espírito não tem nada a ver com temperamento ou personalidade. Algumas pessoas são naturalmente inclinadas a serem calmas e tímidas, enquanto outras são simplesmente mórbidas. Não, o espírito manso e quieto a que Pedro se refere só pode ser implantado em nós pelo Espírito Santo. Ele dá a todos que confiam plenamente no Senhor em todas as coisas. Quando Isaías olhou em volta, viu o povo de Deus fugindo para o Egito em busca de ajuda, confiando nos homens, confiando em cavalos e carros. O profeta advertiu: gora os egípcios são homens, e não Deus; e seus cavalos são carne, e não espírito. Quando o Senhor estender a mão, tanto os que ajudar e os que foram ajudados cairão; todos eles perecerão juntos. Os embaixadores estavam indo e vindo. Os líderes estavam realizando reuniões estratégicas de emergência. Todos estavam em pânico, lamentando. Isaías garantiu a eles que não precisa ser assim. Retorne de seu desvio.

Arrependa-se da sua rebelião de confiar nos outros. Volte-se para o Senhor, e Ele o cobrirá com um cobertor de paz. Ele lhe dará quietude e descanso no meio de tudo o que você enfrentar. Rute é um exemplo desse tipo de confiança. Depois que o marido morreu, Rute morou com sua sogra, Noemi, que era bastante idosa. Noemi estava preocupada com o bem-estar de Rute e queria garantir o futuro de sua nora. Ela aconselhou Rute a deitar-se aos pés do rico Boaz e pedir que ele cumprisse sua obrigação para com ela como seu parente. Naquela noite, depois que a peneira do dia terminou, Boaz se deitou no fim da pilha de grãos; e ,Rute, veio suavemente, descobriu seus pés e deitou-se. Este não foi um esquema manipulador. Rute e Noemi haviam feito tudo em ordem divina. Podemos ter certeza disso, porque a linhagem de Cristo veio através de Rute. Quando Rute voltou para casa mais cedo naquela manhã, Noemi perguntou-lhe: "É você, minha filha?" (3:16). Ela estava perguntando, em outras palavras, "Devo chamá-la de 'noiva Rute'? Ou você ainda é viúva Rute. Rute contou a Noemi tudo o que havia acontecido. Agora ouça o conselho de sua sogra piedosa: Fique tranquila, minha filha, até saber como o assunto vai acabar; pois o homem não descansará até que tenha concluído o assunto hoje. Noemi havia orado sobre o assunto, buscando a direção de Deus, e Deus havia lhe dado conselhos. Ele a lembrou da lei do parente remidor (que era um tipo e prenúncio de Cristo). Noemi estava confiante de que ela e Rute haviam feito a parte delas. Agora era hora de ficar quieta e confiar em Deus para cumprir o que havia prometido. Significa que estava tudo nas mãos do Senhor agora, Rute. Apenas relaxe e fique calma. Deus se moverá sobrenaturalmente por você, para que você não precise se preocupar, se inquietar ou manipular nada. Deixe a quietude e a confiança serem sua força. Deus não deixará Boaz descansar até que ele coloque um anel em seu dedo. Uma calma e paz se estabeleceram sobre a casa de Noemi. Ninguém estava em um frenesi, roendo as unhas e se perguntando: "Deus fará isso? Quando isso acontecerá?". Essas duas mulheres fiéis podiam relaxar, cantar e louvar ao Senhor por sua bondade. E a sua casa? É uma morada calma e pacífica? Ou é um lugar de dúvida, questionamento, ansiedade, inquietação? Você corre aqui e ali, preocupada: "Como vou pagar as contas?" Quando chega o problema, você procura a Deus diligentemente antes de qualquer outra fonte? Então você obedece a tudo o que Ele diz para você fazer? Finalmente, você ainda está descansado, confiando nele para o resultado? Nesse caso, sua casa deve ser calma e pacífica. Tudo isto significa que a forma protege: "Ele é o Deus que me dá forças e me protege aonde quer que eu vá" (Sl 18, 32:35); que a força é instrumento para enfrentar e vencer finfildades os mais variados possíveis: "a esperança e a força de vontade ajudam o homem a vencer dificuldades e doenças" (Pro 18:14) e; que a forma é um forte e valiozo instrumento encorajado para tomar decisões e olhar o outro como filho de Deus: "seja forte e corajoso" (Jos 1:9). portanto, o fenômeno religiosa religioso, sem dúvida alguma, pode ser considerado um dos elementos mais complexos da investigação científica. Isso acontece porque na área da fenomenologia humana ele se manifesta simultaneamente como sendo pertencente a diversos campos, quais sejam, experiencial, filosófico, teológico, antropológico, sociológico e psicológico, entre outros. Por isso, podemos afirmar que ele se apresenta, dada a sua complexidade, como sendo algo de importância fundamental para a compreensão do ser humano. É, portanto, um elemento que confere ao homem um significado marcante e decisivo na construção de sua subjetividade. É uma importante instância de significação e ordenação da vida, de seus reveses e sofrimentos. [...] Como é elemento constitutivo da subjetividade e doador de significado ao sofrimento, defendo que ela deva ser considerada um objeto privilegiado na interlocução com a saúde e os transtornos mentais.Destaca-se, partindo da afirmação acima reproduzida, alguns aspectos de estimada importância para o estudo da religião enquanto fenômeno antropológico. Ela é portadora e, ao mesmo tempo, doadora de sentido para a existência humana, de modo especial naqueles momentos que se apresentam como verdadeiramente determinantes, nosquais toda a solidez parece se diluir e toda referência é vislumbrada na sua mais completa fragilidade. Quando as respostas não parecem oferecer nenhuma segurança,o elemento religioso surge como algo a que se "amparar", desafiando toda e qualquer experiência de desamparo, ainda que seja mesmo aquele desamparo que denominamos "original".Devido a sua importância e pertinência na vida do ser humano, o fenômeno religioso também foi objeto deestudo da área psicanalítica. Embora, frequentemente, seja difundida a concepção de total ruptura e antagonismo entre estes dois campos Ao lado da psicanálise, podemos inferir que foram poucas as verdadeiras contribuições oferecidas à cultura e ao âmbito do conhecimento, que influenciaram de forma significativa o pensamento contemporâneo. Como já mencionado acima, a teoria psicanalítica foi idealizada e forjada por Sigmund Freud, médico da cidade de Viena, que através das construções de seu pensamento conseguiu influir não somente nos meios ditos acadêmicos e científicos sistematizados, mas também nas instâncias do senso comum.

Nota final

A presente nota final é um esboço de retomadas de reflexão dos capítulos anteriores e apontamentos de algumas sujeições que se faz julgar-se ser importante para a psicoterapia. Uma interpretação a necessidade e importância das noções sobre o sagrado para as dimensão psicanalística, psicológicas, cognitivas, das pessoas, sobre as com demência mental, como esquizofrenia e depressão. As verdades das experiências com o sagrado, conforme mencionado acima, resultou para proposto deste incendimento intelectual. Formalmente ele fui iniciado reflexão há trinta e dois anos atrás. Hoje a minha saúde está um pouco debilitado e criei coragem para empreende ideias sobre a importância da Bíblia nas relações sociais, na vida espiritual e no enfezamento e enfretamentos de paciente com demência; sobretudos aqueles elencada nos transtornos mentais, como depressão, esquizofrenia, dentre outras. Este livro, sobretudo, faz-se das análises bibliografara e de pesquisa de observação in natura durante cinco anos em hospitais e clínicas de tratamentos de transtornos mentais, conservadas e avaliadas juntos a doença mental do autor que vos está escrevendo agora. Conforme menciona James (1991), sob a influência do paradigma Newtoniano-Cartesiano, antigo e ultrapassado, esteve em voga, por algum tempo, uma tendência de relegar a experiência religiosa à categoria da mera *fantasia,* para não dizer da *loucura.* Isso explica o fato de a psicologia ter simplesmente não ignorado neste livro: ela própria andava comprometida com essas ideias. No entanto, no que tange ao assunto, esta obra se completa a si mesma, pois começa por considerar a tese psicopatológica e psicoterapêutica a que me referi, para depois, com uma casuística haurida nas principais tradições espirituais, mostrar o que distingue o *santo* e o *místico* do doente mental. Mais: expõe também quais critérios permitem reconhecer, para não dizer "diagnosticar", buscar com amor, a experiência mística legítima. Mas o trabalho segue além e nos leva, a partir de dados experiências, a levantar a questão filosófica da realidade de um poder superior, aventando a hipótese do "self" subconsciente como intermediário entre este poder superior e a natureza propriamente dita. Essa religião o autor considera como sendo a mais elevada de Deus. Numa abordagem original, William James nos dá a conhecer a Psicologia transpessoal e acaba por restituir à psicologia o seu objetivo verdadeiro e último: experienciar o Real. Como vivência intransferível, a resposta só pode ser dada por cada um de nós, a medida em que se possa criar, dentro de si mesmo, as condições necessárias para tanto. E as tradições espirituais propiciaram essas condições ao homem de todas as épocas e de todas as culturas. Futilidade das definições simples da religião. Não existe nenhum "sentimento religioso" específico: a religião institucional e pessoal. Nós nos limitamos ao lado pessoal. Definição da religião para à finalidade destas conferências. Significado do termo "divino". Divino é p que suscita reações solenes. Impossível tiranizar as nossas definições. Precisamos estudar os casos mais extremos. Duas maneiras de aceitar o universo. A religião

é mais entusiasta do que a filosofia.[47] Sua característica é
o entusiasmo na emoção solene. Sua capacidade de
vencer a infelicidade. Necessidade de uma faculdade
Semelhante do ponto de vista biológico. Os conteúdos da
percepção diante dos conceitos abstratos. Influência
destes últimos sobre a crença. As ideais teológicas de
Kant. Temos um sentido da realidade diferente do que é

---

[47] O 'espírito' que eleva o entusiasta de maneira tão espetacular nada
mais é que a flatulência contida no complexo melancólico, e que
ascende do humor hipocondríaco por meio de alguma quentura; esse
vapor é incensado até a cabeça e, tendo sido primeiro acionado e
motivado e, de algum modo, refinado pelo calor, preenche a mente
com imaginação variada, e então acelera e amplia a inventividade,
tornando o entusiasta admiravelmente eloquente e fluente, como se
estivesse bêbado de um vinho novo, trazido de sua adega particular,
que reside na região mais baixa de seu corpo. O pensamento, em que
se funda a filosofia, e a religiosidade, de que a religião recebe o seu
vigor ontológico, podem ser tomados como modulações diversas da
vida. A filosofia emerge da vida como uma modificação da vida.
Ergue-se como busca de um questionamento radical, o mais amplo, o
mais profundo e o mais originário possível. A religião, assim como a
arte, aparece também desde o solo da vida como possibilidade prenhe
de sentido ontológico. A filosofia não pode ignorar a religiosidade e
a religião. Em seu questionamento, vê-se interpelada a questionar a
ordenação (para muitos, essencial) do homem ao sagrado, a Deus. E
isso ela faz por muitas vias, quer tomando em consideração as
investigações do estudo comparado das religiões, quer descrevendo
fenomenologicamente o ato, a vivência ou a experiência religiosa, as
formas fundamentais de culto, as atitudes fundamentais do homem
religioso, as manifestações fundamentais do sagrado, etc. Muitas
vezes este esforço humano toma o caminho de um questionamento a
respeito da essência da religião e da interrogação crítica que pergunta
se esta essência está manifesta ou antes encoberta nas religiões
históricas. Não deixa mesmo de interrogar a respeito da possibilidade
e da necessidade da revelação como consumação e, quiçá, superação
de toda religião dita natural.

dado pelos sentidos especiais. Exemplos do "sentido da presença" . A sensação da irrealidade. Sentido de uma presença divina: exemplos; experiências místicas. Outro caso de sensação da presença de Deus. Força de convicção da experiência não ponderada. Inferioridade do racionalismo no estabelecimento da crença. Ou o entusiasmo ou a solenidade podem prevalecer na atitude religiosa dos indivíduos. A felicidade é o principal escopo do homem. Caracteres "nascidos uma vez" e "nascidos duas vezes". o equilíbrio mental sistemático. O otimismo tal como é estimulado pela Ciência Popular. O movimento da "cura psíquica". Seu credo. Casos. Sua doutrina do mal. Sua analogia com a teologia luterana. A salvação pelo relaxamento. Seus métodos: sugestão; meditação; "recolhimento"; verificação. Diversidade dos esquemas possíveis de adaptação ao universo. Dois casos de cura Psíquica através das noções das dimensões sobre o sagrado. O equilíbrio mental e o arrependimento passa pelo drive da noção sobre as implicações e as importância das pessoas. Pluralismo essencial da filosofia do quilíbrio mental. Morbosidade da mente.[48] O limiar da dor varia de

---

[48] A morbidade psicológica é o desconforto causado pela falta de bem-estar físico e psicológico, o que tem um impacto sobre a saúde do indivíduo. Neste trabalho, o termo morbidade psicológica inclui a combinação de depressão e ansiedade. As doenças, tratamento de doenças e características demográficas estão relacionados a respostas emocionais e cognitivas, bem como *coping*, que preveem consequências psicológicas, físicas e sociais da doença. O *coping* também é influenciado pelos recursos internos e externos do indivíduo. Com base no Modelo de *Coping* de Estresse, neste estudo, a resposta emocional foi analisada como morbidade psicológica, o evento relacionado à saúde considerou a sonolência diurna excessiva e as consequências psicológicas incluíam tanto a

acordo com os indivíduos. A insegurança dos bens naturais. Malogro, ou êxito vão de cada vida. Pessimismo de todo naturalismo puro. Desesperança dos modos de ver grego e romano. Infelicidade patológica. "Anedotiza". Melancolia plangente. O gosto da vida é pura dádiva. A sua perda faz o mundo físico parecer diferente. Casos que necessitam da religião, do sagrado sobrenatural para poderem aliviar-se. Antagonismo entre o equilíbrio mental e a morbosidade. Não há fugir ao problema do mal; mas recorra ao sagrado (COSTA, 2024). Estas acepções psicológica vinculadas à experiência religiosa do sagrado são temáticas latentes na sociedade modernidade líquida, considerandos que estas lógicas estão intimamente relacionada às demências de transtorno mental, como as depressões e as esquizofrenia (COSTA, 2024). Portanto, a psicologia é o único ramo do saber que tenho versado particularmente. Para o psicólogo, as tendências religiosas do homem hão de ser, pelo menos, tão interessantes quanto quaisquer outros fatores pertencentes à sua constituição mental (COSTA, 2024'). Dar-se-á, por conseguinte, que a coisa mais natural para mim, como psicólogo, seja convidá-los a uma resenha descritiva dessas propensões religiosas. Se a indagação for filosófica, o seu tema deverá ser, não as instituições

---

qualidade do sono quanto os comportamentos de saúde. Os hábitos de sono foram considerados um recurso interno que, por meio do *coping*, também poderia influenciar comportamentos de saúde. Com esses objetivos em mente, o foco desta pesquisa foi analisar o possível papel mediador da morbidade psicológica na relação entre a sonolência diurna excessiva e a qualidade do sono, bem como o papel mediador da morbidade psicológica na relação entre hábitos de sono e comportamentos de saúde.

religiosas, senão os sentimentos e impulsos religiosos, e eu terei de limitar-me aos fenômenos subjetivos mais desenvolvidos já registados na literatura produzida por homens perfeitamente evoluídos e conscientes, em obras de piedade e autobiográficas. Por interessantes que sejam sempre as origens e primeiras fases de um assunto, se desejarmos seriamente buscar-lhe a plena significação, deveremos atentar para as suas formas completamente evolvidas e perfeitas. Disso se segue que os documentos mais interessantes para nós serão os dos homens que mais se distinguiram na vida religiosa e se mostraram mais capazes de fazer uma exposição compreensível de suas idéias e motivos. Claro está que esses homens ou serão escritores relativamente modernos, ou autores tão antigos que se tomaram clássicos religiosos. Não deveremos, portanto, procurar os documentos humanos mais instrutivos nos campos da erudição especializada, uma vez que eles jazem ao longo da estrada batida; e essa circunstância, que flui de modo tão natural do caráter do nosso problema, ajusta-se também admiravelmente à ausência de saber teológico deste conferencista. Posso tirar minhas citações, sentenças e parágrafos de confissão pessoal de livros que a maioria dos senhores, em algum momento, talvez tenha tido entre as mãos, mas isso em nada diminuirá valor das minhas conclusões. É verdade que algum leitor e investigador mais corajoso do que eu, pronunciando conferências aqui, no futuro, venha a desenterrar das prateleiras de bibliotecas documentos aptos a proporcionar um entretenimento mais deleitoso e curioso de se ouvir do que os meus. Duvido, contudo, que, pelo controle de um material tão raro, ele chegue, por força, muito mais perto da essência da matéria em apreço.

Faço estes reparos de ordem geral acerca das duas espécies de juízo, porque existem muitas pessoas religiosas, e é possível que algumas delas se encontrem entre os senhores, que ainda não se valem sutilmente de tais distinções e que, portanto, poderão sentir-se, a princípio, um tanto ou quanto perplexas diante do ponto de vista puramente existencial pelo qual, nas conferências que se seguirem, serão considerados os fenômenos da experiência religiosa. Quando os trato biológica e psicologicamente como se fossem meros fatos curiosos de história individual, alguns dos senhores poderão pensar que isso seja uma degradação de assunto tão sublime, e ter suspeitar, enquanto o meu propósito não for plenamente expresso, que eu esteja procurando desacreditar o lado religioso da vida; condizentes as manifestações do sagrado através da relações sociais: o sagrado em manifestação: o sagrado em manifestação. O segundo ponto desta nota final é que, conquanto, a partir da psicanálise, quando fatos rememoram passados, quando interpretamos fatos presentes, quando ouvimos um discurso, quando seguimos o pensamento de alguém e quando escutamos o nosso próprio pensamento, enfim, quando um sistema complexo de representações ocupa nossa inteligência, nós sentimos que podemos tomar duas atitudes diferentes, uma de tensão e outra de relaxamento, que se distinguem sobretudo pela presença do sentimento de esforço em uma e pela sua ausência na outra. O jogo das representações é o mesmo nos dois casos; isto porque os elementos intelectuais são da mesma espécie e mantêm entre si as mesmas relações e; assim, não se encontraria na própria representação, nas suas reações interiores, na forma, no movimento e no agrupamento de estados mais simples que a compõem, tudo o pensamento, é necessário, para distinguir-se deixar viver do pensamento que se concentra e se esforça. Assim, faria parte do próprio sentimento de esforço a consciência de um *movimento de representações* muito particular são as questões que queremos colocar. Todas elas conduzem a uma única questão: *Qual é a característica intelectual do esforço intelectual?*. Em geral, quando decoramos uma lição ou quando procuramos fixar um grupo de impressões em nossa memória, nosso único objetivo é reter bem o que aprendemos. Não nos preocupamos com o que teremos de fazer mais tarde para rememorar. O mecanismo da evocação nos é indiferente. O essencial é que possamos evocar a lembrança, não importa como, quando tivermos necessidade dela. Eis o motivo pelo qual empregamos, simultânea ou sucessivamente, os procedimentos mais diversos, utilizando tanto a memória maquinal quanto a memória inteligente, justapondo entre si as imagens auditivas, visuais e motoras para retê-las tais e quais no estado bruto, ou procurando substitui-las por uma ideia simples, que exprima o seu sentido e que permita, em tal caso, reconstituir-lhes a série. Eis por que, também, no momento da evocação, não recorremos exclusivamente à inteligência ou ao automatismo: automatismo e reflexão misturam-se intimamente, a imagem evocando a imagem ao mesmo tempo em que o espírito trabalha com as representações menos concretas. Daí a extrema dificuldade que experimentamos em definir com precisão a diferença entre as duas atitudes tomadas pelo espírito seja ao evocar maquinalmente todas as partes de uma lembrança complexa seja ao reconstituí-la ativamente. Há, quase sempre, uma parte de evocação mecânica e uma parte de reconstituição inteligente tão bem misturadas que não saberíamos dizer onde começa uma e onde termina a outra. Todavia, apresentam-se casos excepcionais nos quais se propõe a aprender uma lição complicada em vista de uma evocação instantânea e, tanto quanto possível, maquinal. Também existem casos nos quais se sabe que a lição a ser aprendida não terá jamais de ser lembrada de uma só vez; ao contrário, ela deverá ser objeto de uma reconstituição gradual e refletida. Examinemos inicialmente esses casos extremos. Veremos que procedemos diferentemente para reter dependendo da maneira pela qual evocaremos. Enquanto que, tendo adquirido a lembrança, o trabalho *sui generis* que se efetua para favorecer o esforço inteligente de evocação ou para torná-lo inútil nos ensinará sobre a natureza e as condições deste esforço; visto que os tratados de mnemotecnia o dizem e cada um de nós também o adivinha. Lê-se um trecho atentamente, depois se o divide em parágrafos ou secções considerando sua organização interior. Obtém-se, assim, uma visão esquemática do conjunto. Então, no interior do esquema, inserem-se as expressões mais relevantes. Ligam-se à idéia dominante as idéias subordinadas, às idéias subordinadas, as palavras dominadoras e representativas, a essas palavras, enfim, as palavras intermediárias que as ligam como em uma cadeia. Um tratado se exprime do seguinte modo: o talento do mnemonista consiste em apreender em um trecho de prosa essas idéias salientes, essas frases curtas, essas simples palavras que carregam consigo as páginas inteiras. Um outro dá a regra seguinte: reduzir a fórmulas curtas e substanciais; destacar em cada fórmula a palavra sugestiva, associar estas palavras entre si e formar assim uma cadeia lógica de idéias. Nesse caso, não se liga mais mecanicamente imagens a imagens, cada uma restabelecendo a seguinte. Transporta-se para um ponto no qual a multiplicidade das imagens parece se condensar em uma representação única, simples e indivisa. É esta representação que se entrega à sua memória. Então, quando vier o momento da evocação, descer-se-á do cume da pirâmide para a base. Passar-se-á, do plano superior onde tudo estava reunido em uma única representação, a planos cada vez menos elevados, cada vez mais vizinhos da sensação, onde a representação simples está distribuída em imagens, onde as imagens se desdobram em frases e em palavras. É verdade que a evocação não mais será imediata e fácil. Ela será acompanhada pelo esforço. Com este segundo método, é preciso, sem dúvida, mais tempo para se evocar, mas é preciso menos tempo para aprender. O aperfeiçoamento da memória, como observa-se muito frequentemente, é menos um acréscimo de retenção que uma maior habilidade para subdividir, coordenar e encadear as idéias. O pregador, citado por W. James, levava inicialmente três ou quatro dias para decorar um sermão. Mais tarde, ele precisava apenas de dois, depois, de um só, finalmente, uma leitura única, atenta e *analítica* bastava. O progresso aqui é evidentemente apenas uma aptidão crescente para fazer convergir todas as idéias, todas as imagens, todas as palavras para um único ponto. Trata-se de obter a peça única a partir da qual da qual todas as moedas são produzidas. O Terceiro ponto desta nota final é sobre o fundamento importação de operacionalizar a força cognitiva para melhorar a qualidade de vida esta relaciona intelectualidade e aprendizagem cognitivo aplicado e prático. A motivação para aprender envolve características pessoais e socioemocionais, interesses, crenças sobre si e sobre o mundo, fontes de motivação (intrínseca e extrínseca) e o valor que se dá a aprendizagem e à escola. Além disso, engloba a capacidade que cada pessoa tem de estabelecer planos e metas e de construir estratégias de autorregulação da aprendizagem (conseguir se gerenciar e controlar seu desempenho) para alcançar seus objetivos. Sem essa capacidade de autorregulação, aumentam-se as chances de objetivos e aprendizados não serem concretizados. Pensando de forma simples, a motivação para aprender pode ser compreendida por meio do seguinte esquema: desejo, querer, intenção, ação. É importante passar por todas as etapas para que os objetivos e sonhos se materializem. Diversos desses componentes da motivação, descritos no parágrafo anterior, têm sido alvos de iniciativas de desenvolvimento em escolas brasileiras. Contudo, para o alargamento da educação integral em nosso país, o entendimento desses componentes no processo de aprendizagem se torna parte de uma pauta urgente e necessária. A proposição de políticas curriculares e de formação que possibilitem aos professores e gestores não apenas o aprofundamento de seu conhecimento teórico sobre motivação para aprender, mas, principalmente, o desenvolvimento de novas estratégias de ensino e de acompanhamento da aprendizagem, são ações que fortalecem a ponte ciência-escola e o propósito da formação plena dos estudantes. É importante ressaltar que motivação para aprender não é algo inato. Trata-se de uma característica que se desenvolve a partir de experiências de vida. Assim como as competências socioemocionais e cognitivas, a motivação para aprender pode ser impulsionada nas escolas, seja presenciais ou remotas. Um dos passos fundamentais para isso é o de que cada estudante conheça a si mesmo e aprenda estratégias para mobilizar constantemente a sua capacidade de manter-se motivado; para encontrar sentido nas suas atividades; para identificar quando precisa de mais apoio, e como solicitá-lo proativamente, ou quando precisa de novas estratégias para seguir em frente no aprendizado. A promoção da motivação para aprender não deve estar restrita a um componente curricular já existente ou componente específico para o seu desenvolvimento. Ao contrário, é necessário que a motivação para aprender esteja inserida nas estratégias de aprendizagem e práticas pedagógicas de forma transversal no currículo. Nesse sentido, é crucial o compromisso com uma educação integral, que coloque o estudante no centro da aprendizagem, utilizando recursos como metodologias ativas, a flexibilização da grade curricular e o rearranjo dos componentes em torno do projeto de vida de cada aluno. Na prática, a motivação para aprender auxilia no engajamento do estudante com a escola e, quando incluída na jornada formativa do estudante, pode contribuir para dar mais significado à aprendizagem. Esperamos, com este documento, alcançar um público amplo e diverso, em especial educadores, não apenas pesquisadores e especialistas no tema. Assim, neste documento, buscamos dar visibilidade às partes que compõem o todo do que pode ser englobado em motivação para aprender. Pretendemos, ainda, uma reflexão sobre os papéis do professor, dos gestores escolares e da família no desenvolvimento intencional da motivação para aprender, bem como a sua relação com as competências. O quanto ponto nesta nota final está relacionado às informações deste capítulo três é que saber ouvir, ouvir com temperança e sapiência, aos olho da fé é essencial para o bom desenvolvimento da vida do ser humano. A experiência imagética desencadeada pela sinestesia da audição desafia o pensamento educacional a considerar a impossibilidade de cindir sensível e inteligível diante da indivisibilidade da presença que ouvir e escutar suscita no corpo. Tudo acontece nele, o corpo se constitui num processo híbrido com a percepção, pelo qual a experiência do mundo a cada instante se faz em nós. Uma relação de circularidade que constitui a ambiguidade como mistura ou complicação entre corpo e mundo (Merleau-Ponty, 1999). Aqui, a ação educativa ultrapassa a comunicação de significados e torna-se uma experiência de produção de sentido pela disponibilidade em acolher o movimento vital do corpo no mundo como movimento de escuta que integra a relação de sentido. Concebe-se sentido como

> "apresentação ou como vinda à presença", ou seja, como aquilo que tanto preexiste à determinada significação quanto a excede, pois "simplesmente, não há procedência do sentido: ele se apresenta" (NANCY, 2003, p. 66).

Pela experiência estésica do corpo, o interior e o exterior são inseparáveis. O mundo está inteiro dentro de mim e eu estou inteiro fora de mim. Distintos modos do mundo vir sentir-se em nós, são por nós transformados em sentidos compartilhados, ou seja, são por nós organizados, situados e expressos em linguagem. Nesta abordagem, a concepção de linguagem excede o sentido de representação ou identidade de um mundo previamente definido. Por não estar além ou aquém de mim ou de minha ação no mundo, a linguagem ultrapassa a ação de reconhecimento por síntese de identificação de uma mensagem e assume o sentido de uma certa modulação de meu corpo enquanto ser no mundo qual permite abarcar a dimensão como "modulação da existência". Os termos estética e poética convocam campos historicamente marcados por profundos e extensos significados que tensionam debates e opções educacionais. Neste ensaio, os abordamos a partir de noções próximas ao sentido originário de ambas: *aisthesis* e *poiésis*. O princípio de uma palavra não é apenas a origem do seu surgimento, mas o sentido que nela permanece e lhe confere sua especificidade. Em suas antigas raízes gregas, a estética indica a estesia como capacidade primal do humano sentir a si próprio e ao mundo - traduzido por sensação, sensibilidade, ou então pelo que geralmente chamamos o que é percebido pelos cinco sentidos: visão, audição, tato, olfato e paladar. Poética, ao indicar a pluralidade de acepções que dinamizam o estar humano no mundo pelo vigor do agir temporalizado por linguagem; isto é, a vida cotidiana do produzir, criar, traduz o termo poética como ação transfiguradora da pluralidade dos sentidos em experiência de linguagem, a qual simultaneamente nos expõe ao mundo e nele nos situa. Em nossa concepção, é o mistério da linguagem que torna o fenômeno da educação tão instigante e nos faz enfrentar na e com a escrita a fecunda tensão entre filosofia e poética, habitualmente mantidas à distância do pensamento educacional. Assim, a opção pelo ensaio emerge simultaneamente como modo de escrever e como modo de estudar a aproximação entre escuta, ritmo e voz a partir da inseparabilidade entre corpo sensível, mundo e dimensão poética da linguagem. Um tema que não se deixa definir por caminhos previamente demarcados, antes convida ensaiar outros percursos. Nossa expectativa, neste ensaio, é contribuir com um pensamento educacional que não se detenha em uma resposta, nem mesmo uma interrogação, mas se dinamize na abertura à experiência de pensar a disponibilidade pedagógica de estar em presença na coexistência do movimento vital de conviver em linguagem. Movimento que não renuncia a consideração educativa pela experiência estésica do silêncio eloquente, que emerge de um sentir se sentir (*aisthesis*) do corpo sonoro que sempre é, ao mesmo tempo, o corpo que ressoa e meu corpo de ouvinte onde isso ressoa, ou que ressoa por isso;. Implica considerar a relevância educacional da escuta como resistência filosófica ao privilégio do registro teórico fundado na primazia ocidental do modelo óptico. . O movimento da audição acontece com ou sem consentimento. É encontro entre mundo e corpo. Ouço. A vibração sonora não possui face oculta, é e está simultaneamente adiante e atrás, fora e dentro, pois diz respeito a um espaço tempo: se difunde no espaço ou, melhor, abre um espaço que é o seu, o espaçamento mesmo de sua ressonância, sua dilatação e sua reverberação.. A presença sonora, ao mesmo tempo, vibra, estende-se e adentra, fazendo meu corpo coexistir com o acontecimento sonoro. Mesmo que eu não queira, dando-me por conta ou não deste processo, ouço. A presença de alguém que canta desafinadamente ao meu lado, parece frustrar a insistência em querer cantar ordenadamente, pois me perco ao ouvir o outro. Apesar de ter cantado inúmeras vezes e dominar a afinação musical, sigo, neste caso, não um sentido, mas a presença do que está sendo ouvido e não a voz que nasce e vibra em mim. Aqui a presença é majoritária. A potência da presença do que ouço é, primeiramente, um toque no corpo auditivo. Invisível, porém material. E, quando ouço, existe a possibilidade de também escutar. Escutar é ingressar nessa espacialidade que, *ao mesmo tempo*, me penetra: pois ela se abre em mim como em torno a mim, e de mim como em direção a mim", é ao mesmo tempo abertura a mim e ao mundo, "de um a outro, e de um no outro. Nessa compreensão, torna-se importante a consideração educacional da performance vocal como maneira singular de articular sons, na qual importa mais significados pelo modo de fazer ressoar, ou pela relação semântica sonora, do que pela significação linguística que a palavra propõe. Aqui, todos os detalhes importam, pois nos propõem uma gama de sentidos impregnados no corpo. O som ao nosso redor, o som das mídias, as nuances da voz, a trepidação, a respiração, a força, a intensidade, a velocidade, o tempo. Se a voz termina pontuada, cantada alegremente ou puxada, chorada, o ritmo estabelecido por uma projeção vocalizada que escuto torna-se relevante, pois esse ritmo é presença que ultrapassa o significado cultural da palavra ao afirmar-se como materialidade percebida no corpo. Cada detalhe que caracteriza a voz em suas manifestações, sejam agradáveis ou perturbadoras, são modos singulares de perceber e de significar o mundo. Estar em linguagem, equilibrar-se em movimento de presenças e sentidos, é também estar em um ritmo. Abordar o fenômeno da linguagem a partir do ouvir e escutar, e as possibilidades em oralidades nos equilíbrios em movimento, significa também considerar os seus ritmos. Toda e qualquer forma de manifestação linguareiro só pode emergir e ser constituída por e em um ritmo ou ritmos que se intercalam. Um embrião, desde os primeiros instantes da fecundação, já está sendo constituído por um ritmo. Dois corpos. Dois ritmos. O ritmo do encontro de dois ritmos em dois corpos feitos um. A sintonia ou não destes em um único ritmo. Bate um compasso. Desde os primeiros dias de vida no útero da mãe, o embrião de apenas pouquíssimos milímetros de vida já está feito corpo a bater e a pulsar um ritmo. Somos ritmo. O coração, signo maior da amorosidade entre os devires humanos, é justamente aquele que dita o primeiro ritmo próprio. E é por essa presença rítmica que somos tocados primeiramente em nossos sentidos e emoções. Na presença do ritmo e em ritmos vivemos e sentimos, somos constituídos em emoções, saboreamos o mundo e criamos sentidos. Isso é quase como interpelar o paradoxo de o tempo ser simultaneamente familiar a cada um e impossível de ser explicado aos outros. Ao mesmo tempo, ritmo e mundo são por nós sentidos e percebidos e, no entanto, precisamos aprender a sentir e a perceber ambos. Pelo enigma de ser a relação entre as coisas e meu corpo decididamente singular, o mundo é o que percebo, mas sua proximidade absoluta, desde que examinada e expressa, transforma-se também, inexplicavelmente, em distância irremediável. Uma ambivalência que nos faz participar na produção do mundo e de mundos. A única convicção que temos a esse respeito é a de ser pelo ritmo que entramos na linguagem. O ritmo só pode acontecer na emergência temporal de instantes conexos ou desconexos. Instantes que se unem em continuidades e descontinuidades de sons e de silêncios, ou em frações mínimas de percepção de cada um desses instantes. Inscreve-se no tempo. Mas também o tempo é marcado por ele. Tempos no tempo. A linguagem não existe sem movimento do corpo em íntima sedução e emergência que tece o movimento no mundo e do mundo. O ritmo é presença que produz sentido. E conduz sentidos também. A experiência da linguagem engendra um processo histórico particular ao emergir como experiência de temporalização do corpo. O quinto ponto destacado nesta nota está a relação entre fé e suas relações com a neurociência, pesquisaria, psicanálise e com a psicoterapia. A fé é uma forma de "concretizar" a subjetividade: a fé busca compreender como um objeto simbólico (texto, foto, pintura, escultura, etc.) produz sentidos e como este objeto está cheio de significância. Nesta busca, a análise traz à tona o funcionamento da linguagem, no qual o sujeito se constitui pela interpretação que faz. Ao interpretar algo, o sujeito se submete à ideologia e à ilusão de que tudo é transparente, literal, evidente, e de que te temos acesso direto ao sentido completo daquilo que está sendo enunciado. Cabe ao analista de discurso, portanto, compreender como opera o gesto de interpretação do sujeito, os mecanismos de interpretação (como são regulados, o que se interpreta, de que forma, por quem) e mostrar seus efeitos de sentido. Percebemos então a importância do sentido para a análise do discurso. Na verdade, dentro da perspectiva discursiva, é o sentido que fundamenta a linguagem que, por sua vez, só faz sentido porque está inscrita (a linguagem) na história (historicidade). É importante lembrar que, neste olhar, a história não é meramente uma evolução, uma cronologia. São práticas sociais organizadas a partir das relações com o poder. Em outras palavras, ao analista não basta apenas rastrear dados históricos em um texto, mas sim entender de que forma este texto produz sentido levando em conta essas relações com o poder. Para exemplificar esta relação da linguagem com a história e a produção de sentidos e seus deslocamentos em diferentes épocas, basta pensarmos na leitura que você faz de um livro hoje e uma leitura do mesmo livro feita daqui a 20 anos, por exemplo. Esta leitura certamente não será a mesma, pois as condições de leitura não serão as mesmas e você, sujeito-leitor, certamente terá uma diferente relação com a discursividade e com os gestos de interpretação operando nos diferentes momentos. No final das contas, o sujeito-leitor é responsável pelo sentido que constrói ao ler. Por isso é tão comum ouvir de alguém, ao descrever sua experiência com um livro/filme que leu/assistiu mais de uma vez: "Na primeira vez que eu li/assisti eu não gostei tanto" ou "gostei mais". A obra é a mesma! Mas não se pode dizer que o sujeito (e a sua interpretação) também são. O que houve aí foi um deslocamento na produção de sentidos. Para tanto, segue uma interpretação desbodrada em, primeiro, a fé no tratamento de patologia, depois, a fé que equilibra o financeira da pessoa e, terceiro, a fé possibilita ter graça na vida: fé é uma subjetividade. Portanto, o quinto ponto desta nota final está relacionada ao fato da visão integral de que ser humano e da realidade em que se encontra que especialmente inclui a sua dimensão espiritual, portadora deu mais importância especial na nossa temática, sem negar, em momento algum,ainda indispensável atenção que deve ser prestada ato das as demais dimensões.Distinguimos, num primeiro passo, cinco dimensões que chamamos de básicas. A *dimensão física* inclui a corporalidade físico-biológica, da qual, em parte, nem temos percepção. A *dimensão sensorial* é representada pelas nossas sensações físicas, calor-frio, dor-prazer físico, doce-amargo; enfim a percepção que possuímos através dos nossos cinco sentidos: tato, visão, audição, olfato e paladar. A *dimensão emocional* abrange a vida da nossa psique, os estados emocionais (medo, insegurança, euforia, apatia, tristeza, melancolia, impaciência, dispersão, solidão, saudade, indecisão, pessimismo etc.) e suas respectivas movimentações e compensações. A *dimensão mental* do ser humano inclui, em primeiro lugar, o racional e lógico no sentido mais restrito, ou seja, aquilo que compartilhamos em termos de pensamentos com todos os seres humanos, os pensamentos universais, formais (lógica, matemática). Abrange também a capacidade de reflexão- de questionar todas as coisas, inclusive a si mesmo -, a recordação/memória, a imaginação/fantasia, a compreensão/criação de ideias e, finalmente, a nossa intuição, quando sabemos e não podemos justificar, em última instância, por que sabemos. O que é mais difícil identificar é a quinta,*dimensão espiritual*. Não se confunde essa dimensão com a religiosa que, em parte, pode incluir a espiritual, mas que contém algumas características como as da revelação como intervenção direta de Deus e de um tipo de organização social que, dessa forma, são estranhas ou não necessárias à dimensão espiritual. Podemos nos aproximar da dimensão espiritual identificando uma insuficiência das outras dimensões em relação ao homem nas suas possibilidades humanas. Nesse sentido, Podemos chamar essas dimensões de imanentes e a dimensão espiritual de transcendente. Das dimensões imanentes temos evidências constantes. A dimensão espiritual transcende a realidade empiricamente verificável e nem por isso deixa de ser realidade para quem se volta para ela e se compromete come la. Posso viver nas dimensões imanentes sem ser comprometido com nenhum aspecto delas. Percebo a dimensão espiritual no momento em que me identifico com algo, em que eu sinto que isso se torna apelo incondicional para mim incluem-se, dessa forma, todos os valores éticos e metafísicos na dimensão espiritual. Aprofundamos as questões envolvidas nessa breve caracterização da dimensão espiritual, logo após a apresentação da nossa visão sobre a integralidade do ser humano. Segundo a médica Célia Maria Dias Madruga[49], a Fé do doente em si mesmo, no médico, na disposição favorável dos deuses e na piedade de Jesus Cristo. Acreditar na verdade é causa suficiente para muitas curas". Também Albert Einstein, na época, declarou que "Quanto mais acredito na ciência, mais acredito em Deus" .A história desta relação passou por várias fases intercaladas entre distanciamentos e alianças. As grandes evoluções tecnológicas, que hoje ocorrem na área da saúde, exemplificadas com a terapia gênica e a clonagem, têm afastado esta interação. Observa-se, porém que um

---

Acessado em 21/09/2024: https://crmpb.org.br/artigos/importancia-da-fe-na-medicina

segmento da sociedade permanece acreditando na influência da fé na melhora ou até mesmo cura de algumas doenças. Os depoimentos são inúmeros de pessoas que acham ser a fé responsável pelos resultados positivos nos tratamentos de doenças graves. O surgimento de crenças variadas vem preocupando a sociedade pelo abuso e manipulação das emoções do povo, levando ao radicalismo e abandono dos tratamentos médicos, confiando apenas nas falsas promessas de cura. A ciência vem investigando a veracidade destes fatos, com inúmeras pesquisas sobre este tema. Estes estudos visam fundamentos científicos, não apenas para esclarecimento da sociedade, como também, para a provável prática conjunta da fé com a medicina. Na nossa comunidade universitária encontra-se também em curso uma pesquisa sobre a influencia da fé na evolução dos tratamentos dos doentes portadores de patologias crônicas e graves. A ciência biológica nos diz que a fé é o resultado da interconexão de diversas regiões cerebrais. Foi demonstrado que orações repetidas diminuem os batimentos cardíacos e o ritmo da respiração, baixam a pressão sanguínea e reduzem a velocidade das ondas cerebrais. Há evidências que a medicina, a psiquiatria, a psicologia, a psiconeuroimunologia se propõem a respeitar a importância da fé e das crenças, religiosas ou não, do paciente na evolução de sua doença. Acreditamos que diante dos fatos, o bom senso mostra que a fé e a ciência podem se relacionar e se completar. Não importa a religião, e sim a fé de cada pessoa." Tratará tanto melhor as doenças quanto melhor souber, face à situação presente, prever o estado futuro, e ao mesmo tempo discernir se existe algo divino nas doenças, porque é esse também um prognóstico a fazer".São referências de Hipócrates às moléstias da alma; pois "o universo é inexplicável sem Deus". Para Brito (2021), fé e saúde sempre estiveram interligadas desde os princípios da humanidade, na Grécia antiga onde se acreditava que pestes e enfermidades ocorriam em decorrência da insatisfação dos deuses com suas ações, portanto a partir da crença de um ser superior infeliz com um povo na maneira de se portar, desenvolvia-se a fé, ou seja, tinha-se a crença de que arrependimento, mudança de comportamentos e a correção de erros considerados "pecaminosos" abrandaria a ira dos deuses e todos os males cessariam e haveria cura e prosperidades. Deste modo a fé tornou-se um instrumento de confiabilidade, convencimento e aceitação. Apesar da fé durante o século XX e XXI ser considerada uma neurose pela psicologia clássica o que consequentemente gera questionamento sobre sua real efetividade e influência no processo de saúde e doença, há evidências científicas que comprovam intervenções positivas no tratamento de pessoas com distúrbios mentais, pois esta influencia diretamente na forma e aceitação de apoio recebido, nas preocupações e anseios espirituais vivenciados o que gera uma aproximação do indivíduo com o ser transcendental e que resulta em uma visão diferente da situação vivida e muda a maneira de se enfrentar o quadro que se apresenta como também atua como um gatilho de esperança, coragem, significação e aceitação tornando esta uma força intrínseca de transformação pessoal que se reflete no comportamento e modo de se relacionar (BRITO, 2021). Desse modo a fé vem como mediadora que mostra realidade, mas que impõe a esperança, paz, tranquilidade e compreensão, para tanto cabe ao profissional enfermeiro que lida diariamente com a relatividade da saúde e doença em suas dimensões, desenvolver métodos que estimulem o exercício da fé pelos pacientes e pelos próprios profissionais, bem como, evidenciam a influência desta no cotidiano ao cuidar e nos relacionamentos interpessoais dos binômios: profissional-paciente; profissional-profissional e profissional-família. Portanto, asaúde e religião se inter-relacionam a partir da capacidade de enxergar o indivíduo em sua totalidade e dimensões, na arte de promover conforto emocional, fortalecimento pessoal em situações complexas e adversas causadas por condições patológicas e que geram desgaste físico, mental e emocional ao ser humano, atuam ainda na diminuição de ideias e vivências negativas acarretadas pelo processo de adoecimento, significa o adoecimento trazendo novas percepções, ressignifica a vida, traz otimismo, obstinação, esperança e apoio. Como por exemplo, atuar com pessoas com câncer é sempre um desafio devido à complexidade da situação. Exige o trabalho de diferentes profissionais, trabalhando juntos com o mesmo paciente e a família, quando preciso. Sabe-se que a doença - significa uma ameaça à vida, golpeia, atinge cada pessoa envolvida em sua totalidade biopsicossocial, mas, igualmente, nos aspectos espirituais. Portanto, a assistência necessita abranger estas dimensões: afetiva/emocional, psicossocial e espiritual desse paciente e dos cuidadores (familiares e profissionais de saúde). O artigo teve por objetivo, sob a visão da antropologia filosófica de Sberga (2021), apresentar um modo de compreender como os profissionais de saúde (dentista, médicos residentes e contratados, enfermeira, auxiliar de enfermagem, psicóloga) percebem a religiosidade e a espiritualidade de seus pacientes, em tratamento de câncer, e como esses profissionais vivenciam a sua própria espiritualidade.Estudos sobre temas referentes à psico-oncologia, religiosidade e espiritualidade crescendo no Brasil e no exterior (ESPÍDULA, 2010).[50] Estudo qualitativo-descritivo, através de levantamento bibliográfico, enfoca, como objetivo, questões sobre a vida na avaliação bioética, feita pelos profissionais da saúde.[51] significa ressalta que para os estudos aplicados à

---

[50] Acessado em 30/10/2024: https://eventos.galoa.com.br/sbpc-2024/speaker-area/speakers/373327 que também retrata: entendida como o conjunto das declarações e documentos sobre questões sociais feitas pelo Igreja Católica, faz parte da missão evangelizadora da responsabilidade diante da dignidade humana e o bem comum na vida em sociedade. Dentre os principais documentos e pronunciamentos da Igreja na atualidade que atuam neste sentido, podemos destacar as Encíclicas *Laudato si* (2015) e *Fratelli tutti* (2020). Tais textos trazem, em seu conteúdo, aspectos integrativos aos princípios da DSI quando abordam respectivamente, o cuidado da casa comum e à fraternidade e amizade social. Além disso, pode-se citar o projeto de ação conjunta, proposto pelo Papa Francisco, em sua conclamação à um Pacto Educativo Global, onde a educação é entendida como emergência ativa e formativa capaz de intervir em todos os processos da vida pessoal e social. Isto significa dizer sobre a necessidades dos cuidados paliativos: Os cuidados paliativos são um conjunto de práticas destinadas a melhorar a qualidade de vida do paciente, principalmente quando têm doenças graves, incapacitantes ou incuráveis. O principal objetivo dos cuidados paliativos é tornar a fase final do tratamento mais tranquilo, por meio do controle da dor crônica. Assim, os cuidados são centrados em medidas que possam promover o alívio do sofrimento do paciente, por meio do controle de sintomas físicos e emocionais.

[51] Acessado em 16/10/2024: https://anis.org.br

subjetividade relacionada à religião e à psicanálise passa pelas dimensões dos discursos da bioética e;[52] esta se preocupa com os cuidados paliativos; visto que, como exemplo, em bioética, quando presente uma relação entre a vida e uma necessária intervenção dos homens sobre ela, a pessoa que necessita de intervenção precisa ser considerada de acordo com suas particularidades. Precisa ser esclarecida sobre a sua situação em saúde; ter ciência sobre o que pode lhe acontecer no futuro por conta dela; conhecer quais são os tratamentos e as alternativas disponíveis para o que vivencia e, depois destas etapas, ser respeitada com relação à sua opção. Assim sendo, apresenta-se indispensável ao profissional de saúde superar as dificuldades inerentes à relação médico/paciente baseada na "tentação tecnológica", isto é, de ver o paciente apenas por partes. Deve-se buscar reunir os fragmentos e compor, novamente, o todo desse indivíduo, muitas vezes, tão violentado e, desse modo, estabelecer compromisso com a vida, entendida como o bem maior de cada ser e digna de respeito. No entanto, mesmo que a cura não ocorra, os cuidados paliativos podem trazer qualidade ao restante de vida do paciente (ESPÍDULA, 2010). É importante mencionar que a definição de cuidados paliativos da Organização Mundial de Saúde, além da dimensão biopsicossocial, abrange a dimensão espiritual. De acordo com estudos realizados, segundo relatos, as recomendações práticas são melhores com a implementação do cuidado espiritual no tratamento paliativo (ESPÍDULA, 2010). Para muitos, a questão da espiritualidade ocorre dentro do contexto de uma tradição religiosa explícita; para outros pode ser como um jogo de

---

[52] Acessado em 16/10/2024: https://ibcc.org.br/canal-de-bioetica/

princípios filosóficos ou de experiências significativas. Realizado importante estudo para investigar a influência da espiritualidade na saúde, foi aplicada a universitários (dos cursos de medicina e direito) de Pelotas, RS, uma escala sobre bem-estar espiritual (SWBS), por psicólogos ou estudantes de psicologia, levando-se em consideração que, hoje, o bem-estar espiritual é fator de segurança para evitar o desencadeamento de transtornos psiquiátricos menores nesses futuros profissionais (MARQUES, 2009). note-se que os resultados mostraram que 80% dos alunos responderam ter crença religiosa ou espiritual e 86,5% deles faziam uma ou mais atividades espirituais como, por exemplo: oração, meditação, leituras de textos religiosos (cristianismo, judaísmo e islamismo). O estudo destaca que, no grupo dos estudantes de direito e de medicina, frequentam religiões proféticas, monoteístas e espíritas (ESPÍDULA, 2010). A contribuição dessa pesquisa, segundo os autores, foi promover a saúde mental e sugerir aos futuros profissionais exercitar as suas atividades espirituais, o que poderia influenciar, psicodinamicamente, sentimentos positivos como a autoestima, os aspectos psicossociais e espirituais (MARQUES, 2009). Experienciar uma filosofia de vida positiva possibilita à pessoa ter maior consciência e responsabilidade das coisas que tem a fazer, não eliminando os conflitos surgidos, mas, ao mesmo tempo, se não busca resolvê-los não realiza os desejos, as necessidades e as exigências que cada de um tem no mais íntimo de seu ser. Um estudo, feito com psicólogos em atendimento a pacientes com câncer, buscou identificar o significado da fé religiosa para eles em seu trabalho, através de entrevistas semiestruturadas (MARQUES,

2009). Alguns psicólogos, em seus discursos, revelaram que não se pode falar de religião durante a sessão, pois não acreditam que a fé religiosa seja o melhor caminho para proporcionar sentimentos de conforto e bem-estar. Já outros psicólogos valorizaram a fé religiosa, fazendo parte da rotina desse profissional, sendo chamada, pelo autor "energia transformadora, esperança". Pesquisa[53] conclui que metade dos psicólogos acredita que ter fé religiosa seja o melhor recurso para enfrentar a situação de adoecimento e que é possível existir espaço tanto para a ciência como para os aspectos psicoespirituais. Em alguns serviços de oncologia, já se reconhece a necessidade de, além do psicólogo, o capelão fazer parte da equipe, independente de uma ordem religiosa. Estudo qualitativo foi realizado com cinco capelães (dois católicos, dois pastores e um rabino) para identificar o significado da fé religiosa, no seu trabalho com pacientes idosos com câncer, e como veem a fé religiosa dos seus pacientes. Foram realizadas entrevistas semiestruturadas com esses capelães, e o primeiro resultado se apoia na fé, e essa passa a ser a resposta para todas as circunstâncias e instantes da vida, direcionando seu sentido. Foi realizado, de forma sistemática, um método de atendimento ao paciente terminal, servindo de modelo para que outros profissionais da área da saúde pudessem também vir a utilizar essa técnica com seus próprios pacientes. Os profissionais de saúde mostraram melhor enfrentamento do seu luto pessoal e do seu crescimento psicoespiritual, tanto no âmbito profissional como pessoal (ESPÍDULA,

---

[53] Acessado em 15/10/2024:
https://digitalcommons.georgefox.edu/cgi/viewcontent.cgi?article=10
81&context=psyc_fac

2010). Um dado relevante é que essa técnica (RIME) se dirige aos pacientes que acreditam na vida espiritual após a morte (ESPÍDULA, 2010). Pode-se concluir que os estudos apresentam a necessidade de o profissional de saúde estar atento à fé religiosa de seu paciente, ou seja, reconhecer sua dimensão espiritual, na medida em que essa lhe traz estímulo, coragem e esperança para encarar a própria doença. Sinalizam também que é importante ter um psicólogo e um capelão preparados para ouvir os pacientes e procurarem estar em sintonia espiritual (transcendente) com esses, porque essa postura pode ter o papel de auxiliar os pacientes a construir um sentido ao viver um sofrimento inerente à doença, o que poderia facilitar, para os profissionais de saúde, a dimensão do cuidado ao enfermo. Portanto, tudo nos leva a mencionar que os caminhos da psicoterapia para um atendimento proeminente eficaz para com o paciente é essencial. É se estranhar que um psicoterapêutca não passe pela universidade como formação específica aplicada às investigações da mente humana e; ainda, mesmo aqueles forma em psicologia, psiquiatria e neurociência, mesmo sendo academissizado, não possuem nobreza para exercer sua função. Isto está tão evidenda de não deixa de ser vergunho e risco de vida para o paciente sujeitado ao tratamente com esses tipos de profissonais. Correia-Lima (2012) e, sendo e estas questões inicialmente colocadas como forma instrodutória desta sessão sobre os caminho da sugerido para que a os psicoterapêutas, para os desavisdos, passando entender e valorizar a vida do outro como se forma a própria vida.A este respeito este ressalta no seu livro intitulado, "Erro médico e responsabilidade civil"(CORREIA-LIMA, 2012). Este auto colocar a fundamental necessidade de reflexões para o futuro da medicina O médico não é deus. Pelo contrário, é servo. A ele cabe acolher seus semelhantes fragilizados pela doença ou dúvida, examiná-los com rigor, orientá-los em busca da cura e acompanhá-los em sua recuperação. Nesta trajetória ímpar, o médico, humano que é, infelizmente está sujeito às falhas e erros próprios de uma missão que avança sobre a tênue linha que separa a dor do alívio, a vida da morte. Em Erro médico e responsabilidade civil encontramos pertinente reflexão sobre a atuação desses profissionais e as causas das denúncias que chegam aos conselhos de Medicina, não raras vezes, exploradas à exaustão pela mídia. Trata-se de cenário instigante e que nos leva a propor questionamentos cujas respostas estão além do antagonismo entre o bom e o mau, o sim e o não. Convenhamos, o erro médico seria a face mais perversa de uma formação deficiente em escolas de qualidade duvidosa? Ou surge como consequência da falta de políticas públicas que privam o profissional de insumos básicos para bem exercer seu mister? Ou, ainda, apenas demonstra que o paciente atual já retirou os médicos do altar, colocando-os no rol dos profissionais que podem ser questionados? Esses são temas complexos, cuja solução demanda ações em diferentes esferas: na gestão dos serviços públicos e privados, nas salas de aula das escolas médicas, nos plenários e reuniões das entidades médicas e no íntimo de cada profissional – que deve assumir seu real papel com humildade e firmeza em seus compromissos éticos. Independente desses dilemas e possíveis soluções, uma publicação deste nível tem inequívoca importância ao propor aos leitores – de maneira sucinta e objetiva, em linguagem simples e sem apelos para tecnicismos, quer na área médica ou jurídica – uma análise sobre os aspectos vinculados ao erro médico e à responsabilidade civil. Encontramos, assim, obra indispensável tanto para o médico como para os estudantes de Medicina, por conta do progressivo aumento no número de ações buscando condenação por infração ética. Adicionalmente, revela-se preciosa fonte para alunos e operadores do Direito, em decorrência da busca crescente, no Judiciário, por Erro médico e responsabilidade civil reparação frente a denúncias de responsabilidade civil e/ou penal do profissional de saúde consequente a erro médico. De sua leitura, depreende-se que o texto oferece à sociedade uma eficaz ferramenta para a conscientização formal a respeito do erro médico e da responsabilidade civil, tendo em vista a crescente exposição a procedimentos invasivos e não invasivos. Enfim, esperamos que prosperem essa tomada de consciência entre os profissionais, de forma individual e coletiva, e a superação das dificuldades estruturais que afetam o exercício da medicina. Somente assim poderemos ver os médicos, especialmente os mais jovens, contribuindo para resgatar a necessária relação de confiança e respeito de nossa classe junto aos pacientes.isto porque o erro médico é crime, é de responsabilidade. Assim sendo,Correia-Lima ainda ressalta que, o erro médico e responsabilidade civil O tema da responsabilidade civil é um dos mais ricos e complexos do Direito moderno e o erro médico figura como uma das agressões mais graves ao bem jurídico da pessoa. Tratá-los em conjunto, estabelecendo suas interligações, é tarefa difícil pois leva o estudioso a investigações em campos distintos: o campo onde o Direito opera e o campo onde o médico trabalha. Os autores modernos que versam sobre a responsabilidade civil, no seu aspecto mais comum, a responsabilidade subjetiva, realçam a necessidade da reparação dos danos causados, como se lê em B. Starck ao dizer que a atividade dos homens que causa aos outros danos materiais e morais constitui o problema central do Direito contemporâneo. No presente trabalho, seu autor, médico experiente e jovem advogado, lança-se, de modo sucinto e estilo claro, à tarefa de fixar os contornos do erro médico causador do dano e a incidência da responsabilidade civil dele decorrente. Envolve essa relação médico-paciente, dano-responsabilidade, no seu espectro mais amplo, a questão moral que aponta modelos de conduta e traz as regras práticas da ação, daí surgindo o dever ético, tão bem realçado pelo notável médico Arnaldo Pineschi de Azeredo Coutinho, no seu livro Ética na medicina. O Código de Ética Médica traz o ensinamento de que a profissão de médico, sendo desempenhada a serviço da saúde do ser humano, impõe a esse profissional o dever de exercer a medicina com honra e dignidade, aprimorando os seus conhecimentos e utilizando o progresso científico da forma melhor possível, em benefício do paciente. Em linhas gerais, a obra de Fernando Correia-Lima contém essas diretrizes e, por isso, representa valiosa contribuição à área médica, ao lado de tantas outras que valorizam a classe e dignificam o seu trabalho. No tocante à psicanálise, sua inclusão no currículo acadêmico seria motivo de satisfação para um psicanalista, mas, ao mesmo tempo, é evidente que ele pode prescindir da universidade, sem prejuízo para sua formação (FREUD, 1920). Pois o que ele necessita teoricamente pode ser obtido na literatura especializada e aprofundado nas reuniões científicas das sociedades psicanalíticas, assim como na troca de ideias com os membros mais experientes. Quanto à experiência prática, além do que aprende na análise pessoal ele a adquire ao tratar pacientes, sob aconselhamento e supervisão de colegas já reconhecidos. A existência de uma tal organização se deve justamente ao fato de a psicanálise estar excluída das universidades, e ela continuará a exercer uma função decisiva enquanto se mantiver essa exclusão prejudica ainda mais a saúde do pacientes (FREUD, 1920). Outro ponto é uma outra função da psicanálise seria oferecer uma preparação para o estudo da psiquiatria. Em sua forma atual, a psiquiatria é de caráter meramente descritivo; apenas ensina o estudante a reconhecer uma série de quadros clínicos, capacitando-o a distinguir quais deles são incuráveis e quais são perigosos para a comunidade. Seu único vínculo com os outros ramos da ciência médica está na etiologia orgânica, ou seja, no tocante ao organismo e à anato mia. Mas a psiquiatria não proporciona o entendimento dos fatos observados, algo que apenas a psicologia profunda pode fazer.Por fim, cabe considerar a objeção de que dessa forma o estudante de medicina E; jamais aprenderá realmente a psicanálise (FREUD, 1920). Isso é verdadeiro se pensamos no efetivo exercício da psicanálise, mas para os propósitos em vista é suficiente que ele aprenda algo sobre e com a psicanálise. Afinal, tampouco se espera que o estudo universitário transforme o estudante de medicina num cirurgião hábil; quem escolhe a cirurgia como profissão não pode escapar a vários outros anos de trabalho e especialização no departamento cirúrgico de um hospital (FREUD, 1920). Essa outra porção da teoria psicanalítica, não tocada pelo estudo das neur oses de guerra, sustenta que são forças instintuais sexuais que se manifestam na formação de sintomas, e que a neurose nasce do conflito entre o Eu e os instin tos sexuais por ele repudiados. Nisso, "sexualidade" deve ser entendida no sentido lato que é usual na psicanálise, não devendo ser confundida com a noção mais estrita de "genitalidade" (FREUD, 1920). Este auto enumera que, seguindo o exemplo de seus adversários, os psicanalistas, cujos pacientes adoeceram por "frustração amorosa", pelas insatisfeitas exigências da libido, teriam que afirmar que não pode haver "neuroses de perigo", ou que as afecções que surgem após uma vivência aterradora não são neuroses. Jamais lhes ocorreu fazer isso, naturalmente. Veem, isto sim, uma boa oportunidade de reunir numa só concepção os dois fatos que aparentemente divergem. Nas neuroses traumáticas e de guerra, o Eu do indivíduo se defende de um perigo que o ameaça desde fora, ou que é corporificado numa postura do próprio Eu; nas neuroses de transferência, o Eu toma sua própria libido como um inimigo, cujas reivindicações lhe parecem ameaçador (FREUD, 1920). Em ambos os casos o Eu teme ser ferido: neste último, pela libido; naquele, pelos poderes externos. Poderíamos até dizer que nas neuroses de guerra, diferentemente da pura neurose traumática e analogamente às neuroses de transferência, o que se teme é, afinal, um inimigo interno. As dificuldades teóricas que se acham no caminho de uma tal concepção unificadora não pare cem insuperáveis; afinal, a repressão subjacente a toda neurose pode ser entendida, com todo o direito, como reação a um trauma, como neurose traumática elementar.

Referencial Bibliografia

MÁRCIA, M. "Tecnologia e subjetividade". Psicologia em Revista; Belo Horizonte, V.12, N.19, 2006.

BAUMAN, Zygmund. Vida para consumo: a transformação das pessoas em mercadoria. Tradução Carlos Alberto Medeiros. Rio de Janeiro: Zahar, 2008.

DELEUZE, G. "Conversações". Rio de Janeiro: Editora 34, 1992.

BAUMAN, Zygmunt; DONSKIS, Leonidas. Mal líquido: vivendo num mundo sem alternativas. Tradução Carlos Alberto Medeiros. Rio de Janeiro: Zahar, 2019.

COSTA, Gilmar Gonçalves da. "Teologia e cuidado". São Paulo: Uiclap, 2024.

DELOUYA, Daninel. "O método em questão: aspectos relativos à apreensão clínica / Method questioned: aspects of clinical apprehension". Psicanál. univ; V.16, N.39, 2002.

FRAYZE-PEREIRA, J.A. "Entre os sonhos e a interpretação: aparelho psíquico/aparelho simbólico". Psicol. USP, V.10, N.1, 1999.

FOUCALULT. M. "História da sexualidade: o uso dos pra zeres". Rio de Janeiro: Graal.1990.

SILVA, Cyro Marcos da. Do direito ao desejo: subjetividade e legalidade". Florianópolis: Fundação Boiteux, 2002.

KANT, E. "A crítica da razão pura". São Pualo: Nova Culatura, 1999.

CHEMAMA, R. Dicionário de Psicanálise. Porto Alegre: Artes Médicas Sul, 1995.

FRAYZE-PEREIRA, J.A. "Entre os sonhos e a interpretação: aparelho psíquico/aparelho simbólico". Psicol. USP, V.10, N.1, 1999.

DURKHEIN, È. "As formas elementares da vida religiosa". São Paulo: Edipro, 2021.

FREUD, S. "Breves Escritos:*Obras Psicológicas Completas de Sigmund Freud*". Rio de Janeiro: Imago. 1986.

FREUD, S. "Sobre o mecanismo psíquico dos fenômenos histéricos: comunicação preliminar". Rio de Janeiro: Imago, 1893.

FREUD, S. "Inibição, sintoma e angústia". ESB. Rio de Janeiro: Imago, 1976.

FREUD, S. "História de uma neurose infantil". São Paulo: Companhia das Letras, 1920.

FREUD, S. "Caminhos da terapia psicanalítica (1919)". São Paulo: Companhia das Letras, 2010.

FREUD, S. "Obras Completas". Belo Horizonte: Autêntica, 2019a.

FREUD, S. "O Mal-estar na civilização, novas conferências introdutórias à psicanálise e outros textos (1930-1936)". São Paulo: Companhia das Letras, 2010.

FREUD, S. "Análise finita e infinita (1937)". Belo Horizonte: Autêntica, 2019c.

FREUD, S. Fundamentos da clínica psicanalítica. Belo Horizonte: Autêntica, 2019b.

MELTZER, D. "The interaction of visual and verbal language in dreams". Madrid: Tecnopublicaciones, 1984.

JAMES, W. "Variedades da Experiência Religiosa". São Paulo: Cultrix, 1991.

JUAN, F. "A psicanálise: impacto da realidade social". Estudos de Psicanálise, Rio de Janeiro-RJ, N.55, 2021.

JUAN, F. "A psicanálise: impacto da realidade social". Estudos de Psicanálise, Rio de Janeiro-RJ, N.55, 2021.

KANT, É. "Acrítica da razão pura". São Paulo: Nova Cultura, 1999.

KANTE, É. "Metafisca dos costumes". São Paulo: Vozes, 2013.

HARARI, R. "O Seminário "A Angústia" de Lacan: uma introdução". Porto Alegre: Artes e Ofícios, 1997.

LACAN, J. ""O seminário 4". Rio de Janeiro: Jorge Zahar, 1960.

LACAN, J.. "La tercera. In: *Actas de la Escuela Freudiana de Paris*". Barcelona: Ediciones Petrel. 1974.

LACAN, J. "O seminário, livro 7: a ética da psicanálise". Rio de Janeiro: Jorge Zahar, 1968.

LACAN, J. "O seminário, livro 10, a angústia". Rio de Janeiro: Jorge Zahar, 2005.

LACAN, J. "O Tempo lógico e a asserção de certeza antecipada – um novo sofisma". Rio de Janeiro: Zahar, 1998.

LACAN, J. "Função e campo da fala e da linguagem em psicanálise". Rio de Janeiro: Zahar, 1998,

LACAN, J. "O Seminário, livro 1: Os escritos técnicos de Freud (1953-1954)". Rio de Janeiro: Zahar, 2009.

LACAN, J. "O Seminário, livro 11: Os quatro conceitos fundamentais da psicanálise (1959)". Rio de Janeiro: Zahar, 2008.

LACAN, J. "Proposição de 9 de outubro de 1967 sobre o psicanalista da escola (1967)". Rio de Janeiro: Zahar, 2003.

LACAN, J. "O Seminário, livro 17: O avesso da psicanálise (1969-1970)". Rio de Janeiro: Zahar, 1992.

OLIVEIRA, Anna Júlia Braga de. "As socializações primárias e secundárias". Jornal eletrônico, Ano IX, Ed.1, 2017.

RICOEUR, P. "Poétique et symbolique". Francois: Bernard, 1982.

RICOEUR, Paul. "Poétique et symbolique". Paris, Cerf, 1982.

MÁRCIA, M. "Tecnologia e subjetividade". Psicologia em Revista; Belo Horizonte, V.12, N.19, 2006.

MELTZER, D. "The interaction of visual and verbal language in dreams". Madrid: Tecnopublicaciones, 1984.

PORFÍRIO, G. B. "Religião, Espiritualidade e Genética: Possíveis conexões". Research, Society and Development, V.11, N.6, 2022.

RICOEUR, Paul. "L'herméneutique biblique". Paris : Le Cerf, 2001.

RODRIGUES, Gilda Vaz. "Nossos ateus são muito religiosos", nossos psicanalistas também correm o risco de fazer da psicanálise uma religião". Reverso V..37, N.70, Belo Horizonte, 2015.

RIBEIRO, M. de P. "Contribuição da psicanálise par a educação". Psic. da Ed., São Paulo, V.39, N.2 2014.

SANTOS, Luciene dos. "A psicanálise no mundo contemporâneo". Reverso; Belo Horizonte, V.41, N.77, 2019.

SILVA, F. G. "Subjetividade, individualidade, personalidade e identidade: concepções a partir da psicologia histórico-cultural". São Paulo: Picoeduca, 2009.

SAUSSURE, F. "Curso de Lingüística Geral". São Paulo: Cultrix, 2006.

VER, F. e P. SI. "Curso básico de Teorias da Comunicação". Belo Horizonte : Belo Horizonte: Autêntica Editora, 2016.